Designing Web Sites

Illustrated Introductory

Designing Web Sites

Illustrated Introductory

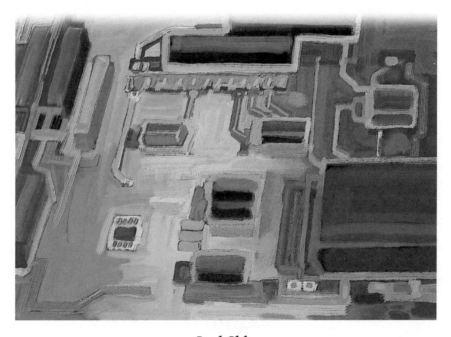

Joel Sklar

COURSE
TECHNOLOGY

THOMSON LEARNING

Australia • Canada • Mexico • Singapore • Spain • United Kingdom • United States

Designing Web Sites – Illustrated Introductory
Joel Sklar

Managing Editor:
Nicole Jones Pinard

Product Manager:
Emily Heberlein

Developmental Editor:
Laurie PiSierra

Composition House:
GEX Publishing Services

Production Editors:
Catherine DiMassa and
Aimee Poirier

Adapting Author:
Rachel Biheller Bunin

Associate Product Manager:
Emeline Elliott

QA Manuscript Reviewers:
John Freitas, Ashlee Welz,
Justin Rand

Text Designer:
Joseph Lee, Black Fish Design

Cover Designer:
Doug Goodman, Doug
Goodman Designs

For more information, contact Course
Technology, 25 Thomson Place,
Boston, Massachusetts, 02210.

Or you can visit us on the World Wide
Web at www.course.com

For permission to use material from
this text or product, contact us by
Tel   (800) 730-2214
Fax (800) 730-2215
www.thomsonrights.com

ISBN 0-619-01821-6

Exciting New Products

Try out Illustrated's New Product Line: Multimedia Tools

Multimedia tools teach students how to create text, graphics, video, animations, and sound, all of which can be incorporated for use in printed materials, Web pages, CD-ROMs, and multimedia presentations.

New Titles

- ▶ Adobe Photoshop 6.0—Illustrated Introductory (0-619-04595-7)

- ▶ Adobe Illustrator 9.0—Illustrated Introductory (0-619-01750-3)

- ▶ Macromedia Director 8 Shockwave Studio— Illustrated Introductory (0-619-01772-4)

- ▶ Macromedia Director 8 Shockwave Studio— Illustrated Complete (0-619-05658-4)

- ▶ Multimedia Concepts—Illustrated Introductory (0-619-01765-1)

- ▶ Macromedia Fireworks 4—Illustrated Essentials (0-619-05657-6)

Check out Multimedia Concepts!

Multimedia Concepts—Illustrated Introductory, by James E. Shuman, is the quick and visual way to learn cutting-edge multimedia concepts. This book studies the growth of multimedia, has an Internet focus in every unit, includes coverage of computer hardware requirements, and teaches students the principles of multimedia design.

This eight-unit book has two hands-on units: Incorporating Multimedia into a Web site and Creating a Multimedia Application Using Macromedia® Director® 8. This book includes a CD-ROM with Macromedia® Director® 8 30-day trial software, and a companion Web site, which bring the concepts to life!

Check out Computer Concepts and E-Commerce Concepts!

Computer Concepts—Illustrated Brief or *Introductory, Third Edition*, is the quick and visual way to learn cutting-edge computer concepts. The third edition has been updated to include advances to the Internet and multimedia, changes to the industry, and an introduction to e-commerce and security.

E-Commerce Concepts—Illustrated Introductory teaches the basic concepts and language of e-commerce. Designed to teach students to explore and evaluate e-commerce technologies, sites, and issues, *E-Commerce* is the ideal introduction to the quickly developing world of e-commerce. The continually updated Student Online Companion allows students to explore relevant sites and articles, ensuring a complete and current learning experience.

Create Your Ideal Course Package with CourseKits™

If one book doesn't offer all the coverage you need, create a course package that does. With Course Technology's CourseKits—our mix-and-match approach to selecting texts—you have the freedom to combine products from more than one series. When you choose any two or more Course Technology products for one course, we'll discount the price and package them together so your students can pick up one convenient bundle at the bookstore.

Preface

Welcome to *Designing Web Sites – Illustrated Introductory*. Whether you are building a site from scratch or redesigning an existing site, the principles presented in this text will help you deliver your Web content in a more interesting, accessible, and visually exciting way.

▶ Intended Audience

Designing Web Sites – Illustrated Introductory is **intended for the individual who has a knowledge of HTML and wants to apply those skills** to the task of designing attractive, informative Web pages. To work effectively with the content of this book, you need to understand the basics of HTML at the code level. You may have taken an introductory class in HTML, or taught yourself HTML with the help of a book or the Web. You should be able to build a simple Web page that includes text, hyperlinks, and graphics. Additionally, you should be comfortable working with computers and know your way around your operating system.

▶ Organization and Coverage

As you progress through the book, you will practice design techniques by studying the supplied coding samples, looking at the example pages and Web sites, and applying the principles to your own work and the exercises at the end of each unit.

The examples and exercises in this book will help you achieve the following objectives:

- ▶ Apply your HTML skills to building well-designed Web pages
- ▶ Effectively use graphics, typography, color, and navigation in your work
- ▶ Understand the effects of browser and computing platform on your design choices
- ▶ Learn to build portable, accessible Web sites that clearly present information
- ▶ Gain a critical eye for evaluating Web site design

Each 2-page spread focuses on a single concept.

Easy-to-follow introductions to every lesson focus on a single concept to help students get the point quickly.

Web Design

Choosing a Graphics Tool

As a Web designer, you may be in the enviable position of having a complete staff of graphic-design professionals creating and preparing graphics for your site. Most Web designers, however, do not have this luxury. Whether you want to or not, you eventually must use a graphics tool. Most of your graphics tasks will be simple, such as resizing an image or converting an image from one file format to another. More complex tasks could include changing color depth or adding transparency to an image. These are tasks that anyone can learn to do, using any of the popular graphics software currently available.

Details

- ▶ Most of your graphics tasks will be simple, such as resizing an image or converting an image from one file to another. More complex tasks could include changing color depth or adding transparency to an image. These are tasks that anyone can learn to do, using any of the popular graphics software currently available.

- ▶ When it comes to creating images, you may want to enlist professional help. Your Web site will not benefit if you choose to create your own graphics and you are really not up to the task. Professional-quality graphics can greatly enhance the look of your Web site. Take an honest look at your skills, and remember that the best Web sites usually are the result of a collaboration of talents.

- ▶ You will use graphics software to create or manipulate graphics. Most Web designers use Adobe Photoshop. This is an expensive and full-featured product that takes time to master. Adobe Illustrator, a high-end drawing/painting tool, also is available. Other commercial tools you can consider include Ulead PhotoImpact and Macromedia Fireworks. Most are available as down-loadable demos, so you can try before you buy. In general, look for a tool that meets your needs and will not take a long time to learn. Table G-1 lists Web sites for the graphic tools mentioned here. This list is not exhaustive, so you may have to try different tools to find the one that suits your needs.

- ▶ Although you also can choose from a variety of shareware graphics tools, such as LView Pro and Graphic Workshop Professional, you may prefer to use a commercial package. Two of the more established tools are Paint Shop Pro 7 and Adobe Photoshop and Illustrator. These tools are each reasonably priced and contain a full range of image-editing features. Like shareware, most graphics tools can be downloaded. Some programs allow you to work with the tools for a trial period before buying and registering.

tip

Although your browser allows you to copy graphics, you should never use someone else's work without permission unless it is a public domain Web site and freely available for use, or you may find yourself in a cyber-lawsuit. New digital watermarking technology lets artists copyright their work with an invisible signature.

TABLE G-1: Graphic tools Web sites

tools you can use are:	you can find graphics tools at:
Adobe Photoshop and Illustrator	www.adobe.com
Graphic Workshop Professional	www.mindworkshop.com/alchemy/gwspro
LView Pro	www.lview.com
Macromedia Fireworks	www.macromedia.com
Paint Shop Pro 7	www.jasc.com
Ulead PhotoImpact	www.ulead.com

▶ 140 **USING GRAPHICS AND COLOR**

Tips provide extra hints and reminders for the concept or lesson.

Tables provide quickly accessible summaries of key terms and technologies, and HTML tags and attributes connected with the lesson material. Students can easily refer to this information when working on their own projects later.

Details provide additional key information on the main concept.

Every lesson features large-size, full-color illustrations, bringing the lesson concepts to life.

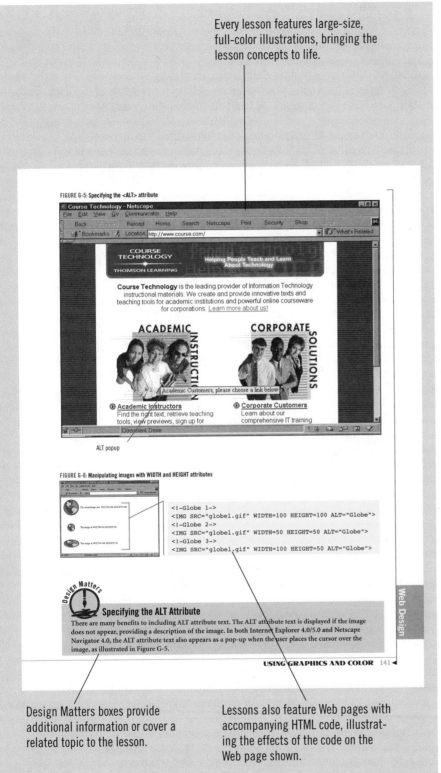

FIGURE G-5: Specifying the <ALT> attribute

ALT popup

FIGURE G-8: Manipulating images with WIDTH and HEIGHT attributes

```
<!-Globe 1->
<IMG SRC="globel.gif" WIDTH=100 HEIGHT=100 ALT="Globe">
<!-Globe 2->
<IMG SRC="globel.gif" WIDTH=50 HEIGHT=50 ALT="Globe">
<!-Globe 3->
<IMG SRC="globel.gif" WIDTH=100 HEIGHT=50 ALT="Globe">
```

Specifying the ALT Attribute

There are many benefits to including ALT attribute text. The ALT attribute text is displayed if the image does not appear, providing a description of the image. In both Internet Explorer 4.0/5.0 and Netscape Navigator 4.0, the ALT attribute text also appears as a pop-up when the user places the cursor over the image, as illustrated in Figure G-5.

USING GRAPHICS AND COLOR   141

Design Matters boxes provide additional information or cover a related topic to the lesson.

Lessons also feature Web pages with accompanying HTML code, illustrating the effects of the code on the Web page shown.

Other Features

Student Online Companion

The Student Online Companion, located at www.course.com/illustrated/designingsites/, contains a wide array of links, HTML code and sample pages, and graphics, to use in completing the end-of-unit material. This innovative online companion enhances and augments the printed page by bringing you onto the Web for a dynamic and continually updated learning experience.

Appendices

The three appendices provide a rich resource. Appendix A provides information on publishing and maintaining a Web site. Appendices B and C contain helpful tables of HTML and CSS references.

End-of-Unit Material

Each unit concludes with a Concepts Review, reinforcing the terms and concepts from the unit, followed by more open-ended objective questions in the Explore Further section. Independent Challenges are hands-on projects involving the concepts and skills covered in the unit. They involve building pages based on unit concepts, and searching the Web for examples of the implementation of concepts. Following the three Independent Challenges, the Web Site Workshop builds through the 8 units. Each unit's Web Site Workshop should be completed in sequence, resulting in an individualized Web site. Each unit concludes with two Visual Workshops, showing existing Web pages that need to be evaluated, compared, recreated, or researched according to the unit concepts.

Instructor's Resource Kit

The Instructor's Resource Kit is Course Technology's way of putting the resources and information needed to teach and learn effectively into your hands. With an integrated array of teaching and learning tools that offers you and your students a broad range of technology-based instructional options, we believe this kit represents the highest quality and most cutting edge resources available to instructors today. Many of these resources are available at **www.course.com**. The resources available with this book are:

Student Online Companion The Student Online Companion, located at *www.course.com/illustrated/designingsites*, contains a wide array of links for students to explore as well as sample HTML code, Web pages and images for students to download and use.

Solution Files Solution Files are sample files illustrating possible solutions to Independent Challenges and Visual Workshops. Use these files to evaluate your students' work. Solution files are available on the Instructor's Resource Kit CD-ROM, or you can download them from www.course.com.

Figure Files Figure Files contain all the figures from the book in bitmap format. Use the figure files to create transparency masters or use them in a PowerPoint presentation.

Instructor's Manual Available as an electronic file, the Instructor's Manual is quality-assurance tested and includes unit overviews, detailed lecture topics for each unit with teaching tips, comprehensive sample solutions to all lessons and end-of-unit material, and extra Independent Challenges. The Instructor's Manual is available on the Instructor's Resource Kit CD-ROM, or you can download it from www.course.com.

Course Test Manager Designed by Course Technology, this Windows-based testing software helps instructors design, administer, and print tests and pre-tests. A full-featured program, Course Test Manager also has an online testing component that allows students to take tests at the computer and have their exams automatically graded.

PowerPoint Presentations Presentations have been created for each unit of the book to assist instructors in classroom lectures or to make available to students. The presentations are located on the Instructor's Resource Kit CD-ROM.

Course Faculty Online Companion You can browse this textbook's password-protected site to obtain the Instructor's Manual, Solution Files, and any updates to the text. Contact your Customer Service Representative for the site address and password.

MyCourse.com MyCourse.com is an easily customizable online syllabus and course enhancement tool. This tool adds value to your class by offering brand new content designed to reinforce what you are already teaching. MyCourse.com even allows you to add your own content, hyperlinks, and assignments. For more information, visit our Web site at www.course.com/at/distancelearning/#mycourse.

WebCT WebCT is a tool used to create Web-based educational environments and also uses Web browsers as the interface for the course-building environment. The site is hosted on your school campus, allowing complete control over the course materials. WebCT has its own internal communication system, offering internal e-mail, a Bulletin Board, and a Chat room. Course Technology offers content for this book to help you create your WebCT class, such as a suggested Syllabus, Lecture Notes, Practice Test questions, Crossword Puzzles, and more. For more information, visit our Web site at www.course.com/at/distancelearning/#webct.

Blackboard Like WebCT, Blackboard is a management tool to help you plan, create, and administer your distance learning class, without knowing HTML. Classes are hosted on Blackboard's or your school's servers. Course Technology offers content for this book to help you create your Blackboard class, such as a suggested Syllabus, Lecture Notes, Practice Test questions, and more. For more information, visit our Web site at www.course.com/at/distancelearning/#blackboard.

Brief Contents

Contents

Web Design

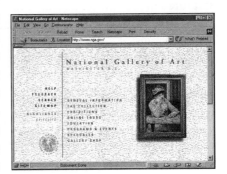

Contents

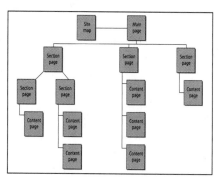

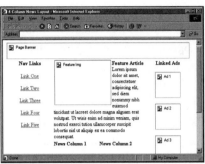

Contents

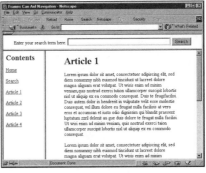

Unit A

Understanding
the Web Design Environment

Objectives

- ► **Understand HTML**
- ► **Create standards**
- ► **Understand XML**
- ► **Design for most browsers**
- ► **Design for state-of-the-art browsers**
- ► **Use an HTML editor**
- ► **Code for multiple screen resolutions**
- ► **Understand bandwidth**

In this unit, you will explore the variables that affect Web design. You will learn how **Hypertext Markup Language (HTML)**, the authoring language used to create documents on the World Wide Web, is constantly evolving and preview the new markup languages that will change how you design for the Web. You will see how Web browsers affect the way users view content and examine whether using an HTML editor can enhance your HTML coding skills. You also will learn how the user's browser choice, screen resolution, and connection speed pose specific challenges to creating Web pages that display properly in different computing platforms.

Understanding HTML

When Tim Berners-Lee first proposed HTML at the European Laboratory for Particle Physics (CERN) in 1989, he was looking for a way to manage and share large amounts of information among colleagues. He proposed a web of documents (which he called a mesh) connected by hypertext links and hosted by computers called hypertext servers. As the idea developed, Berners-Lee named the mesh the **World Wide Web**. He created an application based on the **Standard Generalized Markup Language (SGML)**, a standard system for specifying document structure, and called it the **Hypertext Markup Language (HTML)**. In this lesson, you will explore the roots of HTML, the current design limitations of HTML, and the future of markup languages for creating Web documents.

Details

▶ When Berners-Lee created HTML, he adopted only the necessary elements of SGML for representing basic office documents, such as memos and reports. HTML greatly reduces the complexity of SGML to enhance transmission over the Internet. The first working draft of HTML included elements such as titles, headings, paragraphs, and lists. HTML was intended for simple document structure, not for handling the variety of information needs in use today.

▶ A **markup language** is a structured language that lets you identify common sections of a document such as headings, paragraphs, and lists. An HTML file includes text and HTML markup elements that identify these sections. The HTML markup elements indicate how the document sections display in a browser. The browser interprets the HTML markup elements and displays the results, hiding the actual markup tags from the user. Figure A-1 shows an example of text coded with HTML markup tags.

▶ HTML adopts many features of SGML, including the cross-platform compatibility that allows different computers to download and read the same file from the Web. Because HTML is cross-platform compatible, it does not matter whether you are working on a Windows PC, Macintosh, or UNIX computer. You can create HTML files and view them on any computer platform.

▶ HTML is not a What You See Is What You Get (WYSIWYG) layout tool. It was intended only to express logical document structure, not formatting characteristics. Although many current HTML editors let you work with a graphical interface, the underlying code they create still is basic HTML. Many editing programs use HTML tricks to accomplish certain effects.

▶ You cannot rely on the HTML editor's WYSIWYG view to test your Web pages. Because users can view the same HTML file through different browsers and on different computers, the only way to be sure of what your audience sees is to preview your HTML files through the browsers you anticipate your audience will use.

▶ HTML is ideal for the Web because it is an open, nonproprietary, cross-platform–compatible language. All of the markup tags are included with every document and usually can be viewed through your browser. Once you are familiar with the HTML syntax, you will find that one of the best ways to learn new coding techniques is to find a Web page you like and view the source code. Figure A-2 shows source code for a Web page.

In the above code, the user sees only the text "This is a first-level heading." formatted as a level-one heading

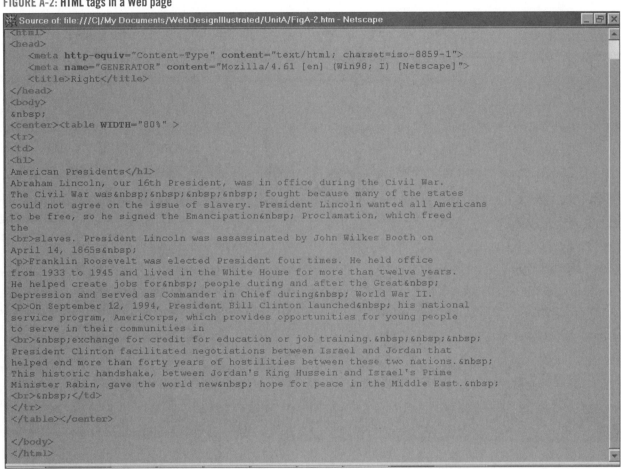

```
<H1>This is a first-level heading.</H1>
```

FIGURE A-2: HTML tags in a Web page

Source of: file:///C|/My Documents/WebDesignIllustrated/UnitA/FigA-2.htm - Netscape

```
<html>
<head>
    <meta http-equiv="Content-Type" content="text/html; charset=iso-8859-1">
    <meta name="GENERATOR" content="Mozilla/4.61 [en] (Win98; I) [Netscape]">
    <title>Right</title>
</head>
<body>
 
<center><table WIDTH="80%" >
<tr>
<td>
<h1>
American Presidents</h1>
Abraham Lincoln, our 16th President, was in office during the Civil War.
The Civil War was     fought because many of the states
could not agree on the issue of slavery. President Lincoln wanted all Americans
to be free, so he signed the Emancipation  Proclamation, which freed
the
<br>slaves. President Lincoln was assassinated by John Wilkes Booth on
April 14, 1865s 
<p>Franklin Roosevelt was elected President four times. He held office
from 1933 to 1945 and lived in the White House for more than twelve years.
He helped create jobs for  people during and after the Great 
Depression and served as Commander in Chief during  World War II.
<p>On September 12, 1994, President Bill Clinton launched  his national
service program, AmeriCorps, which provides opportunities for young people
to serve in their communities in
<br> exchange for credit for education or job training.   
President Clinton facilitated negotiations between Israel and Jordan that
helped end more than forty years of hostilities between these two nations. 
This historic handshake, between Jordan's King Hussein and Israel's Prime
Minister Rabin, gave the world new  hope for peace in the Middle East. 
<br> </td>
</tr>
</table></center>

</body>
</html>
```

Design Matters

Hypertext and Hypermedia

The basic concept of the World Wide Web, and the most revolutionary idea envisioned by Berners-Lee, is the use of hypertext to link information on related topics over the Internet. Hypertext is a nonlinear way of organizing information. When using a hypertext system, you can jump from one related topic to another, quickly find the information that interests you, and return to your starting point or move onto another related topic of interest. As a hypertext author, you determine which terms to create as hypertext links and where users will end up when they click a link.

On the Web, clickable hyperlinks, which can be either text or images, can connect you to another Web page or allow you to open or download a file, such as a sound, image, movie, or executable file. The early Internet consisted of only text and binary files, and when these new hypertext capabilities were introduced, they demanded a new term—hypermedia, the linking of different types of media on the World Wide Web.

Web Design

Creating Standards

HTML has progressed significantly since it was first formalized in 1992. After the initial surge of interest in HTML and the Web, a need arose for a standards organization to set recommended practices to guarantee the open nature of the Web. The **World Wide Web Consortium (W3C)** was founded in 1994 at the Massachusetts Institute of Technology to meet this need. In this lesson, you will explore browser incompatibilities and the use of Cascading Style Sheets (CSS).

Details

tip

Visit the W3C site at *www.w3.org* to find out more about HTML and the history and future of the Web. You can look up individual element definitions, test your code for validity, or keep up to date on the latest Web developments.

► The W3C, led by Tim Berners-Lee, sets standards for HTML and provides an open, nonproprietary forum for industry and academic representatives to add to the evolution of this new medium. The unenviable goal of the W3C is to stay ahead of the development curve in a fast-moving industry. Since its founding, the W3C has set standards for a markup language that is being changed by the evolution of browsers from competing companies, each trying to claim its share of Web users. Figure A-3 shows the W3C homepage.

► As different browsers tried to attract market share, a set of proprietary HTML elements evolved that centered on the use of each particular browser. Some examples of these elements are <FONT> and <CENTER>, which were developed specifically for the Netscape browser. <FONT> eventually became part of the HTML 3.2 specification, but it has been designated as a deprecated element in HTML 4.0.

► **Deprecated elements** are those that the W3C has identified as obsolete and will not be included in future releases of HTML. It is likely, however, that browsers will support these elements and others like them for some time. The browser developers would be doing a disservice to users (and possibly losing customer share) if they removed support for these elements.

► Adding to this confusing compatibility issue are the elements that are strictly proprietary—elements that work only within the browser for which they were designed and are ignored by other browsers. <MARQUEE> creates scrolling text only in Internet Explorer, and <BLINK> makes text blink on and off only in Netscape Navigator. Using proprietary elements like these defeats the open, portable nature of the Web. Avoid using proprietary elements unless you are sure that your audience is using only the browser for which they were designed.

► Opera from *www.operasoftware.com* is an alternative browser. Developed in Norway, Opera is very popular in Europe. Opera is a fast, lean browser that does not include unnecessary add-ons. If you are developing a site that will have international exposure, consider adding Opera to your set of test browsers.

► HTML, like SGML, is intended to represent document structure, not style. Style information should be separate from the structural markup information. Browser developers, in an effort to help HTML authors bypass the design limitations of HTML, introduced style elements such as <FONT>. This separation of style and structure has been accomplished by the W3C, which wrote a specification for a Web style language in 1996.

► The style language, named **Cascading Style Sheets (CSS)**, allows authors to create style rules for elements and express them externally in a document known as a style sheet. CSS rules are easy to create and very powerful. You can place a rule in an external style sheet and then link every page on your site to that style sheet. With a minimum of code you can express the same result, an example of which is shown in Figure A-4.

FIGURE A-3: W3C Web page

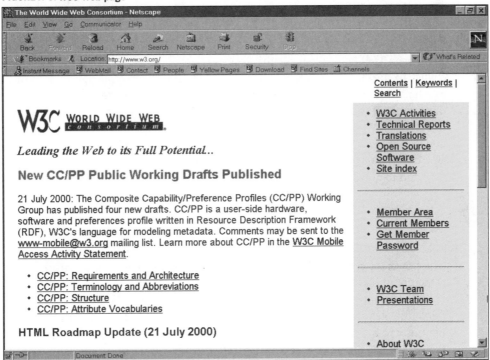

FIGURE A-4: Using CSS

```
<FONT COLOR="GREEN"><H1 ALIGN="CENTER">Some Heading Text</H1></FONT>

              H1 {COLOR: GREEN; TEXT-ALIGN: CENTER}
```

This code in a standard HTML document makes <H1> headings appear green and centered everywhere this code is used

Using a CSS rule, you can express the same style once in an external style sheet

To change the <H1> color to red, you simply change the style sheet rule to change every page on your site

Adopting CSS as a Standard

Mixing of structure and style and the subsequent varied support of different style elements in different browsers threaten to undermine the entire foundation of the Web and to render it useless, as HTML becomes fractured by proprietary elements. Until recently, the adoption of CSS as a standard for style has been limited because of poor support by the major browsers. Both Internet Explorer and Netscape Navigator plan to offer better support for this powerful style language.

Understanding XML

Unlike HTML, **Extensible Markup Language (XML)** is a meta-language—not strictly-speaking a language itself, but a language that lets you describe other languages. With XML, the W3C has a chance to start from scratch in defining a standard markup language, instead of playing catch-up as it had to do with HTML. As a meta-language, XML allows you to create your own elements to meet your information needs, which significantly distinguishes it from the predefined elements of HTML. XML provides a format for describing structured data that can be shared by multiple applications across multiple platforms. In this lesson, you will explore the potential uses of XML and **Extensible Hypertext Markup Language (XHTML)**, which are new markup languages expected to affect the Web's future.

Details

► XML Describes Data

The power of data representation in XML comes from separating display and style from the structure of data. XML elements describe data and structure only and not presentation. Whereas HTML contains elements that describe a word as bold or italic, XML declares an element to be a book title, item price, or product measurement. Once the data is structured in XML, it can be displayed across a variety of media, such as a computer display, television screen, or handheld device, using an associated style sheet that contains the appropriate display information.

Currently, CSS is the only complete style language for XML, though the W3C is working on the **Extensible Style Language (XSL)**, which is derived from XML.

► XML Allows Better Access to Data

HTML elements have no inherent meaning or connection to the data. They simply describe text types and display information. In contrast, the XML code has meaningful element names, which could match the field names in a database. Figure A-5 illustrates this contrast using an example of HTML vs. XML coding. People as well as machines can read XML code. The cross-platform, independent nature of XML markup supports a variety of data applications migrating to the Web. XML lets you display data on many devices without changing the essential data descriptions.

► XML Lends Itself to Customized Information

With the customized elements of XML, standards organizations for various industries and information types can enforce the use of markup constraints with all users.

► XML Improves Data Handling

XML still is under development. Because XML allows better data handling, the new version of XHTML will work better with database and workflow applications. The next generation of HTML will include advanced support for form elements, defining them more for data handling than presentation and allowing data to be passed between applications and devices with greater ease.

► XML Requires Style Sheets

Because XHTML is an application of XML, you must use style sheets to render style in XHTML. Because data is separate from style, the same information can be directed to various display devices simply by changing the style sheet. This data-once, destination-many format liberates the data and structure of XHTML documents to be used in a variety of applications. A script or applet would redesign the data presentation as it is requested from the server and apply the proper style sheet based on the user's choice of device.

```
<BODY>
<H1>Songs of the World</H1>
<H2>Artist: World Singers</H2>
<P>Format: CD</P>
<P>Price: $12.95</P>
<P>Track List</P>
<UL>
<LI>A Song
<LI>Another Song
</UL>
</BODY>
```

```
<RECORDING>
<TITLE>Songs of the World</TITLE>
<ARTIST>Artist: World Singers</ARTIST>
<FORMAT>CD</FORMAT>
<PRICE>12.95</PRICE>
<TRACKLIST>
<TRACKTITLE NUMBER="1">A
Song</TRACKTITLE>
<TRACKTITLE NUMBER="2">Another
Song</TRACKTITLE>
</TRACKLIST>
</RECORDING>
```

Example of the HTML markup code for a page from your online catalog selling audio CDs

If a customer wants to search for a particular recording, the search program must read each line of code to find the title or artist based on the content

Using XML, you could code your catalog this way so the search program could look for a particular element quickly (such as <PRICE>) that matches the user's request because the element names match and describe the data they contain

XHTML: The Future of HTML

HTML has progressed through a number of versions since its inception. The latest standard is version 4.0, which was released by the W3C in late 1997. This probably will be the last version of HTML in its current state. The W3C is working on the next generation, which will be HTML as an application of XML. The W3C decided that the best way to move forward with HTML is to rebuild it as an application of XML. The W3C released the XHTML 1.0 standard in August of 1999. It replaces and extends the capabilities of HTML 4.0. XHTML should display properly in browsers that support HTML 4.0 but will also be XML compliant. XML is extensible, meaning that authors can create their own elements. The next release of HTML will include a base element set for the most common markup elements such as headings, paragraphs, lists, hypertext links, and images. Other facets of HTML, including forms, tables, frames, and multimedia, will be contained in separate element sets. These add-ons will be expressed using XML syntax and can be combined into your document as needed.

Web Design

Web Design

Designing for Most Browsers

One of the greatest challenges facing HTML authors is designing pages that display properly in multiple browsers. Every browser contains a program called a **parser** that interprets the markup tags in an HTML file and displays the results in the canvas area of the browser interface. The logic for interpreting the HTML tags varies from browser to browser, resulting in many possibly conflicting interpretations of the way the HTML file is displayed. In this lesson, you will become familiar with the various techniques Web designers use to ensure that their sites are accessible to as wide an audience as possible.

Details

▶ Most HTML authors do not have the luxury of knowing which browser each person uses to view their Web pages. Browser and version choices can vary widely based on a number of variables. Do not assume that your users always have the latest browser or operating system.

▶ You must test your work in many different browsers, including older browsers, to ensure that the work you create appears as you designed it. Although you may consider your work cross-browser compatible, you may be surprised to see that the results of your HTML code look very different when viewed with different browsers.

▶ Netscape and Microsoft provide easy Web-based upgrades for their browsers, as illustrated for Netscape Communicator in Figure A-6. Many individuals and organizations are reluctant to upgrade software simply because a new version has been released. Other users may have older computers that do not have the processing speed or disk space to handle a newer browser.

▶ New browsers are released frequently, but many Web users still prefer older browsers. The newer browsers support desirable features, such as CSS, that are not supported by older browsers. Including newly supported features in your page design may significantly affect the way your page is viewed if the browser cannot interpret the latest enhancements. Browsers exhibit subtle differences across computing platforms as well. For example, Netscape for Windows is not exactly the same as Netscape for the Macintosh.

FIGURE A-6: Upgrading your browser

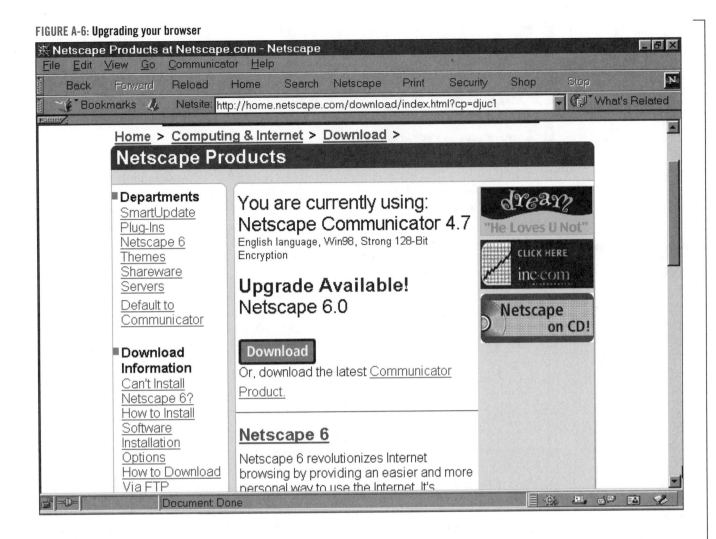

Coding for the Lowest Common Denominator

One way to create portable pages that always display properly is to use a lowest common denominator approach. This approach provides the greatest acceptance across browsers because the authors choose to code their HTML using the next-to-last release of HTML. For example, when the browsers supporting HTML 4.0 were released, many authors continued coding to the HTML 3.2 standard, knowing that their HTML would render more consistently because the browsers understood all of the 3.2 specifications. This safer method of coding is widely supported among sites that are interested in the greatest accessibility.

Web Design

Designing for State-of-the-Art Browsers

Details

You must be able to handle the demands of different browsers while designing attractive Web pages. As you know, some HTML authors suggest that you use an older version of HTML to ensure portability. Others say that you should push the medium forward by coding to the latest standard and using the most recent enhancements. Some Web sites recommend that you use a particular brand and version of browser to access the site. This lesson reviews each of the methods that seek to present the most up-to-date information as part of your site design.

► Another strategy to adopt when designing your Web site is to stay at the cutting edge. Some designers believe that users should be pushed to keep up with the newest browsers and design so the pages always take advantage of the latest technology. This design strategy can result in visually exciting and interactive sites that keep pace with the latest technology. Often the user must not only have the latest browser version but also plug-in enhancements that render certain media types, such as Macromedia Flash animations. **Plug-ins** are helper applications that assist a browser in rendering a special effect. Without the plug-in, your user will not see the results of your work.

► The risk these cutting-edge sites take is that many users may not be able to see the content as it was designed. Sites that use the latest enhancements also may require significant download times for the special effects to load on the user's computer. Sites that adopt the latest technologies must make sure that their user is up to the browser challenge. Otherwise, their information may go unread.

► If you visit a site that states "This site best viewed with Internet Explorer 4.0," you know that the author has decided to forgo the challenge of coding for multiple browsers. The author may have wanted to use some unique enhancement for the site or may have found that the site did not render properly in other browsers. Consider that a site coded for only one browser may alienate a significant number of readers who immediately leave because they do not have the correct browser.

Browser-specific coding may be viable on a company intranet, where you know or you can specify that all users have the same version and brand of browser. For the general Web, it is the least desirable choice because you are limiting the availability of your site.

► Code to the last release of HTML when inaugurating a site, and then slowly add enhancements that move you toward the latest release, testing as you go. This method ensures that you are constructing pages that users can view in both older and newer browsers. If you want to include animations or effects that require a plug-in, use a development tool that already is supported by the major browsers. Make sure that the most important content on your site is rendered in a way that does not rely on the new technology, so users with older browsers still get your message.

► A **sniffer** is a program on the server that detects the user's browser type when they access your site. You then can construct mirrored sets of pages (although this is twice as much work) that are specific to the user's browser.

► You must test your work in as many browsers as possible during and at the end of the development process to make sure that your pages will render properly. Knowing your audience helps you take a major step toward the correct implementation of your site. Table A-1 lists some tips for solving the browser dilemma.

TABLE A-1: Testing for browsers

if you are building a site...	consider...
that discusses the latest in technology trends,	that your users are computer-savvy, so you can code for the latest browsers.
and want to target general Web users,	that general Web users access the Web via America Online, Inc. (AOL), so test your work using their browser as well.
in an academic environment for readers that use Lynx, a text-only browser,	avoiding using too many graphics, and make sure that all of the graphics you include have ALT attributes, which provide alternate text information about images.
for an intranet,	working with one browser in mind if you have the luxury of mandating the type of software your readers use.
for an audience that has physical challenges,	finding out more about this special audience at the W3C accessibility initiative page at *www.w3.org/WAI/*.
and you would like to download a particular browser or find out which browser is currently the most popular,	visiting one of the following Web sites: *www.browsers.com, www.browserwatch.com, www.whichbrowser.com.*

Designing for the Physically Challenged

You can check your Web pages for ease of accessibility to physically challenged people by using Bobby, a Web-based tool developed by the Center for Applied Special Technology (CAST) at *www.cast.org/bobby*. Bobby checks your page by applying the W3C's Web contents accessibility guidelines to your code and recording the number and type of incompatibility problems it finds. Bobby looks for elements such as consistent use of ALT attributes, appropriate color usage, compatibility with screen readers, and ease of navigation. You can use Bobby online if your pages are live, or you can download Bobby to test your work on your own machine. Unfortunately, many mainstream Web sites fail Bobby's requirements for accessibility because they use tables as a page layout device and lack support for CSS.

Web Design

Using an HTML Editor

You can create or generate HTML code to build Web pages in many ways. You may choose to use one of the many editing packages to generate the basic layout or structure for your page or to build a complex table, but be prepared to work with the code and edit at the tag level to fix any discrepancies. You probably will end up working with a combination of tools to create your finished pages. This lesson reviews the many options you have for coding Web pages.

Details

▶ In the short history of the Web, the tool that has gained the greatest universal acceptance is Notepad, the simple text editor that comes with Windows 3.1, 95, 98, and 2000. On the Macintosh, the equivalent tool is Teach Text or Simple Text. Many sites on the Web are coded using these simple text-editing tools. They are easy to use and still relied upon by top-notch HTML authors. They also are the best way to learn HTML because you have to enter every tag by hand.

▶ You can use a number of HTML editing programs to create Web pages. Table A-2 lists some of these programs. Those that forgo a WYSIWYG approach have become popular because they include many powerful enhancements that Notepad lacks, such as multiple search and replace features and syntax checking, while still allowing you to manipulate code at the tag level.

▶ Many of the latest Microsoft Office applications as well as products from other software publishers now convert documents to HTML. For example, you can create a flyer in your word processor and export it to create an HTML page. You can even create slides in Microsoft PowerPoint or Lotus Freelance Graphics and export them to HTML. Figure A-7 shows the dialog box you would use to save a PowerPoint presentation as a Web page. This hands-off approach leaves much to be desired for an HTML author because you give up control over the finished product. This type of HTML conversion also is notorious for creating less-than-standard HTML code. You are better off moving away from one of the office applications to a dedicated HTML authoring package if you are serious about creating attractive, portable Web sites.

▶ As with the browsers, authoring packages interpret tags based on their own built-in logic. Therefore, a page that you create in an editing package may look quite different in the editing interface than it does in a browser. Furthermore, many editing packages create complex, less-than-standard code to achieve an effect specified by the user. The more complex code can cause compatibility problems across different browsers.

▶ Many Web-page designers build complex pages with complex text effects and spacing. When the editing program has to translate this for display with HTML, it must resort to a variety of methods to accomplish the task. These methods may result in code that is difficult to update or debug. HTML authors who are used to coding by hand (in Notepad or another text editor) often are surprised to see what an HTML editing package has generated for code. To really code effectively with HTML, you must be comfortable working directly at the code level.

FIGURE A-7: Saving a PowerPoint presentation as a Web page

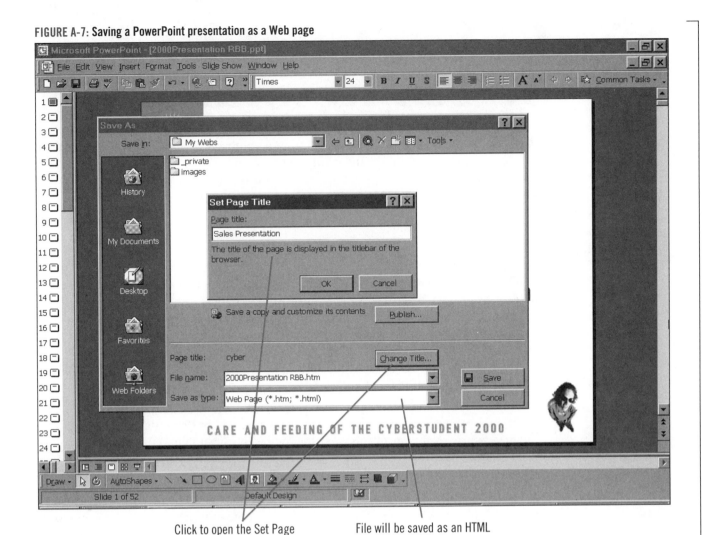

Click to open the Set Page
Title dialog box

File will be saved as an HTML
file, as a Web page

TABLE A-2: HTML editing programs

type of program	program name
HTML WYSIWYG editing programs	Adobe PageMill, NetObjects Fusion, Microsoft FrontPage, and Macromedia Dreamweaver
code-based HTML editors	Allaire, HomeSite, Hot Dog Pro

Web Design

Web Design

Coding for Multiple Screen Resolutions

No matter how carefully you design pages, you can never know how users view your work because you do not know their screen resolution. A computer monitor's **screen resolution** is the horizontal and vertical height and width of the computer screen in pixels. The user's screen resolution is a factor over which you have no control. This lesson discusses how you can compensate for this in the design of your Web pages.

Details

▶ A monitor's range of screen resolution is a function of the monitor's capabilities and the computer's video card. Most monitors can be set to at least two resolutions, whereas larger monitors have a wider range from which to choose. The three most common screen resolutions (traditionally expressed as width × height) are 640 × 480, 800 × 600, and 1024 × 768. Some users choose to use the highest resolution of 1024 × 768, allowing them to display more on the screen. Users at 800 × 600 may maximize their browser to full screen, whereas those working at 640 × 480 may see additional scroll bars if content does not fit on their screen.

▶ Figure A-8 shows the same Web page viewed at different screen resolutions. The page is designed to display its content within 640 × 480 without making the user scroll, thus indicating that 640 × 480 is the base screen resolution of this Web site. As the screen resolution changes, the content remains aligned to the left side of the page. This is known as **fixed resolution design**. The negative background white space on the right side of the page fills in the remainder of the screen.

▶ Figure A-9 shows a Web page that has been designed to adapt to different screen resolutions. As the screen resolution changes, the white space between the columns expands to accommodate the varying screen width. This space between the columns is more active than the white space shown in Figure A-8. The designers accomplished this adaptable solution with variable rather than absolute table widths called **flexible resolution design**.

▶ As a Web designer, you must decide how you will code your Web site to handle different screen resolutions. Some designers believe, and most major Web sites concur, that you always should code your page to the lowest common denominator, which is currently 640 × 480. Most monitors are delivered set to 640 × 480 resolution. Novice users may not know that they can change their screen resolution. Most experienced computer users find they prefer to work at 800 × 600 or better.

▶ Be careful when making the decision to code at higher resolutions. Any content that does not appear with the 640 × 480 window will display additional scroll bars. Although vertical scroll bars are the norm, users consider horizontal scroll bars annoying. Figure A-10 shows a Web page coded at 800 × 600 and viewed at 640 × 480 with horizontal scroll bars.

FIGURE A-8: Fixed resolution design

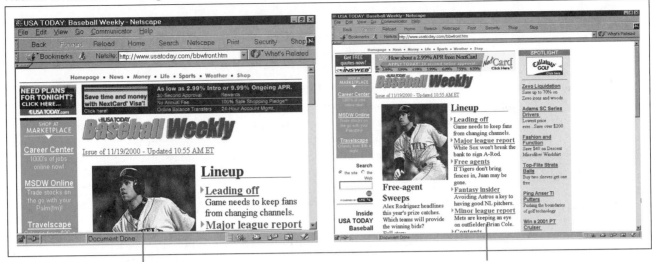

Fixed design at 640 × 480

Fixed design at 1024 × 768

FIGURE A-9: Flexible resolution design

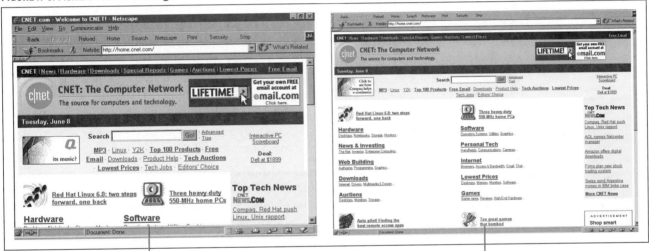

Flexible design at 640 × 480

Flexible design at 1024 × 768

FIGURE A-10: Page designed at 800 × 600 but viewed at 640 × 480

The user must repeatedly scroll from left to right when reading

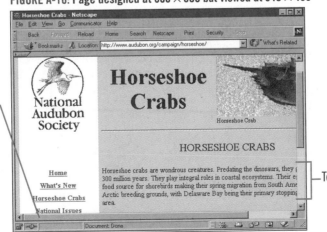

Text extends beyond screen

Web Design

Understanding Bandwidth

Although many cable and media providers would have you believe otherwise, it is a myth that most computer users will soon have fast access to the Web. As such, connection speed must influence your Web-page design. Most users simply will not wait longer than 20 seconds for a page to load. If your pages download slowly, your users probably will click to go to another site before they see even a portion of your content. This lesson introduces the basic concepts and issues concerning bandwidth.

Details

▶ **Bandwidth**, simply defined, is the amount of data that can travel through a communications channel in a given amount of time.

▶ All Web pages are stored on computers called **Web servers**. When you type a **Uniform Resource Locator (URL)** address in your browser, as shown in Figure A-11, it connects to the appropriate Web server and requests the file you specified. The server sends the file to your browser so it can be downloaded. The first time you visit a site, the entire contents of the HTML file (which is plain text) and every image referenced in the HTML code is downloaded to your hard drive.

The next time you visit this site, your browser downloads and parses the HTML file. The browser checks to see if it has any of the specified images stored locally on the computer's hard drive in the cache. The **cache** is the browser's temporary storage area for Web pages and images. The browser always tries to load images from the cache rather than downloading them again from the Web.

▶ Access via cable modem is currently the most reliable high-speed connection to the Web for home users, but less than 20 percent of American households have access to cable modems. Corporations rely primarily on **T1** or **Integrated Services Digital Network (ISDN)** connections. **Digital Subscriber Line (DSL)**, a new technology that allows voice and high-speed Internet access on the same line, is available to only a relatively small percent of all the households in the U.S. Table A-3 describes the more common types of connection technologies.

▶ The single biggest factor influencing the speed at which your pages display is the size and number of graphics on your Web pages. The greater the size and number of graphics, the longer it will take to access your Web site. As a rule of thumb, no single image on your Web site should exceed 10–15k. If you know your users all have faster access, you can design your pages to match. For the general public, you can consider 28.8 Kbps as a base connection speed because many users still use older modems.

▶ A common mistake that many designers make is to omit testing their pages at different connection speeds. If you do not test, you cannot appreciate what it is like for users to connect at different speeds to your site, and you may lose valuable visitors.

TABLE A-3: Common types of connection technologies

technology	speed	notes
regular telephone line	up to 56 Kbps	This is still the most common method of connecting to the Internet. Most people, however, cannot maintain a connection speed over 44 Kbps.
ISDN basic	64–128 Kbps	ISDN offers good speed but is fairly expensive. ISDN is more common in urban areas and primarily used by business.
DSL	512 Kbps to 8 Mbps	For DSL to work well, you must be located within 18,000 feet of your local telephone switching office. DSL uses a single existing phone line to carry both voice and data.
Cable modem	512 Kbps to 52 Mbps	Cable modems are high speed and allow you to stay connected to the Internet. Because you are not using a phone line, you do not have to dial up to connect. Many cable systems are rushing to install Internet access, but most households will have to wait at least 2–5 years.

FIGURE A-11: The URL for a Web page

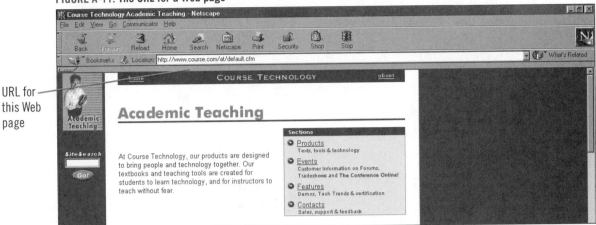

FIGURE A-11: The URL for a Web page

URL for this Web page

Designing around the Cache

Users experience the greatest download times when visiting for the first time. To create the appearance of a first-time visit, you will need to clear your cache of the files and images that the browser has stored there. Figure A-12 shows the Cache Preferences dialog box in Netscape Navigator. The browser's caching mechanism is intended to make the user's browsing experience quicker. As a designer testing your site, however, you want to defeat the natural caching tendencies of the browser. You should design your site with the browser's caching capabilities in mind by reusing graphics as much as possible throughout your site. Once an image is downloaded, it remains in your user's cache for the number of days specified in the user's preference settings. Figure A-13 shows the Internet Options dialog box in Internet Explorer. Most users do not change the settings, so there is a good chance your graphics will remain on the user's hard drive awhile. Leveraging the browser's caching capability is a great argument for standardizing the look of your site by using the same navigation, branding, and background graphics throughout. Not only will the consistency reassure users, your pages will load faster because the browser retrieves the downloaded graphics directly from the cache.

FIGURE A-12: Cache Preferences dialog box

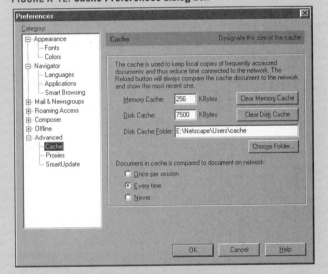

FIGURE A-13: Internet Options dialog box

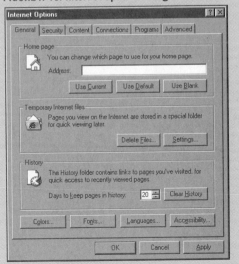

Web Design

Practice

► Concepts Review

Fill in the blank with the best answer.

1. HTML is a subset of the _SGMl_ markup language.

2. _HTML_ is an open, nonproprietary, cross-platform-compatible language that makes it ideal for the World Wide Web.

3. A great way to learn new coding techniques, or to understand how a certain layout was coded, is to view _Source_ on the Web.

4. The _W3C_ is the standards-setting organization for the Web.

5. A _deprecated_ element is an element that is considered obsolete by the W3C.

6. A _proprietary_ element is an element that is created specifically for one browser, such as <MARQUEE> for Internet Explorer or <BLINK> for Netscape Navigator.

7. The _CSS_ style language allows the separation of style from structure in HTML.

8. You can set style rules once for many documents with an _external_ style sheet.

9. _HTML_ has a fixed set of elements, and _XML_ lets you create your own elements.

10. Cascading Style Sheets (CSS) and Extensible Style Language (XSL) are the two types of style languages designed for use with _XML_.

11. XML is designed for describing data. The XML elements can be named to meet any data requirements or match database field names. True/False? _____

12. _Notepad_ and _SimpleText_ are two HTML programs that let you manipulate code at the tag level but forgo a WYSIWYG approach.

13. The most common _screen_ resolution is 800 × 600.

14. _cable_, _DSL_, _phone_, and _ISDN_ are common types of Internet connection technologies.

► Explore Further. . .

1. Describe the characteristics of lowest common denominator coding.

It uses accepted HTML elements that are widely supported, rather than using the latest enhancements.

2. What improvements does XHTML promise over existing HTML?

XHTML has better data structuring and handling, improved forms elements & table elements, more rigid rules.

3. Explain how different browsers affect the display of a Web page.

The logic for interpreting the HTML tags is diff. in every browser, resulting in varying interp. of way the HTML file is displayed

4. Describe how coding that uses the latest technology can prevent users from accessing your site.

The users browser/operating system may not be able to display the results of latest tech. preventing users from accessing info.

5. Explain how screen resolution affects the display of a Web page.

Pages that are coded at a higher resolution greatly affect users who view at lower resolutions. May not be able to view all info

6. Explain how the browser's caching capability improves download time and why an HTML author would clear the browser's cache.

1. browsers store recently downloaded web pages in the cache. When user access pg, the browser checks the cache first to see whether content is stored locally. If so, browser loads the content from the hard drive, rather than down loading again.

2. Clearing the cache lets you test pages as if you were a user visiting for first time.

▶ Independent Challenges

1. You learned about the World Wide Web Consortium (W3C) Web site in this unit. You will explore the Web site further in this Independent Challenge.

a. Log on to the Internet and go to *www.w3.org*.

b. Find the three types of HTML 4.0 (Transitional, Strict, and Frames), and, using your word processor, describe each type and explain why you might use it.

c. Find the CSS specification. Again, using your word processor, list and describe ten style properties that you can affect with a style rule.

d. Examine the Web Accessibility Initiative (WAI). Still using your word processor, write a few sentences that describe how you would design a page that meets the WAI guidelines.

e. Type **Your Name** at the bottom of the document, save the document, print a copy, and then close it.

f. Go to the to *www.w3.org* home page and find the link for the "Getting started with HTML" page. Read through the short introduction for writing HTML. Using what you learned there and what you know from this unit, write a short HTML document that has two heading levels and two paragraphs.

g. Log off the Internet.

2. You don't always have to use an HTML editor to create HTML code when building your Web site. You will explore and test the HTML conversion capabilities of a standard office application in this Independent Challenge.

a. Use your favorite word processing, spreadsheet, or presentation graphics program that supports conversion to HTML.

b. Create a document and export it to HTML.

c. Examine and evaluate the HTML code. Look for nonstandard coding techniques or tricks that the program uses to render content into HTML. Write a detailed description of your findings.

3. Internet Explorer and Netscape Navigator are the two most popular browsers in use today. You will explore and test cross-browser compatibility in this Independent Challenge.

  a. Make sure you have recent versions of both Netscape Navigator and Internet Explorer installed on your computer.

  b. Log on to the Internet.

  c. Browse a variety of Web sites. Make sure to view various pages of the sites in both browsers. If you cannot find a compatible site, go to the Student Online companion site at *www.course.com/illustrated/designingsites* for suggested Web pages.

  d. Use your word processor to write a detailed description of how successfully the various sites appear in both browsers. Look for text, layout, and graphics inconsistencies.

  e. Type **Your Name** at the bottom of the document, save the document, print a copy, and then close it.

  f. Use the Print Screen capability of your computer to print a copy of at least one page as seen in both browsers. (*Hint*: With the Web page on the screen, press [Print Screen] on your keyboard, then open a Word document and click the Paste button on the Standard toolbar to insert the image into the document file.)

  g. Log off the Internet.

To complete the Web Site Workshop for this book, you must create a complete, stand-alone Web site. The site must contain from six to ten pages, displaying at least three levels of information. You can choose your own content. For example, you can do a work-related topic, a personal interest site, or a site for your favorite nonprofit organization. The site will be evaluated for cohesiveness, accessibility, and design. At the end of each unit, you will complete a different section of the project. For Unit A, get started by creating a project proposal, as outlined below. As you progress through the units of the book, you will complete different facets of the Web-site construction, resulting in a complete Web site.

a. Create a one to two page HTML document stating the basic factors or elements you will include in your Web site. Create this document using your favorite HTML editor or Notepad. At this stage, your proposal is primarily a draft that you revise. At the end of the next unit, you will have a chance to modify the proposal and supplement the design details.

b. Include the following items, if applicable:

- Site title—the working title for the site
- Developer—you and anyone else who will work on the site
- Rationale or focus (for example, billboard, customer support, catalog/e-commerce, informational, resource, and so on)—an explanation of the content and goals of the site
- Main elements outline—a list of the main features of the site
- Content—the number of individual Web pages
- Target audience—a description of the typical audience for the site
- Design considerations—a list of the design goals for the site
- Limiting factors—a list of the technical or audience factors that could limit the design goals of the site

▶ Visual Workshop

1. For this Visual Workshop, write a brief paragraph explaining the design issues and differences in the Web pages shown in Figure A-14.

FIGURE A-14

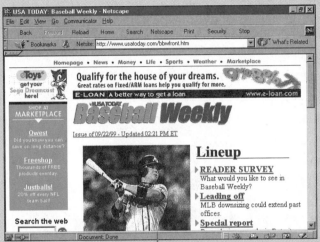

Fixed design 640 × 480

Fixed design 1024 × 768

▶ Visual Workshop

2. As you prepare to complete this Visual Workshop, remember that the most important consideration regarding download times is the size and number of graphics on a page because most users will not wait more than 20 seconds for a page to load before going to another site. Look at the Web site shown in Figure A-15, and name some strategies that the Web developer could use to meet the needs of users with slow connection speeds and older browsers.

FIGURE A-15

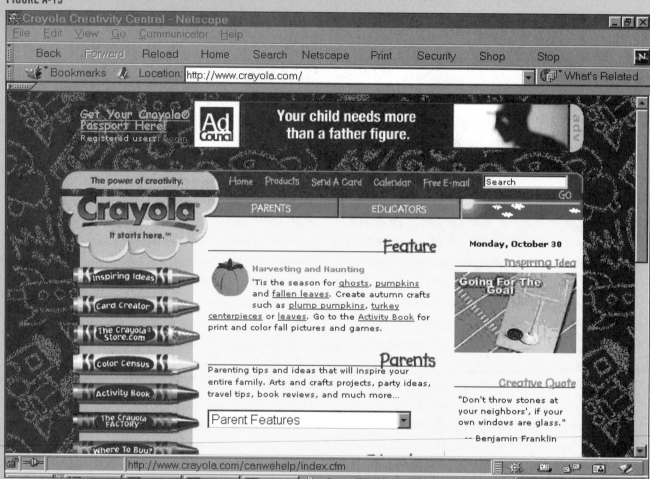

Understanding
Web Design Principles

Objectives

- ► **Design for the medium**
- ► **Design the whole site**
- ► **Focus on white space**
- ► **Design for the user**
- ► **Understand viewing patterns**
- ► **Link with hypertext**
- ► **Restrict the amount of information**
- ► **Design for the screen**

In this unit, you will learn about basic design principles that you should apply as you design Web sites. By examining a variety of Web sites, you will learn to focus on both the user's needs and the information requirements of the content you want to deliver. You should plan a site that is both easy to navigate and quick to download. The sample Web pages in this unit come from a wide range of sites. The Web is so far-reaching in content and design that no collection of pages represents what is typical. Most of the samples illustrate good design principles, although some highlight design defects as well. In truth, almost every site has one flaw or another— whether it is confusing accessibility, over-ambitious design, or poor download time. As you progress through the book, you will practice and apply these principles to your own Web design efforts.

Designing for the Medium

Details

When designing a Web site, remember that the destination is a computer, not the printed page, and the language is hypertext, not linear text. As a Web-page designer, you must create Web pages specifically for the computer screen. You must consider the layout, fonts, and colors and how they will appear. As an HTML author, you must consider the nonlinear nature of hypertext and weave the appropriate links and associations into the information. You should also give users the option to follow the information path they desire by providing appropriate links to related topics, as well as make them feel comfortable at your site by letting them know where they are and where they can go.

▶ Craft the Look and Feel

The interface that the user must navigate often is called the "look and feel" of a Web site. The look and feel is both the way your Web site works and the personality it conveys to the user. Users both "look" and "feel" when they explore the information design of your site. They read text, make associations with links, view graphics, and, depending on the freedom of your design, create their own path through your information.

▶ Make Your Design Portable

Not only should you plan for a deliberate look and feel, but also you must test your design against the variable nature of the Web. You want to ensure that the greatest number of users can navigate your site reliably. Specifically, to be successful, your Web site design must be accessible across different browsers, operating systems, and computer platforms. Many designers make the mistake of testing in only one environment, assuming that their pages look the same to all of their users. Figure B-1 shows a page displayed in Internet Explorer 5.0, and Figure B-2 shows the same page in Netscape Navigator 4.0. The page is coded with standard CSS code that Netscape cannot interpret, so the design does not appear as the designer intended for Navigator users.

▶ Design for Low Bandwidth

If a site contains many separate images, consider that users who connect to the Web with a slow connection may have a long wait before the images download. Figure B-3 shows a site where the designers have made an attempt to accommodate users who have slower connections by providing minimal navigation cues in the alternate text for the images. Another option would have been to design a page that is less graphics-intensive so it would download quickly for all users, rather than only for those with faster connections.

▶ Plan for Clear Presentation and Easy Access

Your information design—the presentation and organization of your information—is the single most important factor in determining the success of your site. Your graphics and navigation options must present a variety of options to the users without detracting from their quest for information. A visitor to your site may choose to browse randomly or look for specific information. Often users arrive at a page looking for information that is low in the hierarchy of information. Sometimes users arrive at your site seeking a specific piece of information, such as a telephone number or order form. Anticipate and plan for the actions and paths that users may choose when they traverse your site. Provide direct links to the areas of your site that you feel will be most in demand.

▶ Present Your Information So It Is Easy to Read

Many Web sites fail these criteria by using too many fonts, colors, and lengthy passages of text. Rather than presenting endlessly scrolling pages, break information into smaller chunks and link them with hypertext. The computer display is a poor reading medium. The low resolution degrades legibility. The light source coming from behind the text tires the eye. Provide contrasting colors that are easy to read and easy on the eye, such as dark colors against a light or white background.

FIGURE B-1: Site in Internet Explorer 5.0

Cursive font

Border on image

Image floats left of text

FIGURE B-2: Site in Netscape Navigator 4.0

Cursive font does not display

Border on image does not display

Image does not float next to text

Text displays further down the page

FIGURE B-3: Web page before images are loaded

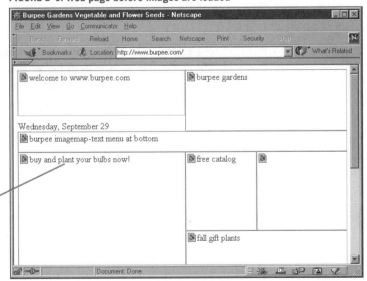

ALT attributes provide users with some information about images that are going to load

Web Design

Designing the Whole Site

When designing your site, plan the unifying themes and structure that will hold the pages together. Your choices of colors, fonts, graphics, and page layout should communicate a visual theme to the users that orients them to your site's content. When you design the whole site, you must consider more than each individual page. For a well-integrated site, create smooth transitions, use a grid to provide visual structure, and use active white space. Plan to create a unified look among the sections and pages of your site. Pages that share the same color scheme, navigation icons, and identifying graphics create a smooth transition from the main page to the secondary page and develop a unified look and feel for the Web site.

▶ Your Web site should reflect the impression that you or your organization wants to convey. For example, Figure B-4 shows the main page of the NASA Web site. The text-based page presents a sober image, and, indeed, the content provides serious scientific information. NASA also maintains a Web site for children, as shown in Figure B-5.

▶ Reinforce the identifying elements of the site and create smooth transitions from one page to another by repeating colors and fonts and by using a page layout that allows various hierarchical levels. Avoid random, jarring changes in your format, unless this is the effect you want to achieve. For example, consider keeping a logo in the same place on all pages for consistency. Consistency creates smooth transition from one page to the next, reassures viewers that they are traveling within the boundaries of your site, and helps them find information. The overall design of a page at any information level should reflect the identity of the site. Think of users turning the pages of a periodical when they browse from Web page to Web page. Although each page should be a complete entity, it also is a part of the whole site.

▶ The grid or page template you choose for your page design imposes the structure of a Web page. The **grid** is a conceptual layout device that organizes the page into columns and rows. You can impose a grid to provide visual consistency throughout your site. You can use the grid to enforce structure, but you also can break out of the grid to provide variety and highlight important information.

▶ HTML authors use the HTML table elements to build the grid for their pages. Although originally designed for tabular data, designers use the table elements as a tool for building the type of columnar grid structure they are accustomed to using in traditional print media. Most well-designed sites use tables in one form or another to provide structure and consistency to their pages. With table borders turned off, users cannot tell a table holds the layout together. What they see is a coherent, well-structured page.

▶ When designing a site, the main page and secondary pages should share a number of characteristics, such as consistent background graphics, consistent placement of navigation information, vertical rule that provides structure, consistent font usage, and a logo that brands the site. The continuity between pages enforces the feeling of a whole piece of work.

tip

Provide grounding for the user by placing navigation elements in the same position on each page. Users will orient themselves quickly to your navigation structure. Use the same navigation graphics throughout the site to provide consistency, and reuse graphics stored in the cache.

FIGURE B-4: NASA Web site

The use of subdued colors, familiar business-oriented fonts, and structured linear columns underscores the content and emphasizes the scientific theme

FIGURE B-5: NASA Web site for kids

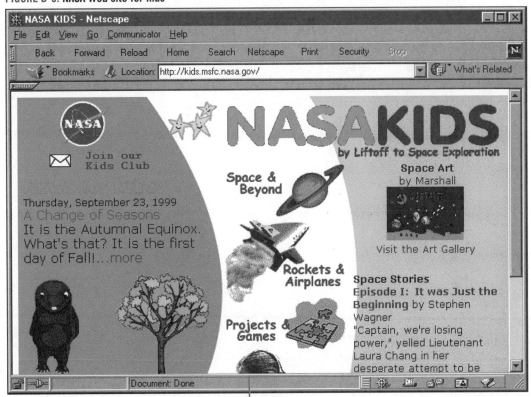

The use of bright colors, an open and friendly font, a dynamic structure, and simple appealing graphics presents a livelier and more playful theme

Focusing on White Space

White space is the blank area of a page. You should use white space deliberately in your design, rather than as an afterthought. Good use of white space guides the reader and defines the areas of your page.

Details

- ▶ White space that is used deliberately is called **active white space**. Active white space is an integral part of your design that structures and separates content. Sometimes the strongest part of a design is the active white space. **Passive white space** is the blank area that borders the screen or results from mismatched shapes. Figure B-6 illustrates active versus passive space.

- ▶ Content presentation can become confused when designers do not use enough active white space to separate and define content. The AOL Web site shown in Figure B-7 would be easier to scan if it used more active white space between the content areas. Notice how the lack of active white space creates the impression that the page contains too much information and that it is difficult to find the piece of information you want.

- ▶ A Web page with generous amounts of active white space makes it much easier to read. Plenty of active white space reduces clutter and clarifies the organization of your ideas. Figure B-8 shows the National Gallery of Art Web site, which has generous areas of active white space.

- ▶ Companies that create design software, such as Adobe, understand that their audience is sensitive to visual design. Because of this, their sites should be visually appealing, adhere to graphic-design rules, and present accessible information. Visit Adobe's site at *www.adobe.com* for an example.

Designing Tips

Keep in mind that readers have different habits when reading online. They scan more and read less, skimming long pages quickly as they scroll through the text. Include plenty of headings so users can find content quickly. Control the horizontal length of your text to provide complete, easy-to-read columns. Keep the seven-plus-or-minus-two rule of information design in mind; that is, users cannot comprehend more than seven plus or minus two steps or segments of information at one time. For example, a well-written procedure would contain no more than nine steps.

FIGURE B-6: Active vs. passive space

Active white space

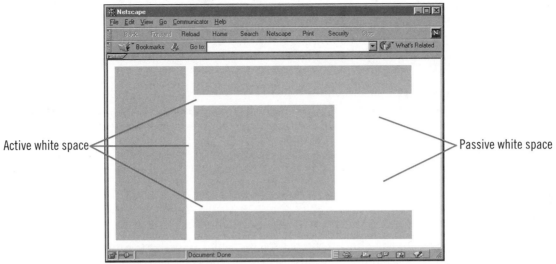

Passive white space

FIGURE B-7: AOL Web page

FIGURE B-8: National Gallery of Art Web page

White space separates columns

White space sets off heading and highlights content descriptions

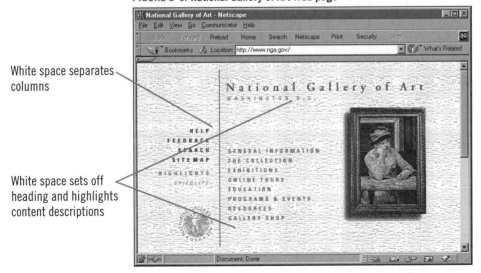

Designing for the User

What do users want when they get to your site? Are they trying to find customer support and troubleshooting help, or do they want to buy something? Do they want to read articles or search for information? Once you know what your users want from your site, you can evaluate how the design reflects the audience profile.

Details

► Keep your design efforts centered solely around your users. Knowing your audience answers almost all design questions—if it serves the audience, keep it; if it is potentially distracting or annoying, eliminate it. Find out what users expect from your site. If you can, survey them with an online form. Create a profile of your average user by compiling responses to basic questions.

► Figure B-9 shows E!online, an entertainment news site. The four-column main page contains competing content that draws the user's eye, such as animations, a Java text scroll, bright colors, and familiar shapes. The overall effect is decidedly similar to television—familiar territory for E!online's audience.

► Pen & Ink's Web site, shown in Figure B-10, projects a strong smell of printer's ink. Other than the black and white photo, the main page components are textual. The prominent logo features a text element—the ampersand. Strong contrasting colors highlight the links. The layout evokes quill pens and lead type, which is exactly what the literary-minded user would like in an online journal.

► Think about how the user wants to interact with the information on your Web page. Design for your content type, and decide if the user will read or scan your pages. For example, suppose your page is a collection of links, such as a main page or section page. Users want to interact with these types of pages by scanning the content, scrolling if necessary, pointing to graphics to see if they are hyperlinked, and clicking linked text. Design for this type of user interaction by using meaningful column headings, linked text, and short descriptions. Organize links into related topic groups, and separate groupings with white space, graphics, or background color.

FIGURE B-9: E!online Web page

Java text scroll

Animated art

Shapes remind you of television sets

FIGURE B-10: Pen & Ink Web page

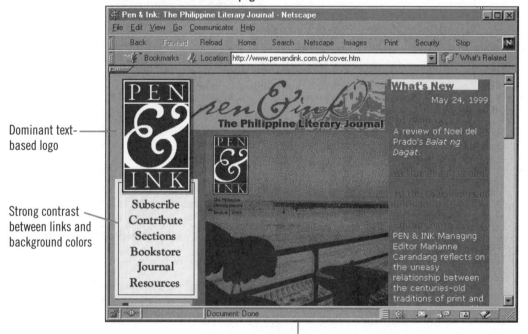

Dominant text-based logo

Strong contrast between links and background colors

Primarily text-based objects

Designing for Text-Intensive Sites

Suppose your Web page is an article that contains large blocks of text. Your user is accustomed to interacting with pages of text by scrolling and possibly clicking hyperlinked words of interest. The links may be in the body of the article or contained in a sidebar. Design your pages for this type of content by keeping paragraphs short for online consumption. Make reading easier by using a text column that is narrower than the width of the screen. Keep your text legible by providing enough contrast between foreground and background colors. Provide links that allow the user to jump quickly to related content.

Understanding Viewing Patterns

Details

It is difficult to predict the user's exact viewing path. There is, however, general agreement on the relative areas of screen importance. Figure B-11 depicts an example of a possible layout. The sections of screen real estate are ranked in order of importance. The user can traverse a page in a variety of ways. Human-engineering studies show a wide range of results when tracking user's eye movements. As you plan your design to guide the user's eye, consider ranking the information you want to display in the following way: Position the most important information in the middle of the window, the next most important across the top, and so on, with the least important or static information in the left margin.

▶ As a function of normal reading habits, the user's eye may move from left to right and back again. Figure B-12 shows this viewing pattern applied to a Pen & Ink Web page. Because this Web site is designed for users who are most comfortable with paper-based information, the page encourages a paper-based reading pattern.

▶ In contrast, when viewing landscape-based displays, such as televisions, users may scan information following a clockwise pattern. Figure B-13 shows this viewing style overlaying the E!online Web site. As the users' eyes sweep over the page, they can take in most of the main content. Because this site is designed for users who are most accustomed to screen-based information, the page encourages a screen-based viewing pattern.

▶ Knowing these common user habits can help you decide where to focus the user's attention by object placement, text weight, and color use. Think about your grid structure and how you want to break out of it to attract attention. Use text weight and size to communicate relative importance of information. Break up sections with rules or active white space. Use shapes and color to reinforce location or topic. Get to know your users, and consider the two sample viewing methods described above as you experiment with content placement based on the way these users will view the page.

▶ Do not make users navigate through too many layers of your Web site to find the information they want. Structure your Web site to include section or topic-level navigation pages so users quickly find their path. Provide prominent navigation cues that quickly take your users to the content they desire. For example, a standard navigation bar consistently placed on every page reassures users that they will not get lost and lets them move through the site with flexibility.

▶ A site map can graphically display a user's location in your Web site.

A graphical view of the Web site can show all the individual pages and the section in which they reside. It can also provide a text box where users can enter keywords to find related information. Another option is to include a page that allows users to orient themselves to the site's content or search the site.

▶ The Web site shown in Figure B-14 displays a clever site map that reflects the target audience of the site. The site uses a house metaphor to organize content. The site map lets you click any room of the house to view that section of content. Text links provide brief descriptions and an alternate navigation method.

FIGURE B-11: Areas of screen importance

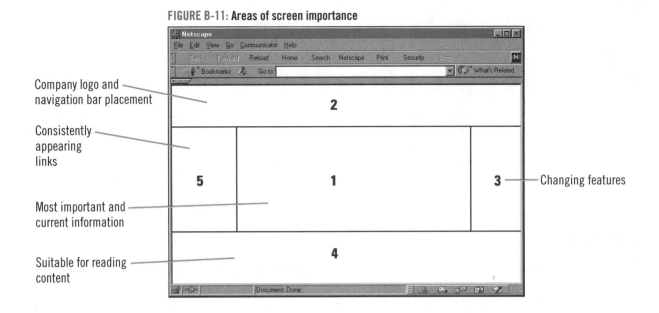

Company logo and navigation bar placement

Consistently appearing links

Most important and current information

Suitable for reading content

2

5   1   3 ——— Changing features

4

FIGURE B-12: Paper-based reading pattern

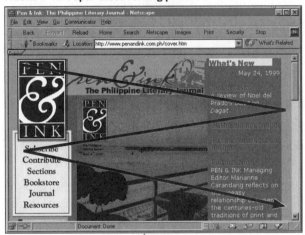

Scanning the Web site

FIGURE B-13: Screen-based reading pattern

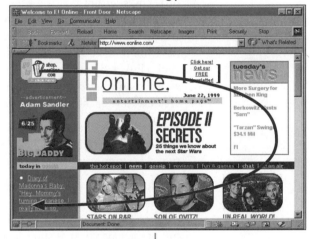

Scanning the Web site

FIGURE B-14: Visual metaphor for the site map

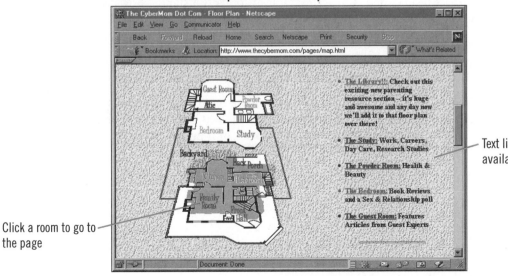

Text links are also available

Click a room to go to the page

Web Design

Linking with Hypertext

Unlike paper-based authors, as a hypertext author you have the luxury of adding clickable text and images where necessary to guide users through your information. This powerful ability comes with a measure of responsibility. You make the decisions that determine how users move through your site and process information.

Details

▶ Readers browsing through magazines can flip to any page in any order they desire. You can replicate this nonlinear reading method on your Web site with links that let users move from page to page or section to section. With thoughtful hypertext writing, you can engage readers in a whole new way.

▶ Many sites have separate columns of links and topics, but many do not provide links within the text. Links within text is a powerful hypertext feature that is not used enough. You can weave your links into your prose to offer a variety of paths. Figure B-15 shows a page from *Arctic Dawn: The Journeys of Samuel Hearne*. This is an online hypertext version of an explorer's journal from the 1700s. Note how the hypertext links are worked directly into the text. When users click a link, they move to another page of information; from that page they either can go back or move to another page of information, and so on. The abundant hypertext links allow users to create a view of the site's information that is uniquely their own.

▶ Avoid the "Click here" syndrome illustrated in Figure B-16. The habit of creating a link that consists of the meaningless "Click here" phrases lacks the power you can apply by using helpful textual clues to move the user to the destination of the link.

▶ Provide plenty of links to let the user get around quickly. Use links to let the user return to the navigation section of your page, to a site map, or to the main page. Do not make the user scroll through lengthy columns. Provide links that let the user jump down the page, jump back to the top of the page, or that show a clear way back to higher levels of your content.

▶ A hypertext table of contents, as shown in Figure B-17, lets the users pick the exact topics they want to view. The benefit of a hypertext table of contents is the color-coding that shows users which pages they have visited. By default, links are blue when new; they change to purple after they have been visited. A hypertext table of contents instantly shows users where they have been and where they have yet to go.

▶ Glossaries and other densely packed documents become much easier to navigate with the addition of hypertext. A hypertext glossary offers an alphabetic listing of easy-to-click letters that link to the section for each specific letter and provides plenty of navigation choices for the user.

▶ A good site provides alternate methods of linking to accommodate a variety of users. It is generally a sound idea to duplicate image links with text links in case users have their images turned off in the browser or use a text-based browser, or if images fail to download.

FIGURE B-15: Good use of textual links

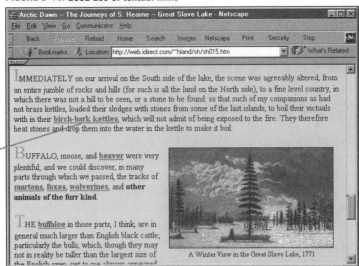

Links in context provide information and allow you to view the site in your own way

FIGURE B-16: "Click here" syndrome

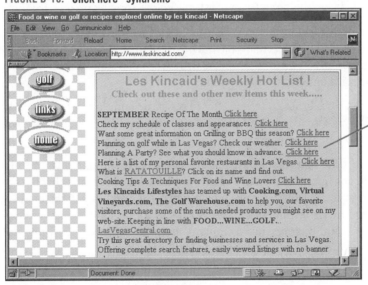

Meaningless navigation clues

FIGURE B-17: Tracking viewed pages

Purple links show users where they have been

Blue links show users where they have yet to go

Web Design

Restricting the Amount of Information

You should always be considerate of your users and not overload the page with unnecessary information. Users should not have to wade through oceans of text and images to find the critical information they seek. Rather than crowding too much information onto any one Web page, you would do better by providing clear links to additional pages to better spread out the content. You must always remain conscious of the cognitive load of the users, who often think that Web pages hold too much information. Remember, the way you choose to present your information directly relates to how accessible the Web page is for users. There are techniques you can use if you have to fill the page up with text or images that can help make it seem less dense.

Details

► AOL's Web site, shown in Figure B-18, offers a dizzying array of Web resources. It is intentionally designed this way because it is intended to be read as a scanning page. The user may spend a few seconds looking for a particular topic before moving on by selecting a link.

► Similarly, the About.com Web site, presented in Figure B-19, squeezes a large amount of varied information into a small space. The more time you spend viewing various Web sites, the better your ability to distinguish those with too much information on each page from those with just the right amount of information.

► When you create a site, you should resist the temptation to overload users with too much information. Provide enough clues to let them find the content they want, and use links to divide content between pages.

► Plan a site that stands out, delivers its message, and presents information that is both accessible and engaging. In this book alone, you have seen Web sites that have a wide variety of looks, so it is easy to see why so many Web designers get caught up in the medium and forget their message. The lure of technology makes it easy to forget that you still are trying to communicate with words and pictures, just as humans have for centuries. Adapting those elements to online display for effective communication is the challenge.

tip

Web pages change frequently, and by the time you read this book, these pages may have changed to present the information in a less dense fashion.

FIGURE B-18: AOL Web site

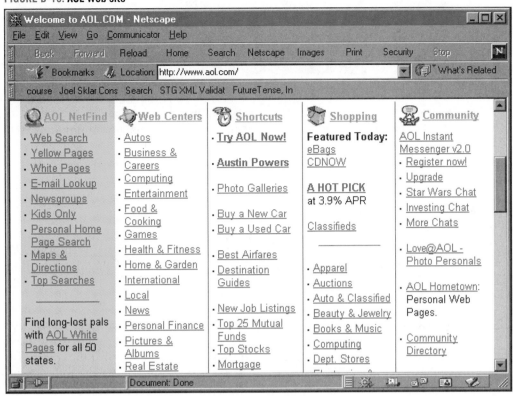

FIGURE B-19: About.com Web site

Designing for the Screen

What the computer displays (in other words, the destination for your Web pages) is very different from print-based media. As such, you must take the shape of the screen, the colors you select, and the varying resolutions available into account when planning your Web site.

Details

► The shape of a computer screen is a critical factor in designing Web pages. Although most paper-based media are portrait oriented, the computer screen is **landscape oriented**—that is, wider than it is tall. Your page design must reflect the space within which it will be displayed and read.

► Whereas a piece of paper reflects light, a computer screen has light passing through it from behind. This changes the nature of the colors and contrasts you choose to use. Design pages that provide enough contrast for the user to read, but not so much that the colors distract from the content easily. Avoid light text on a light background and dark text on dark backgrounds. For example, the Media Center Web site, illustrated in Figure B-20, uses blue links on a black background, making the links illegible.

► Computer screens use a much lower resolution than the printed page. Graphics and text that would look fine on a laser printer at 600 dpi are coarse and grainy at 72 dpi, the typical resolution for a computer monitor. Because of the screen graininess, italic text is especially hard to read in paragraph format.

► Although tempting, it often is a poor choice to take documents that are formatted for print and post them online without considering the destination medium. In most cases, a document that is perfectly legible on paper is hard to negotiate online. The text length, font, and content length will not transfer successfully to the computer screen.

Figure B-21 shows a section of text from Lewis Carroll's *Alice in Wonderland* formatted as if it were a page from a book.

► In contrast, Figure B-22 shows the same section of the text designed for online display. The white space creates a text column that enforces the vertical flow of the page. The illustrations break up the text and relieve the user's eye. The differences between these two pages show that text must be prepared thoughtfully for online display.

FIGURE B-20: Hard-to-read links

Lack of color contrast with background makes links hard to read

FIGURE B-21: Text formatted for paper

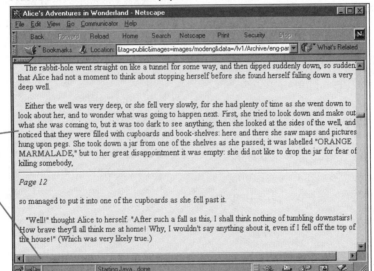

Text is dense and fills screen in large gray blocks

User must scroll from left to right to read an entire line because text does not fit screen resolution of 640 × 480

FIGURE B-22: Text formatted for the screen

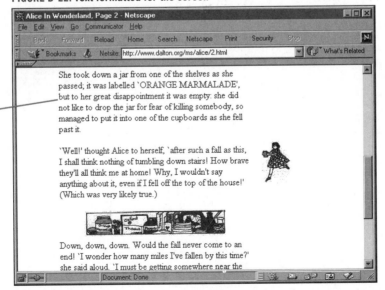

The text width is short and easy to read without horizontal scrolling

Web Design

Practice

► Concepts Review

Fill in the blank with the best answer.

1. The _look/feel_ refers to the interface the user must navigate in a Web site.
2. Hypertext links are the color _Blue_ by default in a Web page.
3. Create smooth ~~transitions~~ to move from one page to the next and reassure viewers that they are traveling within the boundaries of your site.
4. White space that is used deliberately is called _active white space_.
5. _Passive whites_ is the blank area that borders the screen or results from mismatched shapes.
6. The computer monitor as display medium has no effect on the legibility of the information in a Web site. True/(False) _____
7. You should use _Links_ to divide content between pages.
8. Using a _grid_ layout enhances Web design and enforces a structure and visual consistency.
9. What are three ways to focus a user's attention on your Web site? _____, _____, and _____.

10. A _hypertext_ (glossary) offers an alphabetic listing of easy-to-click letters that link to the section for each specific letter and provides plenty of navigation choices for the user.
11. Use the same navigation graphics throughout the site to provide consistency, and reuse graphics stored in the _cache_.
12. Use a _hypertext_ table of contents so that the built-in color properties of the link instantly show users the contents they have visited already.
13. One of the benefits of _textual linking_ is that users can choose links within the context of the information they desire, allowing them to create their own path through the site.
14. Using ~~hypertext~~ _click here_ as link text is ineffective because it provides the user with no clues to the destination content.
15. Computer screens use a much _lower_ resolution than the printed page.

1. create smooth transitions between pg's.
2. use grid to provide visual structure.
3. use white space actively.

► Explore Further. . .

1. Describe the difference between reading and scanning a page.

Users read when they find info they want, they scan when they're looking for links that interest them.

2. Describe at least three differences between paper-based and screen-based design.

1. Comp display = landscape paper disp. = portrait

2. Comp. disp. affect the colour/contrast of web pages

3. Users tire easily when reading online.

3. Describe the three ways to create a unified look for your site.

1. Use white space actively   3. Use grid to provide visual structure.

2. Provide consistency for user

4. Describe how to create a smooth transition between pages of a Web site.

1. consistent placement of navigation info   3. Cons. grid usage.

2. " typeface usage.

5. Describe a good strategy to format text for online display.

1. Avoid lrg blocks of italic text   3. Use plenty of white space

2. Use shorter text width.   4. Chunk text into smaller segments.

▶ Independent Challenges

1. As you become more familiar with different Web sites based on your experience on the Internet, you will become more aware of those sites that are easy to use and are well designed. Of course, there is a lot of subjectivity in determining good design, but your experience and the principles of design that you have learned in this unit should help you find those sites that appear to be designed well.

a. Log on to the Internet, and browse the Web for examples of good Web design. Find one site that you want to use for this Independent Challenge. Or, you can use the Student Online Companion site at *www.course.com/ illustrated/designingsites* and review the sites suggested there.

b. Using a screen-capture program, capture screens that show two levels of information from that Web site. You can capture a screen by pressing [Print Screen] on your keyboard. Then insert the screen in a document by opening your word-processing program, and then pressing [Ctrl][V] on the keyboard, clicking the Paste button, or clicking the Paste command on a menu.

c. Print the document with the images of the screens from the Web pages.

d. On the printout, draw lines to indicate the unifying characteristics of the pages.

e. Indicate the areas of active and passive white space.

f. Use your word processor to write a short essay critiquing the Web site's design. Be sure to describe the structural layout of the site and determine whether the information is presented clearly and is easily accessible. Type **Your Name** at the bottom of the document, save the document, print a copy, and then close it.

g. Attach this essay to the printout of the good Web-design images.

2. As you become more familiar with different Web sites based on your experience on the Internet, you will become more aware of those sites that have good navigation systems and those that do not. Of course, there is a lot of subjectivity in determining good navigation, and you may have different preferences than other users. Your experience and what you have learned in this unit about design principles should help you find those sites that generally result in a site that is easy to navigate.

a. Log on to the Internet, and browse the Web for examples of sites that use unique navigation methods. Find one site that you want to use for this Independent Challenge. Or, you can use the Student Online Companion site at *www.course.com/illustrated/designingsites* and review the sites suggested there.

b. Using a screen-capture program, capture one screen, then navigate to the next screen, remember what you used to get there, and capture the second screen. (You can capture a screen by pressing [Print Screen] on your keyboard. Then insert the screen in a document by opening your word-processing program, and then pressing [Ctrl][V] on the keyboard, clicking the Paste button, or clicking the Paste command on a menu.)

c. If you find that the site uses more than one method to get to different content levels or pages, capture and print those sequences of screens too.

d. Insert the screens in a document showing the levels of information from the Web site.

e. Print the images of the screens from the Web pages from the site.

f. Indicate on the printout how you went from one screen to the next.

g. Use your word processor to write a short essay describing why the navigation is unique and why it is or is not successful. Type **Your Name** at the bottom of the document, save the document, print a copy, and then close it.

h. Attach your printouts to the essay.

3. As you become more familiar with different Web sites based on your experience on the Internet, you will become more aware of those sites that are not designed well and are difficult to use. Of course, there is a lot of subjectivity in determining good design, but your experience and what you have learned in this unit about which design issues to avoid should help you find those sites that are not designed well.

a. Log on to the Internet, and browse the Web for examples of sites that you think could benefit from changes in design. Find one site that you want to use for this Independent Challenge.

b. Using a screen-capture program, capture screens that show two levels of information from the Web site.

c. Print two copies of the two pages with the images of the screens from the Web pages from the site. You will work with one copy and set the originals aside.

d. On the printout, draw lines to indicate the jarring or distracting inconsistencies of the site.

e. On the same printout, write notes that make recommendations for improving the site design.

f. Using scissors, take the second copy of the images and cut out the main elements of each page. Rearrange the elements and paste them in a design that you feel improves the site. Use tape to put it back together.

g. Use your word processor to write a short essay critiquing the Web site's design. Describe the structural layout of the site, and describe why you feel that the information is not presented clearly and is not easily accessible. Explain your reasons for the way you have rearranged the elements of the site. Compare and contrast the original to your improved design. Type **Your Name** at the bottom of the document, save the document, print a copy, and then close it.

h. Attach this essay to the printout of the poorly designed Web images with your notes.

You will continue to work on the site you began in Unit A. You will recall that to complete the ongoing case study for this book, you must create a complete, stand-alone Web site. The site must contain from six to ten pages, displaying at least three levels of information. You already have selected your own content in Unit A. As you progress through the units of the book, you will complete different facets of the Web site construction, resulting in a complete Web site.

a. Visualize the page design for your site by sketching a number of page layouts for different information levels of the site. For example, sketch the main page, a secondary page, and a content page. You do not have to be concerned with the exact look of the elements.

b. Indicate the main components of the pages, such as headings, navigation cues, links, text areas, and so on.

c. Start to organize your site. Create a visual diagram that indicates the main page, section pages, content pages, etc. Indicate the links between the pages. Indicate whether you will provide alternate navigation choices, such as a table of contents and site map.

▶ Visual Workshop

1. In the following Visual Workshop you will write a short essay explaining the design issues in the main and secondary Web pages from the site shown in Figure B-23. Include a discussion about the navigation, as well as the elements that create a unifying look.

FIGURE B-23

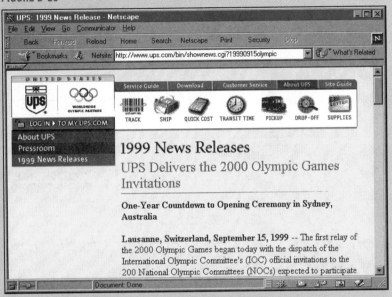

► # Visual Workshop

2. This Visual Workshop deals with the AOL Web site. You may already be familiar with it. Figure B-24 shows the first part of the page at 800 × 600 resolution. The page extends down to several sections of links not visible in this screen. If you can, go to the site at *www.aol.com* to see how this is organized. Then write a short essay discussing how the information on this Web page could have been arranged better. Identify all the various links and areas on the page, include a discussion about the navigation, and cite any additional elements that could be created to present a clearer, easier way to move around and find information in this Web site.

FIGURE B-24

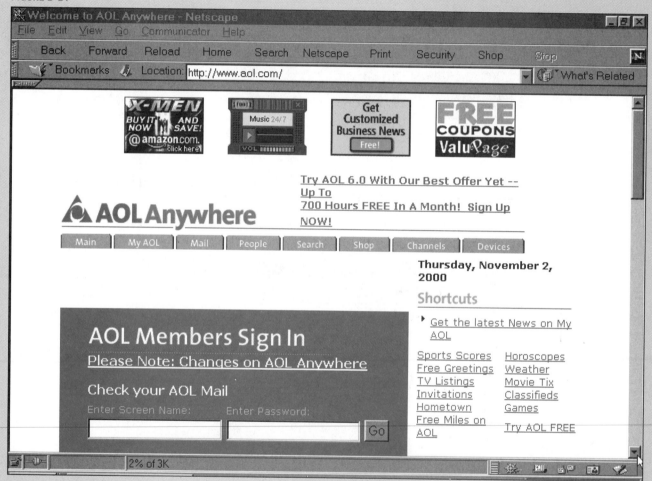

Unit C

Planning
the Site

When faced with the daunting task of building or restructuring a Web site, many designers simply do not know where to begin. Rather than rushing straight to the computer and coding your site, the best way to start is by picking up a pencil and paper and sketching out your site design. This unit walks you through the planning process, allowing you to set a framework for development. If you incorporate planning into the site-development process, you will have to do less recoding when you actually sit down at the computer.

Creating a Site Specification

As you start, it is important to determine your objectives for building a Web site. You may want to increase communication among employees, gain visibility, provide a service, attract new customers, or simply show the world you can code HTML. Properly maintained Web sites take a lot of work. Make sure you have a valid justification for building your site, other than just to say that you have a Web site.

Details

▶ Start your planning by creating a site specification. A **site specification** is the design document for your site. This document will enable you to answer a number of additional questions about your site. You can return to the site specification as you build your site to help maintain your focus. Figure C-1 shows a sample site specification.

▶ Answer the following questions in your site specification:

- Why are you building the Web site? Can you write a two- or three-paragraph mission statement that briefly defines the site?

- What do you envision as the goal of the site? What do you, your company, or your organization hope to gain from creating and maintaining a Web site?

- How will you judge the success of the site? What are the measuring factors you can use to assess the effectiveness of the site?

- Who is the target audience? What characteristics do they share? How will you find out more about them?

- What are the limiting technical factors affecting your site?

Design Matters

Using Shareware

Shareware are programs that users download and use for a trial period. Shareware programs, including all types of software that can help you with your Web site development, are readily available for you to try before you buy. Users then can register the software for a relatively small fee. Individuals or very small software companies usually develop shareware, so registering the software is important to support future development efforts. A popular and commonly used shareware program is WinZip. WinZip, which is available at *www.winzip.com*, lets you work with ZIP archive files, which is the PC defacto standard for file compression and archiving. If you are sending or receiving files via e-mail, you will need WinZip to compress and uncompress these files. If you are working with a Macintosh computer, you can use Stuffit to compress your files. Stuffit Deluxe and Stuffit Lite, created by Aladdin Systems, Inc., are available in shareware versions at *www.aladdinsys.com* or *www.shareware.com*. If you are a PC user and someone sends you a Stuffit file, you can expand it with Aladdin's Expander program, which also is available freely at the Aladdin site.

FIGURE C-1: Sample site specification

Web Site Proposal for The Parenting Resource Center

Site Developer: Emily Heberlein
Total pages: 20

- **Why is the site necessary?**
- **Who is the audience? Who will maintain the site?**
- **What is the proposed site structure?**

Why is the site necessary?

Developing a Web site for this organization fills two needs:

1. Educating those in need of services on what services are available and how to get them — Goals of the site
2. Publicizing the organization to potential donors and/or volunteers, and letting them know how they can get involved

Who is the audience? Who will maintain the site?

The Parenting Resource Center (PRC) is a non-profit organization in Chicago that provides programs — Defines the target audience
and services to single parents and their families. While their target audience is all single parents, the
largest population they serve is single women with children, who experience poverty, substance
abuse/addiction, and incarceration. Their annual budget is about 1 million dollars, which they raise
through the efforts of their Board of Directors.

The intended audience of the site can be broken down to two groups:

1. single parents who need assistance
2. potential donors and volunteers

From my experience in the non-profit world, organizations and those who need services do not have the
latest technology or the time to learn it; it's peripheral to their goals and needs. Therefore, I anticipate
that this site's audience will be varied in their experience, connection speed, and browser choice. I plan
to make the site very accessible:

- Have a simple and intuitive design so inexperienced users can find information they need quickly — Technical considerations
- Make the download time quick by using a few simple, common graphics

Because PRC will ultimately maintain the site, I plan to use basic CSS to keep the content of the site
separate from the design. This will allow PRC to update the information easily without being concerned
with the design; so, anyone with basic computer skills will be able to update site content quickly and
easily.

According to Charles A Upsdell's Browser News , the overv
Netscape Navigator 4.0+ and IE 4.0+. While using CSS may
design optimally, they will still be able to access the content,
think the need to make the site easy to maintain by SPRC ou
without CSS compatible browsers.

What is the proposed site structure?

Here is an overview of the content that will be included. The navigation bar will always appear on the
left side of the Web page. The Home Page will be a clean, simple page, and will let users know what
PRC is, how they can get in touch, and what else is in the site. From the home page, users will have
links to the following main categories:

- About Us (overview of organization, staff, mission statement)
- What's New? (new programs, special events, etc.)
- Programs (services that are available, when, where, to who, etc.)
  - There will be one page for each program (totalling 8 pages).
- Donate
  From the donate page, visitors can link to:
  - Donate your time (information on volunteering, contact info, and a form to request information)
  - Help fund the programs (form to request information, link to demographic and budget allocation information, which can also be accessed from About Us)
- Resources and Links

Preliminary plan for the site

Web Design

Identifying the Content Goal

Your objectives and your users' objectives—what you want the Web site to accomplish and what your users want from your site—may differ. Examine closely what type of site you are building. For example, site designers often are more concerned with the visual aspects of a Web site, such as the quality of the graphics and the use of animation. Your users probably care more about how quickly they can find information. Adopt your users' perspective. Think about the type of content you are presenting and look to the Web for examples of how best to present it. The following types of Web sites demonstrate ways to focus your content.

Details

▶ **Billboard**

These sites establish a Web presence for a business or commercial venture. In many cases, they are informational and offer no true Web-based content, acting as an online brochure rather than offering Web-based interaction. Many businesses build this type of site first, then slowly add functions, such as online ordering and product demonstrations, as they become more comfortable with the medium. The WAVE Web site shown in Figure C-2 is an example of a billboard site.

▶ **Publishing**

Most major newspapers and periodicals now boast an online counterpart. *The New York Times* home page is shown in Figure C-3. These are some of the most ambitious sites on the Web in the breadth and depth of content, usually containing multiple levels of information with many page templates. Many publishing sites use special software that enables them to publish Web pages by drawing the content from the same databases as the paper-based versions.

▶ **Special Interest, Public Interest, and Nonprofit Organization**

No matter what your special interest, there is a Web site devoted to it, including news and current information for volunteers, devotees, novices, a specific audience, or the general public. Public service Web sites contain links, information, downloadable files, addresses, and telephone numbers that can help you solve a problem. Nonprofit organizations can state their manifesto, seek volunteers, and foster a grass-roots virtual community. See Figure C-4.

▶ **Virtual Gallery**

The Web is a great place to show off samples of all types of art and design. Photographers and artists can display samples of their work; musicians can post audio files of their songs on a site; and writers and poets can offer sections of text or complete manuscripts on various sites as well.

tip

Any copyrighted material you display on a Web site can be downloaded to a user's machine without your permission. Software companies such as Digimarc (*www.digimarc.com*) offer digital watermarking technology that lets artists embed digital copyright information in their electronic files as a deterrent to piracy of proprietary content. This information cannot be seen or altered by the user.

▶ **E-commerce, Catalog, and Online Shopping**

The Web has become a viable shopping medium that will continue to expand as more users improve their Internet access and learn to trust the security of online commerce. Many software vendors offer turnkey systems that can integrate with existing databases to speed the development of a commerce site. Web commerce already has begun to make inroads on traditional retailing, and it offers many advantages over mail-order shopping, such as letting the customer know immediately if an item is in stock. Other types of commerce on the Web include stock trading, airline ticketing, and auctions. A good e-commerce site provides users with quick access to the item they want, detailed product descriptions, and easy secure ordering.

▶ **Product Support**

The Web is a boon to consumers who need help with a product. Manufacturers can disseminate information, upgrades, troubleshooting advice, documentation, and online tutorials on their Web site. Companies that provide product help information on the Web often find that their customer support calls decrease. Software companies especially benefit from the Web. Users can download patches and upgrades and use trial versions of software before they buy.

FIGURE C-2: WAVE billboard site

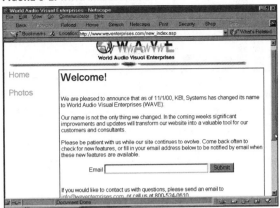

FIGURE C-3: The New York Times online

FIGURE C-4: Gilda's Club home page

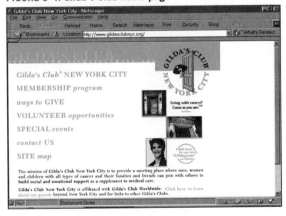

Intranets and Extranets

An intranet is a private computer network contained within an organization. An intranet works like the Internet, and many companies build Web sites that are accessible only to those who have access to their intranet. Additionally, many companies have telecommuting employees who need access to company policies, documentation, parts lists, pricing information, and other materials. These employees can be reached via an extranet, which is a part of the private intranet extended outside the organization using the Internet. Many organizations mandate a particular browser for employee use, making the Web designer's job a little bit easier because they only have to code and test for one browser.

Analyzing the Audience

If at all possible, analyze your audience and produce an audience definition—a profile of your average user. Contact your typical users or those who work with them, and try to find out the following information: What do users want when they come to your site? How do you attract them and entice them to return for repeat visits? What types of computers and connection speeds do your typical visitors use?

Details

► Finding answers to these questions is especially difficult when your medium is the Web. Even though you may find that your users fit no common profile, there are ways to gather useful information about them. One way is to create an online survey as part of your site. Enticements often help get responses. If possible, offer an incentive for filling out the survey, such as a product giveaway, t-shirt, or imprinted mouse pad. Figures C-5 and C-6 show a portion of an online survey from the Millipore Corporation. The questions survey Millipore's customers on whether they would purchase products online, and Millipore provides an incentive to fill out the form—they will send a baseball cap to the first 500 respondents. This is well worth Millipore's investment if they get quality information from the survey results.

► If you cannot survey your users, or if you feel you are not getting good survey results, try to imagine yourself as a member of your audience and adopt their perspective as you complete the survey. Table C-1 organizes questions to consider in a survey.

► You should continue soliciting user feedback to keep your site focused and the content fresh, and you may find you need to refine your content and presentation even after your site is built and running.

► Make your best effort to identify any limiting or universal technological factors that are particular to your audience. For example, if the audience is simply the typical Web surfer, then you may have to design for the lowest common denominator, using fewer graphics and considering 640 × 480 as the base screen resolution. If you primarily have a high-tech audience, a higher resolution or connection speed may apply. If you are designing an intranet site, you may have the luxury of knowing your users' exact operating systems and browser versions. Whatever the particulars, make sure to design at the correct level, or you will risk losing visitors.

FIGURE C-5: Online survey part 1

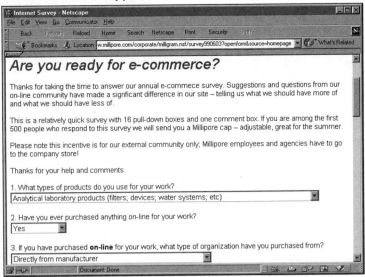

FIGURE C-6: Online survey part 2

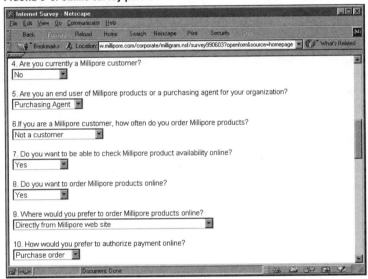

TABLE C-1: Creating survey questions

what you need to know	typical questions
Who are the typical members of your audience?	Male or female? Level of education? Reading and vocabulary level? Level of technical aptitude?
Why do people come to your site?	Seeking information? Needing to download files? Looking for links to other Web sites?
Do you have a captive audience?	Is there a base of loyal customers that want up-to-date information? Are you designing for an intranet, where users are employees of an organization? How often will users return to your site? Is there a reason to come back?
Will other sites link to your site?	What links would you like to see?
What computing platform do your users have?	Typical connection speed? Type of browser? If on an intranet, is there a standard for browsers, connection, and screen resolution?

Building the Web Site Development Team

Although one person can maintain small Web sites, larger sites require a group of personnel filling a variety of roles. The line can be blurred between the roles, and, of course, many aspects of site design require more than one head to solve a problem. The following roles are examples of the types of talent necessary to build a larger, well-conceived site.

Details

▶ **Server Administrators**

Get to know and appreciate the technical people that run your Web server. They take care of the sticky technical issues like firewalls, modem ports, internal security, file administration, and back-up procedures. Consult with them to determine your Web site's default filename and directory structure. They also can generate reports that will tell you how many visitors your site is attracting, where the visitors are coming from, and what pages they like best. There are many companies that offer Web-tracking software as shown in Figure C-7.

▶ **HTML Coders**

These are the people responsible for creating the HTML code and troubleshooting the site. Most HTML coders now are using HTML editors to create code, but any self-respecting HTML coder knows how to open the HTML file in a text editor and code by hand. The coders also are responsible for testing and evaluating the site across various operating systems and Web browsers.

▶ **Designers**

Designers are the graphic artists responsible for the look of the site. Many will use design software, such as Adobe PhotoShop, the industry standard graphic-design program. Designers contribute to the page template design, navigation icons, color scheme, and logos. If your site uses photographic content, the designers will be called upon to prepare the photos for online display.

▶ **Writers and Information Designers**

Writers prepare content for online display, which includes designing hypertext information and navigation paths. Additionally, writers should be responsible for creating a site style guide and typographic conventions. The writers are responsible for consistency, grammar, spelling, and tone. They also work closely with the designers to develop the page templates to create a consistent design through the site. Web development tools often come with predefined templates; Figure C-8 shows the general templates available with FrontPage 2000.

▶ **Software Programmers**

Programmers write the programs you need to build interaction into your site. They may write a variety of applications, including Common Gateway Interface (CGI) scripts, Java scripts, and back-end applications that interact with a database. Commerce sites will especially need the talents of a programming staff.

▶ **Database Administrators**

The people who are responsible for maintaining the databases play an important role in commercial Web sites. They make sure that your data is accessible and safe as well as accurate and up-to-date.

▶ **Marketing**

The marketing department can generate content and provide exposure for the site. Promoting the site, researching competitors, establishing strategic partners, and maintaining the company profile are all roles that are critical to the success of the site.

FIGURE C-7: Web-tracking software

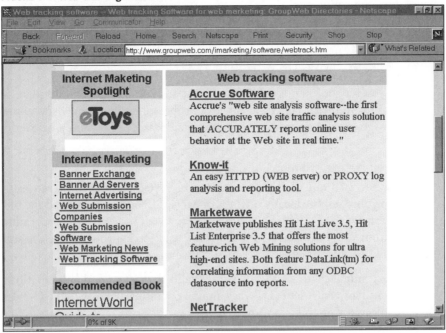

FIGURE C-8: Web templates

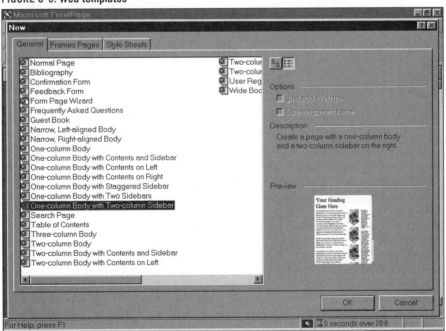

Web Design

Understanding Filenames

Before you set your hands on the keyboard and mouse, you should plan the file-naming conventions for your site. The importance of proper planning for how you name the files you create for the Web site and where and how you organize these files cannot be overlooked or overstated.

► **The Importance of Following File-Naming Conventions**

You have to find out what type of operating system your Web server uses. Typically, you will develop your Web site locally on a PC or Macintosh and then upload the files to the Web server as the last step in the publishing process. If the Web server runs an operating system that is different from your local development system, transferring your files to the server may break local URL links because of either filename or directory structure inconsistencies.

The maximum length of the filename, valid characters and punctuation, and sensitivity to upper- and lowercase letters all vary among operating systems. Table C-2 describes file-naming conventions for several operating systems.

► **Case Sensitivity**

If you have an image file named *Picture.gif*, for example, and you reference that file as <IMG SRC="picture.gif">, the image will display properly on a Macintosh or Windows machine. On a UNIX server, however, the image will not load properly because UNIX is case sensitive. To a UNIX machine, *Picture.gif* and *picture.gif* are two different files.

► **Character Exceptions**

Character use also is incompatible between operating systems. For example, the filename *my stuff.htm* is valid on a PC or Macintosh but not on a UNIX machine because of the space in the filename. If you transfer a Web site containing *my stuff.htm* to a UNIX server, the links to the file will not work. As another example, the filename *<section2>.htm* is valid on a Macintosh or UNIX machine, but if you transfer the files to a Windows NT server, the < > characters are not allowed.

► **File Extensions**

You should be careful and use the correct file extensions to identify your file to the browser. HTML text files must end in *.htm* or *.html*. You must be sure to add this extension when you are working in Notepad, which defaults to saving as *.txt*. You also must correctly specify image file formats in the file extensions. Joint Photographic Experts Group (JPEG) files must end in *.jpg* or *.jpeg*. Graphics Interchange Format (GIF) files must end in *.gif*. Portable Network Graphic (PNG) files must end in *.png*. There are many ways to learn about Web graphics, as you can see from the Web Graphics 101 Web page shown in Figure C-9.

► **The Default Main Page Name**

Every Web site has a default main page that displays when the browser requests the directory of the site rather than a specific file. This is indicated by a trailing slash in the URL, such as *http://www.mysite.com/*. In this instance, the Web server provides the index file, which usually is named *index.htm*. Windows NT, however, defaults to an index filename of *default.htm*, and other servers may be set to other names such as *main.htm* or *home.htm*. Before you start coding, check with your system administrator to verify the main page filename.

tip

It is best always to use lowercase letters for all filenames. Remember to use lowercase letters in filenames in your HTML code as well. Also, when naming your files, leave out special characters such as /, \, &, *, and blank spaces.

FIGURE C-9: Learning about Web graphics

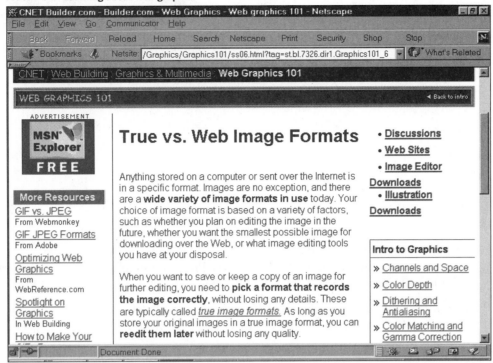

TABLE C-2: File naming conventions

operating system	file naming conventions
ISO 9660 standard	The filename consists of a maximum of eight letters followed by a period and a three-letter extension. Allowed characters are letters, numbers, and the underscore (_).
DOS and Windows 3.x (FAT file system)	The same as ISO 9660 but with these additional characters allowed: $ % ' ` - @ ^ ! & [ ] ( ) #
Microsoft Windows/NT, NTFS, and Windows 95 VFAT, Windows 98 FAT32	Maximum 255 letters, all characters allowed except: \ / * " < > |
Macintosh	Maximum 31 letters, all characters allowed except the colon (:)
UNIX	Maximum 255 letters, all characters allowed except the forward slash (/) and spaces

Solving the Filename Dilemma

The best way to overcome the restrictions of case sensitivity, character exceptions, and file extensions is to use the convention specified by the International Standards Organization (ISO) for all your files. This standardized naming convention (often called 8.3) specifies a maximum of eight letters followed by a period and a three-letter extension. Allowed characters are letters, numbers, and the underscore character. Thus, a filename in 8.3 means an eight-letter filename with a three-letter file extension, such as *mypage.htm* or chap_1.htm.

If you use the 8.3 file-naming convention on your development system, you will have little or no filename problems when you transfer your files to the Web server, regardless of the server's operating system. By sticking with this filename format, you ensure that your files will be portable across the greatest number of operating systems. Do not forget to use lowercase characters and omit special characters from your filenames to ensure compatibility.

Understanding URLs

A **Uniform Resource Locator (URL)** is the unique address of a file's location on the World Wide Web. Although you may know that URLs are the addresses you type into your browser to access a site, you may not realize that there are two types of URLs: complete and partial. This lesson discusses the importance of planning the URL for your site.

Details

▶ **Complete URLs**

A **complete URL** includes the protocol the browser uses to access the file; the server or domain name; the relative path; and the filename. Figure C-10 shows an example of a complete URL.

In the URL shown in Figure C-10, *http* is the protocol, and *www.mysite.com* is the domain name. The path shows that the destination file, *laptop.htm*, resides in the *business/trends* folder.

▶ **Partial URLs**

Use a partial URL when you are linking to a file that resides on your own computer. **Partial URLs** omit the protocol and domain or server name and specify the path to the file relative to one another on the same server. Files that reside in the same directory need no path information other than the filename. Figure C-11 shows an example of a partial URL.

▶ **Determining URLs**

The URL you chose will be your address on the Web. It is how your clients, customers, friends, family, students, or colleagues will find your site. You have to consider how you want to be identified. Obviously, you should not select a URL that might be offensive or inappropriate in any way. Additionally, you should consider that the URL has to be simple to type, fairly short, and also representative of the site. You do not want it to be too similar to commonly known sites so that a user will inadvertently type the wrong URL. Many common domain names are already registered, so the exact domain you want may not be available.

Use complete URLs in your HTML code when linking to another server. Use partial URLs when you link to files within your own site.

tip

When you are browsing the Web, you do not need to enter the protocol because the browser defaults to *http://*. However, in your code you must always include the protocol with a complete URL, otherwise the browser will not know how to connect to the location you specify.

FIGURE C-10: A complete URL

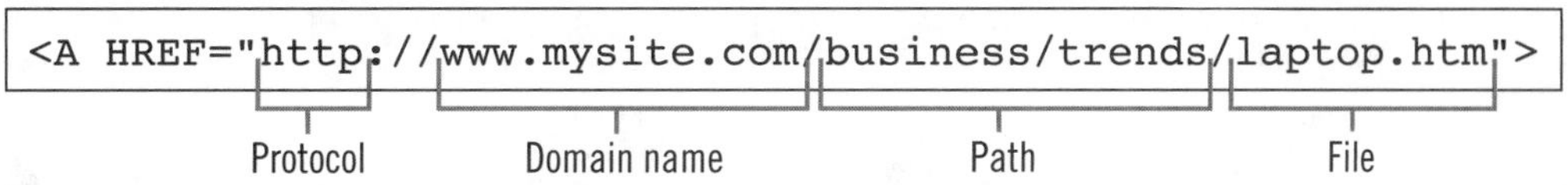

```
<A HREF="http://www.mysite.com/business/trends/laptop.htm">
```

Protocol   Domain name   Path   File

FIGURE C-11: A partial URL

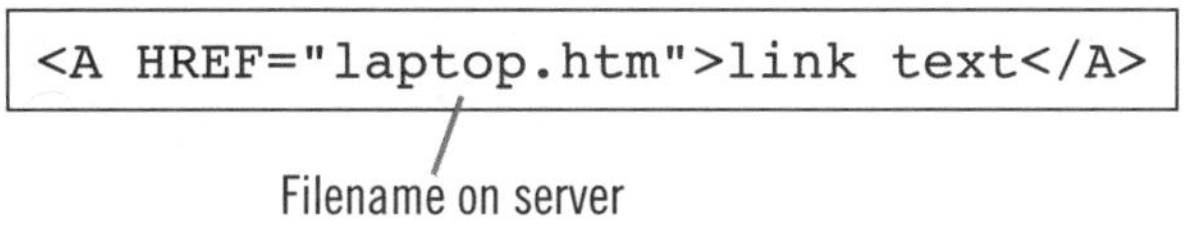

```
<A HREF="laptop.htm">link text</A>
```

Filename on server

Availability of Domain Names

If you want to see if a domain name is available, or to register your own domain name, visit Network Solutions at *www.networksolutions.com*. Network Solutions is the company responsible for registering *.com*, *.net*, and *.org* domain names and works in cooperation with the U.S. government. The Network Solutions home page is shown in Figure C-12. Over 5 million business and personal domain names are currently registered. The site contains a simple form that lets you enter the domain so that you can see if it is already registered.

FIGURE C-12: Network Solutions home page

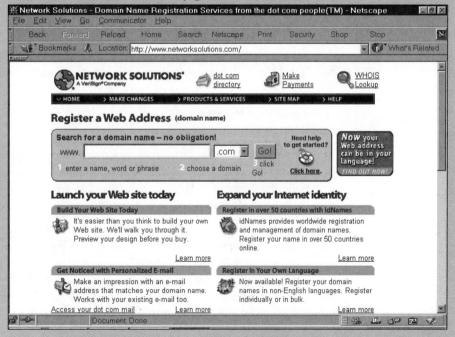

Web Design

Unit
C
Web Design

Understanding Directory Structure

You most likely will build your Web site on a computer that is different from the computer that will be hosting your site. Keep this in mind when you are designing the directory and file structure. When you complete your site, you will publish your files on the Web by transferring them to a Web server. A typical Web server has a user area that contains folders for each user. Your files are stored in your user area, along with other files from other Web sites stored in their respective user areas. The directory structure of the Web server affects the format of your site's URL.

Details

▶ Figure C-13 shows a typical Web server directory structure. If you do not register and pay for a domain name for your site, you will have a URL that reflects your path in the public area of the Web server. When you buy a domain name, the name you choose is an alias that points to your actual location on the Web server, as shown in Figure C-14. The figure shows that User2 has purchased *www.mysite.com* for a domain name. The actual path to User2's content has not changed, but the visitor to the site only sees the domain name. Now User2 can advertise the Web site with an easy-to-remember URL.

▶ Because your files will be transferred to another computer, any URLs you specify to link to other pages in your site must include paths that are transferable. This is why you should never specify an absolute path in your partial URLs. An **absolute path** points to the computer's root directory. The **root directory** is indicated by a leading slash in the file path: */graphics/logo.gif*.

If you include the root directory in your partial URLs, you are basing your file structure on your development machine. If the files are moved to another machine, the same path to your files will not apply, and your site will include links that do not work because the browser cannot find the files.

▶ **Relative paths** tell the browser where a file is located relative to the document the browser currently is viewing. Because the paths are not based on the root directory, they are transferable to other computers.

Figure C-15 takes a closer look at User2's folder on the Web server. Examine the relative file structure for User2's Web site. Notice that User2's Web folder contains three HTML files and two subfolders. The two subfolders, *Graphics* and *Pictures*, contain the graphics and pictures for the Web site.

To include the file *logo.gif* in the file *index.htm*, User2 adds the following code to *index.htm*: <IMG SRC="graphics/logo.gif">.

The path in the SRC value tells the browser to look down one level in the directory structure for the *Graphics* folder and find the file *logo.gif*. The path to the file is relative to the file the browser is viewing. This type of relative file structure can be moved to different machines—the relationship between the files will not change because everything is relative within the Web folder.

▶ Of course, the easiest way to ensure that all your path names are correct is to keep all of your HTML and image files in the same directory. Because all files are kept together, the only information you need to put in the SRC or HREF attribute is the filename itself. In Figure C-16, User2 has simplified the directory structure. To reference the file *logo.gif*, User2 adds the following code in one of the HTML files: <IMG SRC="logo.gif">.

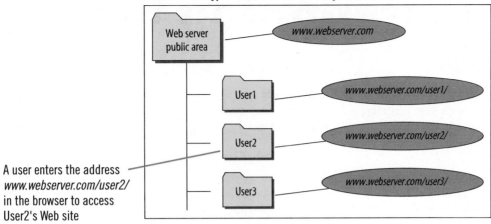

FIGURE C-13: Typical Web server directory structure

A user enters the address *www.webserver.com/user2/* in the browser to access User2's Web site

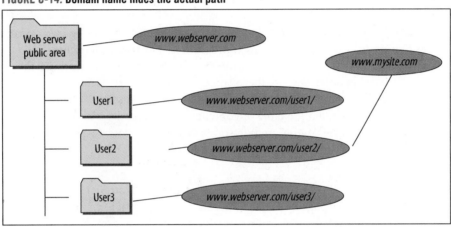

FIGURE C-14: Domain name hides the actual path

FIGURE C-15: Relative file structure

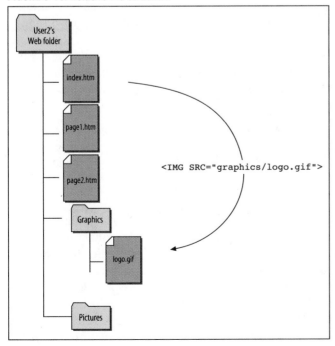

FIGURE C-16: Simplified single-folder file structure

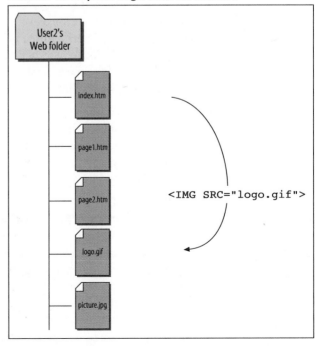

Diagramming the Site

Creating a flowchart that shows the structure and logic behind the content presentation and navigation choices you offer will help you plan your site. Whether you use sophisticated flow-charting software or sticky notes, this preliminary planning step is one of the most important that you take in planning your site.

Details

► Linear Structure

The linear information structure is illustrated in Figure C-17. This structure lends itself to book-type presentations or content that requires the user to follow a predefined path. Once into the content, users can navigate backward or forward within the content path. Each page can contain a link back to the main page if desired. Pages may contain links to a related subtopic. If the users jump to the subtopic page, they only can return to the page that contains the subtopic link.

► Tutorial Structure

The tutorial structure illustrated in Figure C-18 is perfect for computer-based training content, such as lessons, tutorials, or task-oriented procedures. The tutorial structure builds on the simple linear structure. The user navigates in a linear manner, progressing through the concept, lesson, and review pages in order. Because the lesson exists in hypertext, users can leave the lesson structure and return at any time. They also can choose the order of lessons and start at any main concept point they wish. Notice that the table of contents, index, and site map pages are linked to and from all pages in the course. Within each lesson, users can navigate as necessary to familiarize themselves with the content before they review. This structure can be adapted to fit the content needs.

► Web Structure

Many smaller Web sites follow the content structure illustrated in Figure C-19, which offers links to and from every page in the site. This allows the user to jump freely to any page from any other page. Be sure each page includes clear location information and a standardized navigation bar that not only tells the user where they are, but where they can go.

► Hierarchical Structure

The hierarchical structure illustrated in Figure C-20 is probably the most common information design. It lends itself to larger content collections because the section pages break up and orga-nize the content at various levels throughout the site. Navigation primarily is linear within the content sections. Users can scan the content on the section page and then choose the content page of their choice. When they finish reading the content, they can return to the section page. The site map allows users to navigate freely throughout the site. Include a navigation bar on each page that lets the user jump to any section page, the main page, and the site map.

► Cluster Structure

The cluster structure is similar to the hierarchical structure, except that every topic area is an island of information, with all pages in each cluster linked to each other. This structure encourages explo-ration within a topic area. All pages contain a navigation bar with links to the section pages, main page, and site map.

► Catalog Structure

The catalog structure illustrated in Figure C-21 accommodates electronic shopping. The user can browse or search for items and view specific information about each product on the item pages. Users can add items to their shopping cart as they shop. When they are finished, they can review the items in their shopping cart and then proceed to checkout, where they can enter credit card information and finalize the order. This type of Web site requires sophisticated back-end transaction processing to handle the shopping cart tally, process credit card information, and generate an order for the warehouse. Businesses that want to set up an electronic commerce site can purchase ready-made commerce software packages or develop their own from scratch.

FIGURE C-17: Linear information structure

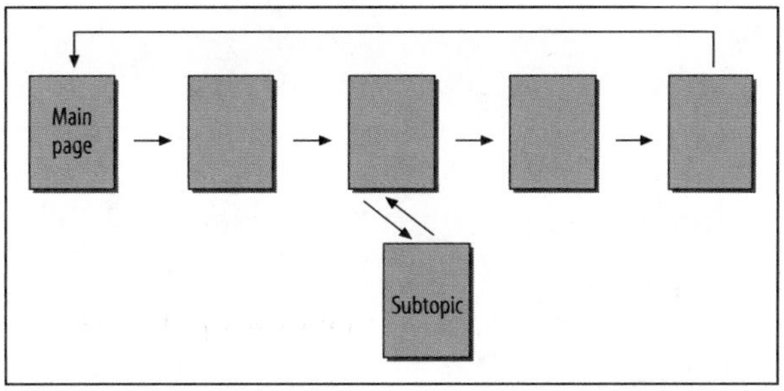

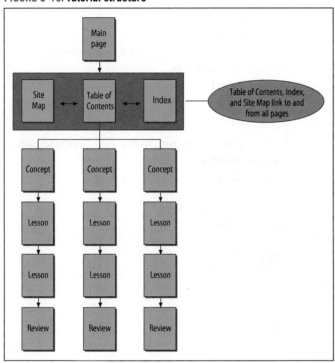

FIGURE C-18: Tutorial structure

FIGURE C-19: Web structure

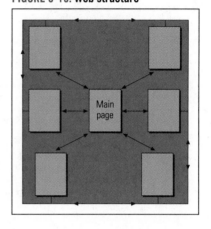

FIGURE C-20: Hierarchical structure

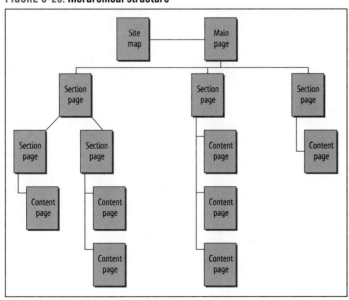

FIGURE C-21: Catalog structure

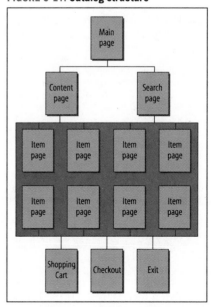

Practice

► Concepts Review

 # theory test

Fill in the blank with the best answer.

1. Three technology constraints that can affect the way a user views your Web site content are *connection speed* , *browser type* , and *display type*.

2. The *site specification* document that you've created helps you to maintain focus as you design your site.

3. The goal of a *billboard* site is to establish a Web presence for a business.

4. *Server Admin* take care of technical issues like fire-walls, modem ports, internal security, and back-up procedures.

5. Consult with your Web server administrator when you need to determine the *default filename* and *directory structure* for your site.

6. Two inconsistencies that can cause broken links when you upload your files to a Web server are *Filename* and *directory*.

7. Three characteristics of filenames that vary by operating system are *length of filename* *valid characters + punctuation* and *sensitivity to upper / lowercase letters*.

8. The international standard for filenames often is called *8.3*.

9. The computer operating system that is case sensitive is *UNIX*.

10. *index.htm* is the default main page name for a Web site.

11. The four parts of a complete URL are *protocol browser uses to access file*, *server/domain name*, *relative path*, and *Filename*.

12. A *Partial* URL links within a server.

13. *directory structure* affects the format of the URL for your Web site.

14. The *leading slash* symbol indicates an absolute path.

15. Files that reside in the same directory need only the *Partial URL* *Filename* to refer to each other.

▶ Explore Further...

1. Explain why it is so important to have a mission statement for your Web site.

— set framework = make sure you have a valid justification for building site.

2. Rename the following files so that they are compatible across all operating systems. Explain the changes.
   My file.htm, case:1.htm, #3rdpage.htm

   myfile.htm   case_1.htm   3rdpage.htm

3. What is the benefit of building a site with relative paths?

   Not based on the root directory, they are transferable to other computers

4. Explain and list the four parts of a complete URL.

   ① the protocol the browser uses to access the file, ② the server or domain name, ③ relative path, ④ filename.

5. Explain why it is so important to use relative file paths when setting up the directory structure for your Web site.

   Files are portable to another computer.

6. Explain two benefits of diagramming your site before you start coding.

   Diagramming enables you to experiment w site structures and standardize filenames.

▶ Independent Challenges

1. As you spend more time on the Web, you will notice that some Web sites would benefit from user feedback. This independent challenge will help you assess what information would be most helpful in improving the performance, navigation, and manageability of a Web site through information obtained from your user base.

   a. Browse the Web and find a site that does not contain a user survey form. Or, you can use the Student Online Companion site at *www.course.com/illustrated/designingsites* and review the sites suggested there.

   b. Write a 10–15-question user survey that you would use on the site. Tailor the questions to the site's content and goals.

   c. Keeping in mind the type of site for which you are creating a survey, determine what kind of incentive you would offer to encourage user feedback.

   d. Include **Your Name** on the printouts.

   e. Log off the Internet.

2. As you become more familiar with different Web sites based on your experience on the Internet, you will begin to notice different styles and content types. Depending on what you are looking for, you will find different types of sites.

   a. Log on to the Internet and browse the Web for different types of sites. Find Web sites that fit each of the following four content types: virtual gallery, publishing, special interest, and product support. Or, you can use the Student Online Companion site at *www.course.com/illustrated/designingsites* and review the sites suggested there.

   b. Either print directly from your browser or use a screen-capture program to capture and print the home page from each of the sites you selected.

   c. Use your word processor to write a short summary of how the content is presented at each of the four Web sites and describe how the site focuses on its users' needs.

   d. Type **Your Name** at the bottom of the document, save the document, print a copy, and then close it.

3. As you surf the Web and move from one page to another, you will begin to recognize and become familiar with different site structures. This independent challenge will help you gain even more experience in identifying the differences. If you have difficulty finding sites, you can go to the Student Online Companion Web site for this unit and find sample links.

a. Browse the Web to find examples of linear and catalog site structures. Or, you can use the Student Online Companion site at *www.course.com/illustrated/designingsites* and review the sites suggested there.

b. Print a few pages from each site that you find and draw a diagram explaining how the pages make up the structure.

c. Use your word processor to describe how the content fits the structure.

d. Type **Your Name** at the bottom of the document, save the document, print a copy, and then close it.

e. Browse the Web to find a site that uses more than one structure type.

f. Print a few pages from the site that you find and draw a diagram explaining how the pages make up the structure.

g. Use your word processor to describe why you think the site's content benefits from multiple structures.

h. Type **Your Name** at the bottom of the document, save the document, print a copy, and then close it.

You will continue to work on the site you began in Unit A. You will recall that to complete the ongoing Web Site Workshop for this book, you must create a complete, stand-alone Web site. The site must contain from six to ten pages, displaying at least three levels of information. You already have selected your own content and started to organize your site. You should have created a visual diagram that indicates the main page, section pages, and content pages as well as indicated the links between the pages.

a. Write a site specification for the site.

b. Include as much information as possible from the project proposal you completed at the end of Unit B.

c. Include a mission statement that defines the goals for the site. Consider audience, technological issues, and how you will evaluate the site's success in meeting its goals.

d. Prepare a detailed flowchart for your site using the preliminary flowchart you created at the end of Unit B. Create a filename for each page.

e. Indicate all links between pages. Write a short summary that describes the flowchart. Describe why you chose the particular structure, how it suits your content, and how it benefits the user.

► Visual Workshop

1. In this Visual Workshop, design a Web site using the structure shown in Figure C-22. Using this book as a guide, use the lesson titles and summarized text from this unit to complete your work. Give details for each of the pages shown in the diagram below.

FIGURE C-22

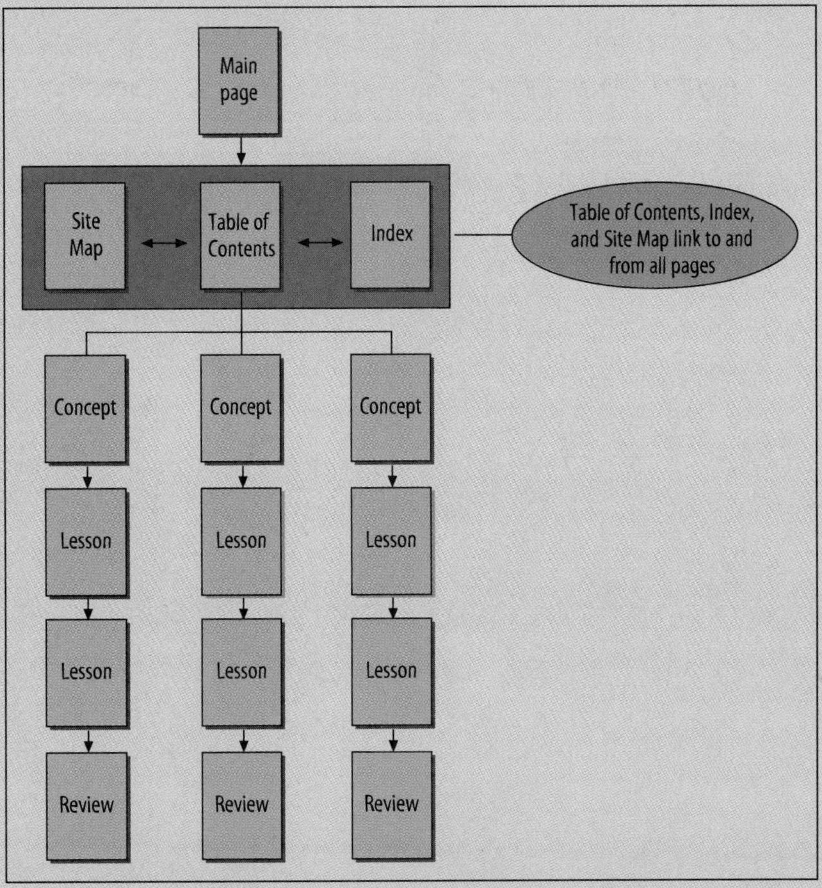

Web Design

▶ Visual Workshop

2. This Visual Workshop illustrates that the Web site shown in Figure C-23 is designed for a very specific special interest audience. Based on what you read in the unit about nonprofit special interest sites, write a brief essay that explains the type of information, downloads, and links you would expect to find at this site.

FIGURE C-23

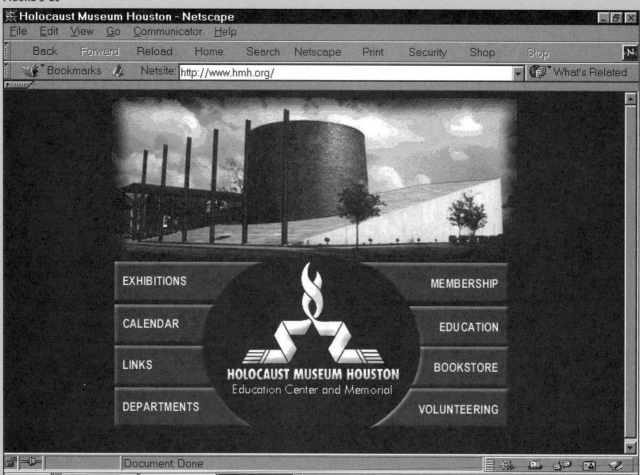

Planning

Site Navigation

Objectives

- ► **Understand navigation principles**
- ► **Introduce text-based navigation**
- ► **Link with a text-based navigation bar**
- ► **Link to document fragments**
- ► **Link to external document fragments**
- ► **Add contextual links**
- ► **Use graphics-based navigation**
- ► **Use the ALT attribute**

The free-flowing nature of information in a nonlinear hypertext environment can be confusing to navigate. Helping your users find content easily, rather than making them hunt through a maze of choices, and reassuring your users, by letting them know where they are at all times and where they can go, will help you succeed with your Web site. In this unit, you will learn to build user-focused navigation within the hypertext environment to accomplish these goals.

Understanding
Navigation Principles

The PC Webopaedia defines hypertext as a system "in which objects (text, pictures, music, programs, and so on) can be creatively linked to each other…You can move from one object to another even though they might have very different forms." Ted Nelson, who described it as nonsequential writing in his book *Literary Machines*, envisioned the idea of hypertext in the 1960s. Nelson's basic idea of connecting content through the use of hypertext linking influenced the creators of the Web. With hypertext-linked content, users can traverse information in any order or method they choose, creating their own unique view.

Details

▶ **Hypertext** is a rich environment in which to write and structure information. In traditional paper-based media, users navigate by turning pages. To find where they want to go, users can refer to a table of contents or index separate from the information they are reading. In a hypertext document, users can connect instantly to related information. In hypertext, forms of traditional navigation devices, such as tables of contents and cross-references, can be consistently displayed alongside related content. The user can explore at will, jumping from one point of interest to another. Of course, this capability is dependent on the hypertext author adding enough links to facilitate navigation.

tip

Use an alternate set of text links in the event that the user cannot or will not view your graphics.

▶ Hyperlinks are easy to create in HTML. When hyperlinks are text based, they do not add to the user's download time. However, graphics-based hyperlinks increase the download time for the user.

Unfortunately, many sites fail to provide even the most basic navigation options to the user. When you are planning your site navigation, do not skimp on navigation cues, options, and contextual links. You can add graphics easily to create attractive navigation elements. Be cautioned that you should keep your navigation graphics simple, and reuse the same graphics throughout your Web site. Once the navigation graphics are loaded in the user's cache, the server does not have to download them again.

▶ Effective navigation includes providing cues to the user's location, not only links to other pages in the Web site. Provide enough location information to let users answer the navigation questions listed in Table D-1.

▶ The navigation cues on a page should give users many options without disorienting them. Figure D-1 shows a page from the Snap Web site that displays a number of user-orienting features. A linked path at the top of the page shows the user's location within the Web hierarchy. Users can see they are on the Web Authoring page, which is contained in the Web Building section, which is part of the Internet section, and so on. Users can click any of the links in the path to move through the content structure. This location device is especially effective in guiding users who may have arrived at this page from somewhere other than within this Web site. A significant, eye-catching banner also identifies the page, and meaningful headings break up the content. Using these navigation devices, users can choose to jump directly to a page, search for information, or move back up through the information hierarchy.

Figure D-2 shows a section page from the AOL Web site, which also offers the same types of helpful navigation devices as the page from the Snap Web site. The location information on this page includes a "You are here" navigation path that tells users the page they are viewing and the path back up through the hierarchy. The navigation path indicates the current page is the Pictures & Albums page, which is a subtopic of the Web Centers page. Web Centers is one of the main topics on the Home page. A banner in large, dark text identifies the page. Even though this page contains many choices, logical headings break up the lists of single-word, meaningful links.

FIGURE D-1: Providing user location cues

Location path

Page banner

Meaningful headings

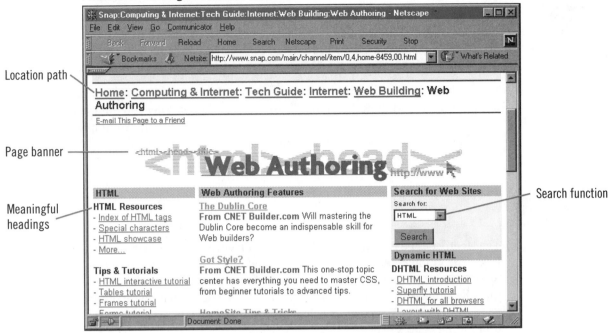

Search function

FIGURE D-2: Helpful navigation devices

Location path

Page banner

Meaningful links

Useful headings

TABLE D-1: Planning for navigation

allow users to answer these questions	provide the following information
Where am I?	Let the users know their current page and what type of content they are viewing
Where can I go?	Let users know where they are in relation to the rest of the Web site
How do I get there?	Provide consistent, easy-to-understand links
How do I get back to where I started?	Provide alternatives to the browser's Back button that lets users return to their starting point

Introducing Text-Based Navigation

Text-based linking often is the most effective way to provide navigation on your site. It can work in both text-only and graphical browsers and does not depend on users choosing to turn on graphics in their browser. Although you may want to use linked graphics for navigation, including a text-based set of links as an alternate means of navigation will make the site available for all users.

Details

▶ The Hoeffler Type Foundry Web site shown in Figure D-3 uses identical text-based and graphic links. The graphic links on this page are listed in a column along the left margin so they stand out. They also are separated visually from the text-based links, which are easy to find under the main heading. Instead of seeming repetitive, the text links provide an alternate means of navigation and a quick list of contents for users who cannot view graphics or who are not willing to wait for the images to download.

▶ Figure D-4 diagrams an example of effective hypertext linking using a collection of HTML documents that includes a Home page, Table of Contents page, Index page, and Chapter pages. The focus is on the Table of Contents page, toc.htm, and how it relates to the rest of the content in the collection. Think about how a table of contents works in a paper-based book. You can see the tremendous advantage that a table of contents could have in a Web site if it is skillfully hyperlinked. In the hypertext environment, the user should be able to select links in the table of contents to jump to any document in the collection.

▶ Figure D-5 shows how the HTML document toc.htm looks in the browser. Users expect a table of contents to list the main topics covered in the document or Web site and to indicate how to find those topics. This sample page contains no hypertext links, and as you can see, the text is for example only and does not contain real words. Instead, the emphasis of the figure is on the concept of linking text-based documents.

Using Navigation to Limit Information Overload

Many Web sites tend to present too much information at one time. Lengthy files that scroll on and on or arrays of links and buttons can frustrate and overwhelm the user. There are several ways you can limit information overload.

Create manageable information segments by breaking your content into smaller files, and then link them together to provide logical groupings of choices. Control page length. Do not make users scroll through never-ending pages. Long files also can mean long downloads. Provide plenty of internal links to help users get around or keep the pages short. You can judge your page length by pressing [PageDown]. If you have to press [PageDown] more than two or three times to move from the top to the bottom of your page, break up the file. Use hypertext to connect facts, relationships, and concepts. Provide contextual linking to related concepts, facts, or definitions, letting the users make the choices they want. Know your material, and try to anticipate the user's information needs.

FIGURE D-3: **Identical text-based and graphic links**

Graphic links —

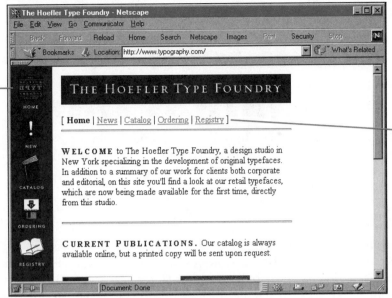

— Text-based links

FIGURE D-4: **Diagram of Web site**

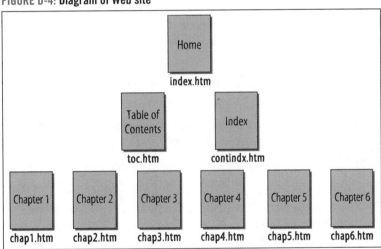

FIGURE D-5: **toc.htm in browser**

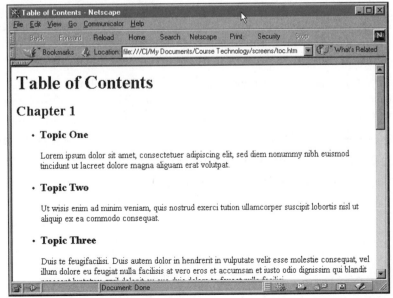

Linking with a Text-Based Navigation Bar

The table of contents page must link to the other main pages of the Web site so that users can click the links to go directly to the pages they want. You can meet this need by adding a simple text-based navigation bar.

Details

▶ Figure D-6 shows the Table of Contents page with a navigation bar at the top. The navigation bar includes links for Home, Table of Contents, and Index. Viewers can click the Home link in the navigation bar to go to the Web site's Home page and the Index link to see an index of keywords they can use to find information. Because this is the Table of Contents page, the Table of Contents text is not a hypertext link but is bold to designate the user's location.

▶ Navigation bars should be clearly available on the page. You can add a navigation bar to the top of every page in the collection, and you may want to add one at the bottom of every page as well. If a user scrolls down the page, they can still have the necessary links available to navigate through the site.

▶ The code to create the navigation bar shown in Figure D-6 is:

```
<DIV ALIGN=CENTER>
<A HREF="index.htm">Home</A> | <B>Table of Contents</B> |
<A HREF="contindx.htm">Index</A>
</DIV>
```

The <DIV> element centers the navigation bar on the page, taking the place of the more common, but deprecated, <CENTER> element. Use <DIV> instead of <P> in the navigation bar because <DIV> has no leading or trailing vertical white space like <P>. <P> is the tag commonly used to mark the beginning and end of a new block of text. Spaces and the vertical bar character separate the links in the code. Notice that the HTML files referenced in the HREF attributes have no path attributes; they reside in the same directory as toc.htm.

▶ Whereas the navigation bar lets users access the main pages in the Web site, the table of contents lets users access the exact topic they want. The Table of Contents page, therefore, needs links to the individual chapter files in the Web site. For example, you can add separate links to each chapter heading in the file, as shown in Figure D-7.

This linking method lets the users scroll through the table of contents to scan the chapters and topics and then jump to the chapter they want. The link colors—by default, blue for new and purple for visited—allow the user to keep track of which chapters they already have visited.

▶ The code to create chapter links is standard hypertext. You make <A> the innermost set of tags to avoid extra space in the hypertext link.

```
<H2><A HREF="chapter1.htm">Chapter 1</A></H2>
```

FIGURE D-6: Text-based navigation bar

Navigation bar at top of Table of Contents page

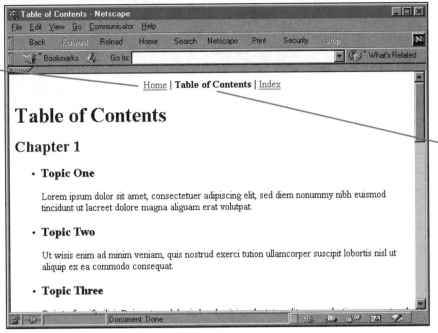

Unlinked text shows user's location

FIGURE D-7: Individual file links

Link to chapter

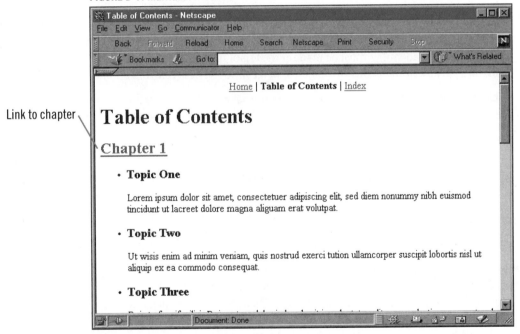

Using the <DIV> Tag

In this and some other code examples in this book, you will notice the use of the <DIV> tag. <DIV> indicates a logical division in a document. You can use it to specify characteristics for the division, such as ALIGN=CENTER, and especially with CSS. Using <DIV> lets the browser display the navigation bar as close to the top of the page as possible. In general, you can replace the deprecated <CENTER> tag with <DIV ALIGN=CENTER> in almost every situation.

Web Design

Linking to Document Fragments

Besides linking to documents, you also can add links for navigating within the table of contents itself. In most Web sites, users can drag the scroll bar to view the rest of the page's content and then click a link to view the desired material. If they scroll to the bottom of the Web page without clicking a link, they must scroll back up to the top to review the content again and, perhaps, choose a different link. Instead of making users scroll, you can provide links to navigate the document using hypertext. You can add a top link that lets users return to the top of the page from many points within the file.

▶ The Top link lets the user jump back to the top of the file from any point in the file. Figure D-8 shows a Top link in the middle (notice the scroll bar shows there is more to the page) of the Table of Contents page. Adding a Top link requires two <A> anchor elements: one uses the NAME attribute to name a **fragment** of the document; the other targets the fragment name in the HREF attribute. The two <A> elements that create a Top link are <A NAME="top">any character</A>. This is the destination anchor of the Top link. The value of the NAME attribute can be any alphanumeric combination you choose, so make it something meaningful to indicate the top of the page.

Add a standard anchor tag later in the file where you want the link to appear. This is the source anchor. Reference the destination fragment by using the number sign (#) in the HREF attribute like this: <A HREF="#top">Top</A>

▶ Where you place the fragment identifier in your code is important. When the user clicks the word Top, the browser opens to the exact spot in the file designated by the NAME attribute. Figure D-9 shows the result of users clicking the Top link when the fragment identifier is placed incorrectly. The placement of the fragment identifier must be made at the top of the file. The navigation bar is the first item in the file and already contains anchor elements, so it cannot be nested within another anchor element.

Use the NAME attribute in the anchor tag to make the link text, Home, both a source and destination anchor. With the code shown below, the browser will open to the very top of the page as shown in Figure D-10.

```
<BODY>
<DIV ALIGN=CENTER><A HREF="index.htm" NAME="top">Home</A>
| <B>Table of Contents</B> | <A HREF="contindx.htm ">
Index of Contents</A></DIV>
<BR>
<H1>Table of Contents</H1>
```

▶ You can use additional fragment identifiers to add more user-focused navigation choices. You can add an internal navigation bar that lets users link to topics within the list of chapters. Figure D-11 shows the addition of an internal navigation bar. When users click one of the linked chapter numbers, they jump to the specific chapter they want to view within the table of contents. The fragment identifier must contain at least one character to work properly in all browsers. Use HREF attributes to point to fragment identifiers. Constructing an empty fragment identifier is not a valid link destination. If you have no characters to bracket with <A> tags, use a nonbreaking space character entity that will work as an invisible link destination: <A NAME="top"> </A>

To ensure that this internal linking works properly, add the fragment identifiers to the file for each chapter heading. These headings are linked already to each of their respective chapter files. <H2><A HREF="chapter2.htm">Chapter 2</A></H2>

Because the text already is contained in an anchor element, use the NAME attribute to name the fragment. Now users can click one of the links in the internal navigation bar and jump directly to that place in the file. As you can see with this code: <A HREF="chapter2.htm" NAME="chapter2">Chapter 2</A>

FIGURE D-8: Adding a Top link

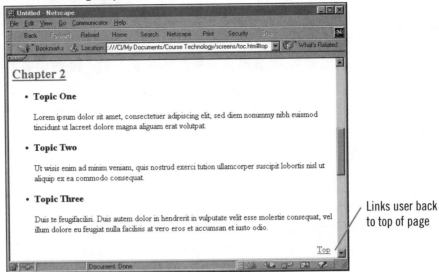

Links user back
to top of page

FIGURE D-9: Incorrect placement of fragment identifier

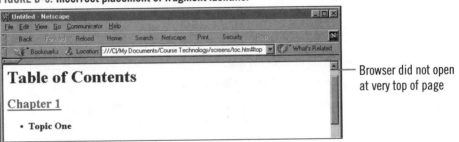

Browser did not open
at very top of page

FIGURE D-10: Correct placement of fragment identifier

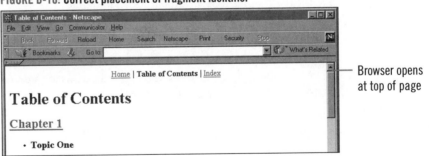

Browser opens
at top of page

FIGURE D-11: Internal navigation bar added to table of contents

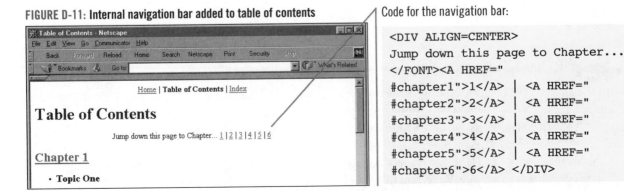

Code for the navigation bar:

```
<DIV ALIGN=CENTER>
Jump down this page to Chapter...
</FONT><A HREF="
#chapter1">1</A> | <A HREF="
#chapter2">2</A> | <A HREF="
#chapter3">3</A> | <A HREF="
#chapter4">4</A> | <A HREF="
#chapter5">5</A> | <A HREF="
#chapter6">6</A> </DIV>
```

Web Design

Linking to External Document Fragments

A well-designed Web page provides the user with plenty of internal navigation choices. To create these extra links, you have to understand how the table of contents is linked to the chapter files.

Details

▶ With the basic design, each chapter has one link in the table of contents. Users click the chapter link and the browser opens the chapter file at the top. However, each chapter also contains multiple topics. It is possible to let users jump to the exact topic they want within each chapter. This requires marking up the chapter documents with topic fragment identifiers.

Figure D-12 illustrates what happens when users click the topic link in the table of contents; the browser opens the destination file and displays the fragment.

▶ Each chapter file currently contains a navigation bar and fragment identifiers for each topic within the chapter. In this page collection, the user can jump to any file and topic within a file, though some users may want to read the pages sequentially. You can enhance the navigation bar in the chapter pages by adding page-turner links. **Page turners** let you move either to the previous or next page in the collection. These work well in a linear structure of pages as shown in the diagram in Figure D-13. Note that Chapter 1 includes the Table of Contents as the previous page, while Chapter 6 uses the Index as the next page. Figure D-14 shows the enhanced navigation bar at the top of the page.

tip

Using the <P> element instead of <DIV> provides extra white space above and below the navigation bar.

▶ Once you establish links for the larger content pages, you can examine the individual chapter files to see if they can use any additional links. Finally, you can make double use of the fragment identifiers that name each topic within the chapter by adding an internal navigation bar to each chapter. This is the same type of navigation you added to the table of contents, but it helps users navigate from topic to topic within a chapter.

The code for the chapter navigation bar looks like this:

```
<P ALIGN=CENTER>
<A HREF="#topic1">Topic One</A> | <A HREF="#topic2.htm">
Topic Two</A> | <A HREF="#topic3">Topic Three</A> |
<A HREF="#topic4">Topic Four</A> </P>
```

You can place one of these navigation bars in each chapter and adjust the number of topic links appropriately.

Using the ID Attribute

With the advent of HTML 4.0, you have the option of adding the ID attribute. You can use ID to identify a fragment, just as NAME does. The advantage of working with ID is that you can use it with almost any element. If you want to identify an <H1> heading as a fragment, add the ID attribute to the <H1> tag:
```
<H1 ID="topic1">Topic One</H1>
```
The disadvantage of using ID is that it is not supported in all browsers. Netscape 4.08 and Internet Explorer 5.0 do support the ID attribute. Be certain to test in multiple browsers if you choose to use ID.

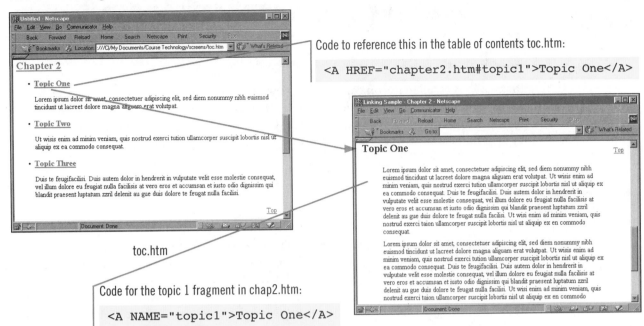

Code to reference this in the table of contents toc.htm:

```
<A HREF="chapter2.htm#topic1">Topic One</A>
```

toc.htm

Code for the topic 1 fragment in chap2.htm:

```
<A NAME="topic1">Topic One</A>
```

chapter2.htm

FIGURE D-13: **Sequential page turning**

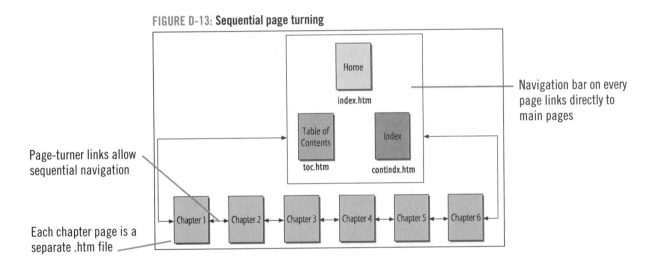

Navigation bar on every page links directly to main pages

Page-turner links allow sequential navigation

Each chapter page is a separate .htm file

FIGURE D-14: **Adding page turners to the navigation bar**

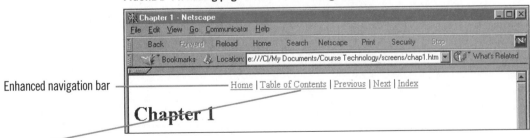

Enhanced navigation bar

Code for the navigation bar:

```
<DIV ALIGN=CENTER>
<A HREF="index.htm" NAME="top">Home</A> | <A HREF="toc.htm">Table of Contents</A> |
<AHREF="toc.htm">Previous</A> | <A HREF="chapter2.htm">Next</A> | <A HREF="index.htm">
Index</A>
</DIV>
```

Adding Contextual Links

Many Web sites fail to use one of the most powerful hypertext capabilities—the contextual link. **Contextual links** allow users to jump to related ideas or cross-references by clicking the word or item that interests them. These are links that you can embed directly in the flow of your content by choosing the key terms and concepts that you anticipate your users will want to follow.

Details

► Figure D-15 shows a page from the W3C HTML specification that contains contextual linking. Note the links within the lines of text, which let the user view related information in context. For example, as users read the first bulleted item, "May leave <u>white</u> <u>space</u> intact," they can click the "white space" link to see a definition of that term. Including the link within a line of text is more effective than including a list of keywords because users can see related information within the context of the sentence they are reading.

► Users also can see that repeated words are linked no matter how many times they appear within the browser window, offering users the opportunity to access additional information at any time.

► Figure D-16 shows a page from the site *www.olympics.com* that makes excellent use of contextual links. You can click the name of the athlete or the event. The site takes advantage of contextual links to guide the viewer to the relevant pages. Some contextual links will open a new window, others will navigate you to another page within the site. Figure D-17 shows a page from the site *www.howthingswork.com* where you can click terms in articles to open pages that give you more information about what you are reading.

FIGURE D-15: Contextual linking

Contextual link ─────

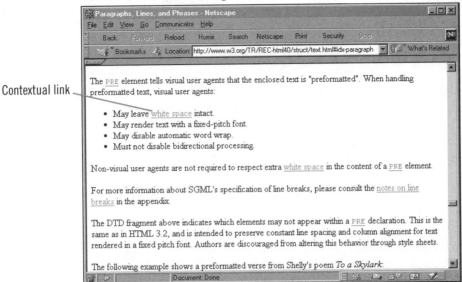

FIGURE D-16: Olympics Web site

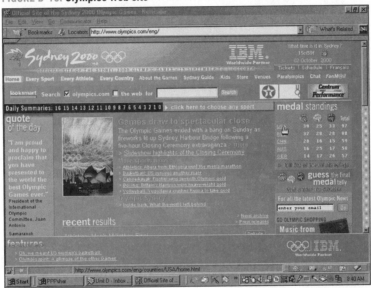

FIGURE D-17: How Things Work Web site

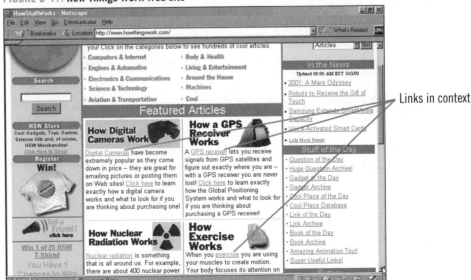

───── Links in context

Using Graphics-Based Navigation

Similar to most Web-site designers, you probably want to use graphics for some of your navigation cues. As you have learned, navigation graphics on the Web come in every imaginable style. The ability to use graphics is one of the most appealing aspects of the Web, but too many graphics used inconsistently will confuse the users. To make sure your navigation graphics help rather than hinder your users, you should standardize your navigation graphics throughout your Web site.

Details

▶ Once users learn where to find navigation icons and how to use them, they anticipate them on every page. Consistent placement and design also build trust in your users and help them feel confident that they can find the information they want.

▶ Design graphics to minimize download time. Once the graphic is downloaded, the browser will retrieve it from the cache for subsequent pages rather than downloading it every time it appears.

▶ Many sites use text images, rather than HTML text, for navigation graphics. **Text images** are text created as graphics, usually as labels within the graphic. Many Web designers prefer text images because they have more typeface and design choices when creating their own graphics. Figure D-18 shows the top navigation bars from a standard page of *The Sydney Morning Herald* Web site. Notice that this text uses graphics instead of HTML text. The navigation bar builds the page name, Web site name, main sections, and page turners into a unified graphic that serves as the banner for the top of the page. The banner creates a unified look to all of their content, while providing a variety of useful navigation choices. Note that what appears to be a single graphic actually is composed of different graphics held together by a table.

▶ Figure D-19 shows the main page navigation bar from Travelocity, a travel Web site that uses icons and text-based links. The text-based links serve a dual purpose: If the graphics for the icon do not appear, the user still can navigate, and the text describes each icon. When coded appropriately, the design would carry these icons through to each of the destination pages, in addition to displaying them on the main page of the Web site to provide consistent identifying navigation graphics.

▶ The text that labels each image in the Travelocity Web site points out one of the main problems with icons: Not everyone agrees on their meaning. Especially with a worldwide audience, you never can be sure exactly how your audience will interpret your iconic graphics. This is why so many Web sites choose text-based links, even if they are text as graphics. If you do use navigation icons, be sure to define them; that is, possibly use a table that lists each icon and describes its meaning.

▶ You also can use navigation graphics to indicate location within a site. For example, you can change the color or shading to indicate which page the user currently is viewing. At the Empire State Building Web site, illustrated in Figure D-20, the navigation graphic includes an arrow to indicate which section of the site the user currently is viewing.

FIGURE D-18: Text images used for navigation bars

Page name

Web site name

Main sections

Page turners

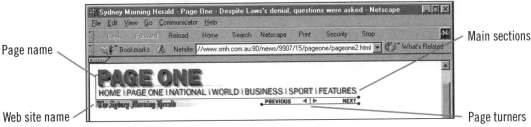

FIGURE D-19: Icons for navigation

Text-based links

Navigation icons

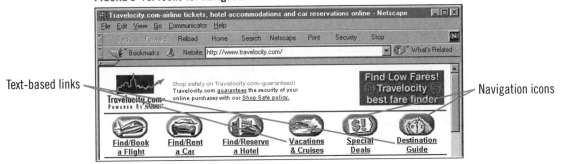

FIGURE D-20: Navigation graphic indicates location

Location in page

Design Matters

Designing for a Universal Audience

No matter what type of graphics you choose as icons, make sure that all your users will understand their meaning. Test your navigation graphics with people from your target audience and ask them to interpret the icons and directional graphics you want to use. The most obvious type of graphics to avoid are symbols that are culturally specific, especially hand gestures (such as thumbs-up) that may be misinterpreted in other cultures. Other graphics, such as directional arrows, are more likely to be interpreted correctly. For example, the up arrow universally is interpreted as "top," the left arrow as "previous," and the right arrow as "next" for navigation within a site.

Web Design

Using the ALT Attribute

As you read earlier, you should provide alternate text-based links in addition to graphical links. You can do so by including an ALT attribute in the <IMG> tag of the HTML code for the graphic. Repeating navigation options ensures you meet the needs of a wide range of users. Some sites choose not to offer a text-based alternative, and this makes it difficult for users who cannot view graphics in their browsers.

Details

▶ If you are creating a site that consists almost entirely of graphics, you must take advantage of techniques that help users. For example, if the site you create uses navigation images in the left column as the only way to navigate the site, users will not be able to clearly navigate from the main page if graphics are turned off or do not download.

Figure D-21 shows a sample Web page designed like this with images turned off. Without the graphics, this site offers no navigation information. Even though graphics are turned off, they retain their hypertext characteristics as shown by the hypertext pointer, but the user does not have any destination information.

▶ By adding descriptive ALT text, nongraphical browser users can navigate your site. Figure D-22 shows a sample elementary school Web site with the ALT attributes added. With the graphics turned off, users still can navigate the Web site because the ALT attribute values appear in the image space. The user finds navigation cues by reading the ALT text and pointing to the image areas to find the clickable spots.

▶ The code for a navigation button in a sample elementary school site for the Parent's Page that has the ALT attribute may look like this:

```
<A HREF="parent.htm"><IMG border=0 height=35 src="smparent.gif"
width=113 ALT="Parent's Page"></A>
```

While the ALT attribute provides valuable navigation information to users who are not displaying graphics or are waiting for graphics to download, it does have some limitations. If your graphics are small, the ALT text may not appear because it needs more room for the text in the graphic area.

▶ Both Internet Explorer 4.0/5.0 and Netscape 4.0 display pop-up text boxes if the ALT attribute is included. Figure D-23 shows an example of a pop-up text box. When the user points to a graphic, the pop-up text box containing the ALT attribute appears, even if the browser does not display graphics. Not only is this effective if graphics are turned off, but you can add descriptive text that helps the user navigate. For example, pointing to the navigation arrow could display additional navigation information, such as "You are here."

tip

You must specify the image width and height in the <IMG> tag to reserve the image space in the browser.

tip

If you omit ALT attributes and rely on graphics for navigation, the user cannot effectively navigate the site.

FIGURE D-21: No ALT values in <IMG> tags

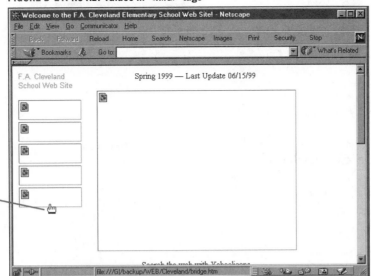

Insertion point turns to hypertext pointer when scrolled over image areas

FIGURE D-22: ALT values in <IMG> tags

ALT text provides navigation information

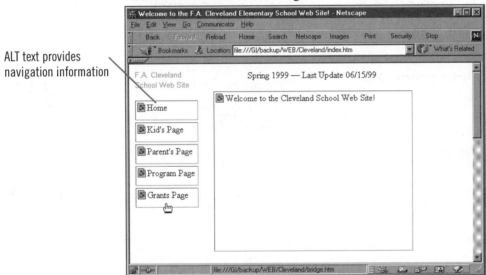

FIGURE D-23: Value of ALT attribute displays in pop-up text box

ALT pop-up text box

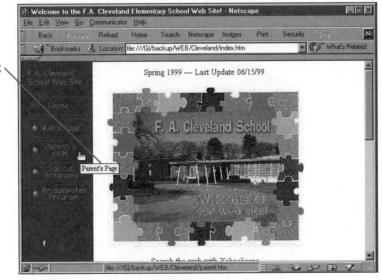

Practice

▶ Concepts Review

Fill in the blank with the best answer.

1. Use links within the _Table of Contents_ page to jump to chapter descriptions and from that page to specific topics within each chapter.

2. In _linked_ documents, users can connect instantly to related information.

3. Two reasons for standardizing graphics are _download time_ and _consistency of navigation cues_.

4. Three types of navigation cues are _meaningful links_, _locate refer_, and _pg identifiers_

5. Two navigation cues you can add to a text-based navigation bar are _links to main pg_ and _user-location info_.

6. The deprecated element you can replace with <DIV ALIGN=CENTER> is _<center>_

7. It is best to make <A> the innermost element to a piece of text because you avoid extra white space in the linked text. True/**False**? _____

8. The _href_ <A> tag attribute is associated with fragment identifiers.

9. The _ _ character entity is useful as an invisible link destination.

10. The _name_ attribute is used to make an <A> tag both a source and destination anchor.

11. The HTML 4.0 attribute _id_ allows you to create fragment identifiers.

12. _Pg turners_ such as Top, Next, and Previous, work best in sequential structure.

13. Links are embedded in the flow of the content and allow users to jump to related ideas or information through _contextual linking_.

14. _text img's_ used as navigation tools are appealing to HTML authors and help with and offer a variety of typefaces and font sizes.

15. If you use navigation icons, you never have to worry that their meaning will be misunderstood. True/**False**? _____

16. By adding descriptive _alt_ text, nongraphical browser users can navigate your site.

▶ Explore Further...

1. Describe two ways to break up lengthy HTML pages.

1. Break content into separate documents.
2. Use internal linking to fragments of doc.

2. What navigation questions should you consider when planning a Web site?

Where am I?   How do I get there?
Where can I go?   How do I get back?

3. Explain three ways to control information overload.

1. create manageable info segments. 2. Control pg. length.
3. Use hypertext to connect facts

4. Explain how you would link to a fragment in an external file and provide sample code.

/ fragment identifier
<a href="unit2.htm#topic1">topic one </a>

5. Explain why you would include both graphic and text-based links on a Web page, and then explain the advantages of linking by using text instead of graphics.

If the graphics for icon don't appear, user still can navigate, and text describes each icon. Don't know how audience will interpret iconic graphics. (worldwide audience).

6. Describe the benefits of using the ALT attribute.

provides valuable navigation info to users who aren't displaying graphics or are waiting for graphics to download

▶ Independent Challenges

1. Your experience browsing the Web has taken you to sites with various types of navigation designs. Although a successful design can be subjective, most certainly you have visited sites that you found easier to navigate than others. Also, the user's success at navigation also is dependent on the audience you are addressing and the type of site you are visiting. You will be able to develop designs of your own based on how you feel about sites you have visited.

a. Log onto the Internet and find a Web site that you feel has a successful navigation design. Or, you can use the Student Online Companion site at *www.course.com/illustrated/designingsites* and review the sites suggested there. You can select from any type of site, such as shopping, research, search engine, or general interest.

b. Use your word processor to write a short summary of why the navigation is effective and how it fits the user's needs. If you feel that the navigation can be improved, describe how to change the navigation to increase its effectiveness.

c. Type **Your Name** at the bottom of the document, save the document, print a copy, and then close it.

d. Next, go to the Web and find an online shopping Web site. You can see how navigation differs for online shopping than for other sites. Examine the navigation options and determine whether you think the navigation adds to or detracts from the online shopping experience.

e. Use your word processor to write a short summary of why the navigation at this online shopping site is effective and how it fits the user's needs. If you feel that the navigation can be improved, describe how to change the navigation to increase its effectiveness.

f. Type **Your Name** at the bottom of the document, save the document, print a copy, and then close it.

g. Next, go to the Web and find an online information resource that likely would be used for research.

h. Examine the navigation options and write a short summary that describes how the navigation aids or hinders the user's information-searching process. If you feel that the navigation can be improved, describe how to change the navigation to increase its effectiveness.

i. Type **Your Name** at the bottom of the document, save the document, print a copy, and then close it.

2. Icons have become ubiquitous in our society. As a computer user, you see them on toolbars, and as a consumer, you see them on packaging. You use icons to navigate the Web as well as many other computer applications in electronic devices. You are familiar with hand-held devices such as Palm Pilots; you work with icons each day. Even if you only use a hand-held calculator, an ATM machine, or even a cell phone, you have certainly worked with icons.

a. Log on to the Internet and then use your favorite Web search engine to search for navigation icons on the Web.

b. When you find sites that use icons, print the page of each Web site with the icons. Use your favorite screen-capture program or you can use [Print Screen] to capture the screen, then paste the screen into your word processor for printing.

c. Assemble a set of icons that would be suitable for international audiences.

d. Assemble a second set of icons that only would be understood by a local population.

e. Write a summary explaining your selections for steps c and d.

f. Type **Your Name** at the bottom of the document, save the document, print a copy, and then close it.

3. The code provided in this chapter gives you the information you need to change a text-based paper document into a hypertext one. If a project that you created has a table of contents, more than one chapter, embedded topics, and/or an index, you can take an existing paper-based project and turn it into a hypertext document.

a. Use a term paper or report that you prepared for a previous class using a word processor and that is available in electronic format. Preferably, the document should contain a table of contents and topics.

b. Convert the document to HTML if the program allows, or save the document as ASCII text and paste it into Notepad or an HTML editor.

c. Mark up the document for Web presentation. Include a linked table of contents, topic links, content links, footnote links, and top links. You may find it best to break the single document into a few HTML files and then link them together.

d. Test your document in multiple browsers to ensure its portability.

e. This book's Student Online Companion Web site at *www.course.com/illustrated/designingsites* contains all the HTML files for the sample Web site illustrated in Figure D-24. Use these sample HTML files to recreate the examples in this chapter or practice different types of hypertext linking.

f. Type **Your Name** in the document, save the document, print a copy, and then close it.

FIGURE D-24

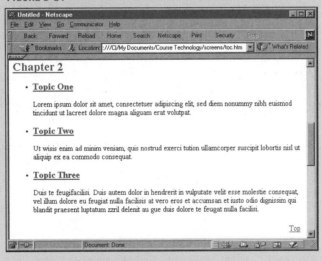

toc.htm

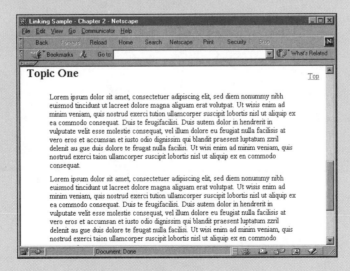

chapter2.htm

You will continue to work on the site you began in Unit A. You will recall that to complete the ongoing case study for this book, you must create a complete, stand-alone Web site. The site must contain from six to ten pages and display at least three levels of information. By this point, you should have selected your own content and started to organize your site. You should have created a visual diagram that indicates the main page, section pages, and content pages, as well as indicating the links between the pages.

a. Examine the flowchart you created for your Web site. Consider the requirements of both internal and external navigation. Create a revised flowchart that shows the variety of navigation options you are planning for the Web site.

b. Using your HTML editor, mark up examples of navigation bars for your content. Make sure your filenames are intact before you start coding. Save the various navigation bars as separate HTML files for later inclusion in your Web pages.

c. Plan the types of navigation graphics you want to create. Sketch page banners, navigation buttons, and related graphics.

d. Find sources from where you will acquire your navigation graphics. For example, you can use public domain (non-copyrighted) clip art collections on the Web, such as *www.microsoft.com/clipgallerylive* for basic navigation arrows and other graphics.

e. Remember to code the necessary ALT attribute elements so the navigation graphics will display the appropriate alternate text.

▶ Visual Workshop

1. In this Visual Workshop the image shown in Figure D-25 is from the Empire State Building Web site at *www.esbnyc.com*. Identify at least four words in the text about the tower lights for which you could create contextual links. Write a brief paragraph about what each linked page might include for each of the links.

FIGURE D-25

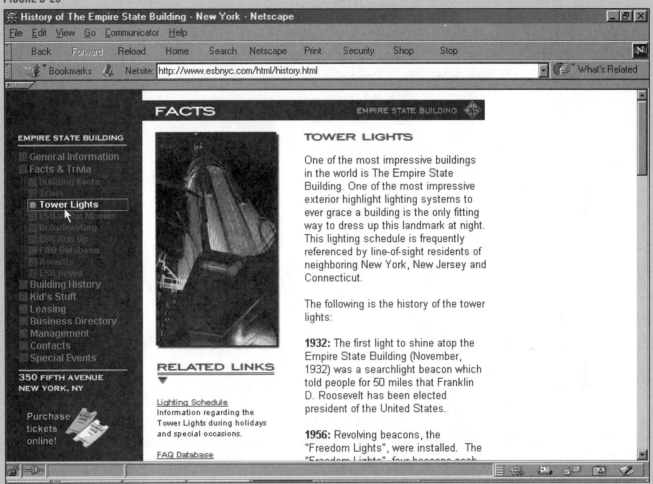

▶Visual Workshop

2. In the Visual Workshop the images shown in Figures D-26 and D-27 show the main page and a secondary page from the Seussville Web site. Write a brief paragraph on how graphics are used in navigation through the site. Be sure to include information about the target audience in your discussion.

FIGURE D-26

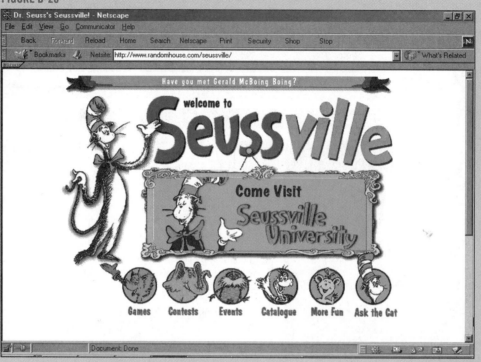

FIGURE D-27

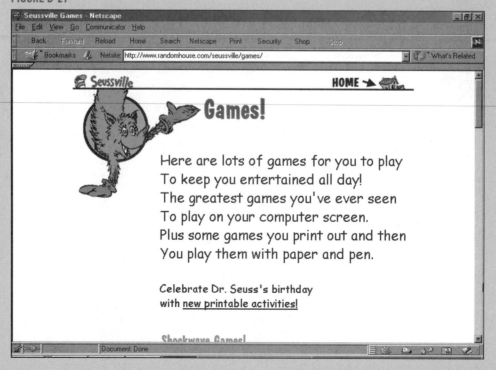

Understanding
Tables

Objectives

► **Understand table basics**
► **Define and use table attributes**
► **Work with table widths and spacing**
► **Use design rules**
► **Create a basic page template**
► **Create page banners and feature cells**
► **Work with columns and cells**
► **Review template examples**

HTML table elements allow Web designers to create grid-based layouts. You can use tables to create templates and to solve design problems. This unit explains how to manipulate the most commonly used table elements and attributes to create templates. Once you understand tables, you can create and use templates to gain more control over how your content displays in the browser, while building more visually interesting pages.

Understanding Table Basics

To build effective page templates, you must be familiar with the HTML table elements and attributes. With tables, Web designers have the control and the tools to build columnar layouts, align text, create margins, and structure pages. Tables currently are used as the primary design tool throughout the World Wide Web. This lesson describes the most commonly used table elements and attributes.

Details

▶ When HTML was introduced, tables were used only for tabular data. After examining tables, Web designers realized they could build print-like design structures that allowed them to break away from the left-alignment constraints of basic HTML.

▶ Although CSS provides an alternate method of controlling page display, it will not replace tables until all browsers provide more complete CSS support. There are some discrepancies across browsers in table support, especially with the HTML 4.0 table enhancements, but tables currently are supported enough to make them the page-design method of choice for some time to come.

▶ The HTML <TABLE> element contains the table information, which consists of table row elements <TR> and individual table data cells <TD>. These are the three elements used most frequently when you are building tables. Figure E-1 shows a basic table that uses these three table elements and the code that created the table.

The <TABLE> element contains the rows and cells that make up the table. The <TR> tag signifies the three rows of the table. Notice that the <TR> tag contains the table cells but no content of its own. The BORDER attribute displays the default border around the table and between each cell.

▶ You may occasionally use the <CAPTION> and <TH> elements when creating tables. <CAPTION> lets you add a caption to the top or bottom of the table. By default, captions display at the top of the table. You can use the ALIGN=BOTTOM attribute to align the caption at the bottom of the table. The <TH> tag lets you create a table header cell that presents the cell content as bold and centered. Figure E-2 shows the same table with a caption and table header cells.

▶ The HTML 4.0 table model adds a number of new table elements that are not supported in all browsers. As late as 1999, only Internet Explorer supported the following elements: <COL> specifies column properties, <COLGROUP> specifies multiple column properties, <THEAD> signifies table header, <TBODY> signifies table body, and <TFOOT> signifies table footer.

tip

Remember to always close the <TABLE> element properly. Netscape Navigator does not display a table or any of the contained data if the closing </TABLE> tag is missing. However, Internet Explorer ignores this omission and displays the table.

FIGURE E-1: **Basic table**

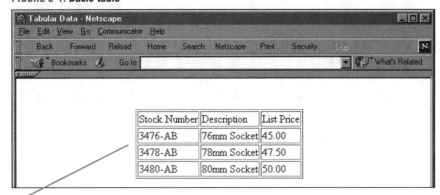

Code for the table:

```
<TABLE BORDER>
<TR><TD>Stock Number</TD><TD>Description</TD><TD>
List Price</TD></TR>
<TR><TD>3476-AB</TD>
<TD>76mm Socket</TD><TD>45.00</TD></TR>
<TR><TD>3478-AB</TD>
<TD>78mm Socket</TD><TD>47.50</TD></TR>
<TR><TD>3480-AB</TD>
<TD>80mm Socket</TD><TD>50.00</TD></TR>
</TABLE>
```

FIGURE E-2: **Table with caption and header row**

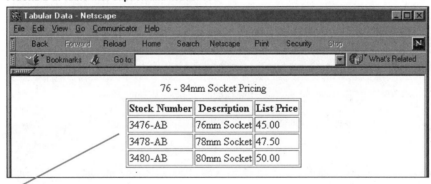

Code for the table:

```
<TABLE BORDER>
<CAPTION>76 - 84mm Socket Pricing</CAPTION>
<TR><TH>Stock Number</TH><TH>Description</TH>
<TH>List Price </TH></TR>
<TR><TD>3476-AB</TD><TD>76mm Socket</TD><TD>45.00</TD></TR>
<TR><TD>3478-AB</TD><TD>78mm Socket</TD><TD>47.50</TD></TR>
<TR><TD>3480-AB</TD><TD>80mm Socket</TD><TD>50.00</TD></TR>
</TABLE>
```

Web Design

Defining and Using Table Attributes

Table attributes let you further define a number of table characteristics. You can apply attributes at three levels of table structure: global, row level, or cell level.

► **Global attributes** affect the entire table. Place these attributes in the initial <TABLE> tag. Global table attributes are listed in Table E-1.

► **Row-level attributes** affect an entire row. These attributes are placed in the beginning <TR> tag. Row-level attributes are listed in Table E-2.

► **Cell-level attributes** affect only the contents of one cell. These attributes are placed in the beginning <TD> tag. Cell-level attributes are listed in Table E-3. Cell-level attributes take precedence over row-level attributes. The following code for a single table row has conflicting ALIGN attributes: The ALIGN=RIGHT value in the <TD> tag overrides the ALIGN=CENTER in the <TR> tag.

```
<TR ALIGN=CENTER><TD>Center-aligned text.</TD><TD ALIGN=
RIGHT>Right-aligned text.</TD></TR>
```

TABLE E-1: Global table attributes

attribute	description
ALIGN	Floats the table to the left or right of the text; this is a deprecated attribute in HTML 4.0
BACKGROUND	Specifies a background image that tiles the background of the cell; this is a deprecated attribute in HTML 4.0
BGCOLOR	Specifies a color for the table background; this is a deprecated attribute in HTML 4.0
BORDER	Displays a border around the table and each cell within the table
CELLPADDING	Inserts spacing within the table cells on all four sides; the value for this attribute is a pixel count
CELLSPACING	Inserts spacing between the table cells on all four sides; the value for this attribute is a pixel count
HEIGHT	Adjusts the height of the table; the value either can be a percentage relative to the browser window size or a fixed pixel amount; this is a deprecated attribute in HTML 4.0
WIDTH	Adjusts the width of the table; the value either can be a percentage relative to the browser window size or a fixed pixel amount; this is a deprecated attribute in HTML 4.0

TABLE E-2: Row-level table attributes

attribute	description
ALIGN	Horizontally aligns the contents of the cells within the row; use LEFT, CENTER, or RIGHT values; LEFT is the default; this is a deprecated attribute in HTML 4.0
BGCOLOR	Specifies a background color for the cells within the row; this is a deprecated attribute in HTML 4.0
VALIGN	Vertically aligns the contents of the cells within the row; use TOP, MIDDLE, or BOTTOM values; MIDDLE is the default

FIGURE E-3: Table with column and row span

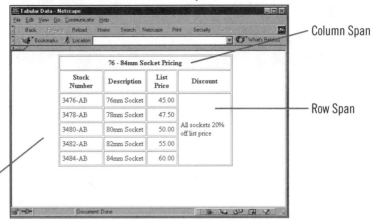

Column Span

Row Span

Excerpt of code for column and row span:

```
<TABLE BORDER>
<!-- Row 1 contains the column span -->
<TR><TH COLSPAN=4>76 - 84mm Socket Pricing</TH></TR>
<TR><TH>Stock Number</TH><TH>Description</TH><TH>List
Price</TH><TH>Discount</TH></TR>
<!-- Row 3 contains the row span in the 4th cell-->
<TR><TD>3476-AB</TD><TD>76mm Socket</TD><TD ALIGN=RIGHT>
45.00</TD> <TD ROWSPAN=5>All sockets 20% off list price
</TD><TR>
```

TABLE E-3: Cell-level table attributes

attribute	description
ALIGN	Horizontally aligns the contents of the cell; use LEFT, CENTER, or RIGHT values; LEFT is the default; this is a deprecated attribute in HTML 4.0
BGCOLOR	Specifies a background color for the cell; this is a deprecated attribute in HTML 4.0
COLSPAN	Specifies the number of columns a cell spans
HEIGHT	Adjusts the height of the cell; the value either can be a percentage relative to the table size or a fixed pixel amount; this is a deprecated attribute in HTML 4.0
ROWSPAN	Specifies the number of rows a cell spans
VALIGN	Vertically aligns the contents of the cell; use TOP, MIDDLE, or BOTTOM values; MIDDLE is the default
WIDTH	Adjusts the width of the cell; the value either can be a percentage relative to the table size or a fixed pixel amount; this is a deprecated attribute in HTML 4.0

Spanning Columns and Rows

The COLSPAN attribute lets you create cells that span multiple columns of a table. Column cells always span to the right. When you build column spans, make sure that all of your columns add up to the correct number of cells. In Figure E-3, because each row has three cells, the COLSPAN attribute is set to span all four columns of the table; thus, the COLSPAN value in the first row is four. The ROWSPAN attribute lets you create cells that span multiple rows of a table. Rows always span down. The table in Figure E-3 has a row span added to the right column. The code displayed with the figure shows the new cell that contains the ROWSPAN attribute and the extra column cell in the table header row. Note that the row span cell is the fourth cell in the third row. It spans down across five rows of the table.

Web Design

Working with Table Widths and Spacing

Whether you choose to use relative or fixed tables depends on your content and the amount of control you want over the result. Many Web designers prefer fixed tables because they can be sure that their view of the content will be the same as the user's view. The current trend is to provide content in relative tables that adapt to various screen resolutions.

Details

▶ You can set relative table widths as percentages in the table WIDTH attribute. If you choose relative table widths, your tables resize based on the size of the browser window. Figure E-4 shows a table with the WIDTH attribute set to 100%. The browser will try to fit the content into the window, wrapping text as necessary. The advantage to using a relative width is that the resulting table is more compatible across various browser window sizes and screen resolutions. The disadvantage is that you have little control over the way the user sees the result because your content can shift from user to user based on browser window size.

▶ You can set absolute table widths as pixel values in the table WIDTH attribute. Fixed tables remain constant regardless of the browser window size. The advantage to using a fixed table is that you can gain greater control over the result the user sees. The user's browser size and screen resolution have no affect on the display of the page. Figure E-5 shows a table with the WIDTH attribute set to a fixed width of 600 pixels. Notice that the table extends beyond the browser window.

▶ When creating a table that will be used for a Web site, consider that the most common width for tables is between 580 and 600 pixels. This width supports the current lowest common denominator—640 × 480 screen resolution—to which most mainstream Web sites still adhere. You should set the width to approximately 600 pixels, not 640.

▶ The width of the page margin on the left of the screen is approximately 10 pixels and is built into the browser. The scroll bar on the right of the screen is approximately 20 pixels. If your table extends into this area, the horizontal scroll bar will appear. You have to allow approximately another 10 pixels for a right page margin. Subtracting all of these values from 640 equals an approximate table width of 600 pixels.

▶ Default spacing values are included in the table even when you do not specify values for the table's BORDER, CELLPADDING, or CELLSPACING attributes. Without the default spacing values, the table cells would have no built-in white space between them, and the contents of adjoining cells would run together. Depending on the browser, approximately 2 pixels are reserved for each of these values. Figure E-6 shows five images assembled in a table with the default spacing. The default cell padding and cell spacing also are adding to the white space between the images. Even though borders are turned off, their default space remains in the table.

▶ You can remove the default spacing by explicitly stating a zero value for each attribute. This very useful technique lets you join the contents of adjacent cells. You can take an image, break it into separate pieces, and then rejoin the pieces in a table by removing the default spacing. Because the image is composed of separate parts, you can link individual parts of the image or include animated GIFs in the image. Figure E-7 shows the same table with BORDER, CELLPADDING, and CELLSPACING attributes set to zero.

FIGURE E-4: Table with WIDTH attribute set to 100%

Table resizes to window size

FIGURE E-5: Table with WIDTH attribute set to 600 pixels

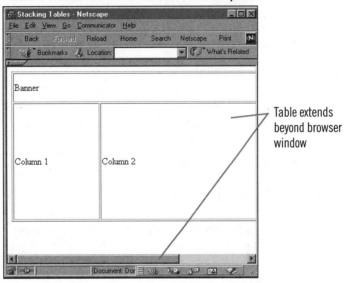

Table extends beyond browser window

FIGURE E-6: Default table spacing

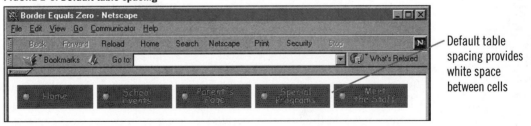

Default table spacing provides white space between cells

FIGURE E-7: Default table spacing removed

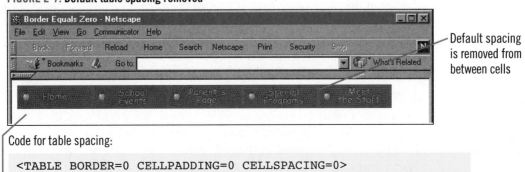

Default spacing is removed from between cells

Code for table spacing:

```
<TABLE BORDER=0 CELLPADDING=0 CELLSPACING=0>
```

Web Design

Using Design Rules

When designing HTML tables, observe the following guidelines to create effective tables: Write easy-to-read code, remove extra spaces, center tables, stack tables, and nest tables. This lesson summarizes these simple points for creating effective tables.

Details

► Write Easy-to-Read Code

The HTML table code can get complicated when you add content to your tables. Not only do you have to manage all the table tags and attributes but also the text, images, and links in your cells. One small error in your code can cause unpredictable results in the browser.

You can simplify your table creation and maintenance tasks by writing clean, commented code. If you have to go back into the code at a later date, comments will help you remember why you did what you did or provide information if someone else has to review your code. If you use plenty of white space in the code, you will find your tables are easier to access and change. Adding comments helps you quickly find the code you want.

► Remove Extra Spaces

Always remove any leading or trailing spaces in your table cell content. In some browsers, the extra spaces create white space in the table cells. These spaces cause problems if you are trying to join the contents of adjacent cells. Even though the default spacing has been removed, there still is space between the images.

The code shows the extra spaces after the <IMG> element within each cell.

```
<TABLE BORDER=0 CELLPADDING=0 CELLSPACING=0>
<TR>
<TD><IMG SRC="smhome.GIF" WIDTH=113 HEIGHT=35 ALT=""
border="0">        </TD>
```

► Center Tables

You can center tables on the page using either the <CENTER> or <DIV> elements. Centering a fixed table makes the table independent of resolution changes because the table always is centered in the browser window. Because <CENTER> is deprecated, using the ALIGN=CENTER attribute is the preferred coding method. Figure E-8 shows a centered table at 800 × 600 resolution and highlights the code to show the use of the <DIV> element to center the table.

► Stack Tables

Browsers must read the entire table code before displaying the table. Any text outside of a table displays first. If you build long tables, they increase the time the user has to wait before the tables appear in the browser. Because of the way browsers display tables, build several small tables rather than a single large one. This technique also can simplify your table design task because smaller tables are easier to work with. Another benefit of stacking tables is that they display in the same order they appear in the code. This means the user can start reading the contents of your first table while the next one downloads. Also, more complex layouts are easier to build if you break them into multiple tables. Figure E-9 shows a page built with two stacked tables. Notice that the top table has five columns, whereas the second has three. It would be much harder to build this layout using a single table.

► Nest Tables

You can nest tables by placing an entire table within a table cell. Both Netscape Navigator and Internet Explorer support table nesting. Figure E-10 shows an example of a two-column table with a second table nested in the right column. The code for the nested tables is shown in the figure; the nested table code in the right column is highlighted.

tip

Although HTML 4.0 allows you to use the ALIGN=CENTER attribute in the <TABLE> element, most browsers do not support it, so you should use the <DIV> element as a container for the table.

FIGURE E-8: **Centered table**

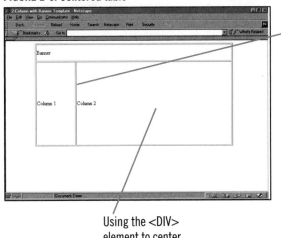

Code for a centered table using the <DIV> element:

```
<DIV ALIGN=CENTER>
<TABLE WIDTH=590 BORDER>
<TR><TD COLSPAN=2 HEIGHT=50>Banner</TD></TR>
<TR><TD HEIGHT=250 WIDTH=20%>Column 1</TD>
<TD>Column2</TD></TR>
</TABLE>
</DIV>
```

Using the <DIV> element to center the table

FIGURE E-9: **Stacked tables**

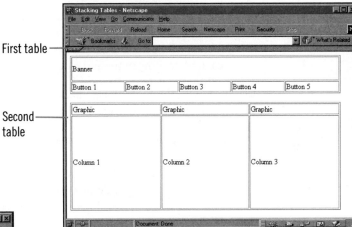

First table

Second table

FIGURE E-10: **Nesting tables**

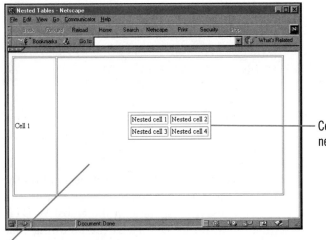

Cell 2 contains nested table — *rarely used*

Code for nested table:

```
<TABLE WIDTH=590 BORDER HEIGHT=300>
<TR><TD>Cell 1</TD>
<TD ALIGN=CENTER>
<!-- Nested table starts here -->
<TABLE BORDER CELLSPACING=5>
<TR><TD>nested cell 1</TD><TD>nested cell 2</TD></TR>
<TR><TD>nested cell 3</TD><TD>nested cell 4</TD></TR>
</TABLE>
<!-- Nested table ends here -->
</TD>
</TR>
</TABLE>
```

Web Design

Web Design

Creating a Basic Page Template

Now that you understand the mechanics of building tables, you can apply your knowledge to creating a page template. A **page template** is a form that you can use to standardize the placement of objects, images, and text on your pages throughout the Web site. You may be familiar with templates in other application packages such as your spreadsheet or word processor software. This example demonstrates how to take a design sketch for a Web page and build a template for the page layout.

Details

▶ Figure E-11 shows a sketch of the desired Web page layout. This layout is designed for a base screen resolution of 640 × 480, so the table will be fixed at a width of 590 pixels. Notice that the basic structure of the table is three rows by four columns. Each column uses 25% of the total width of the template. Row spans and column spans break across the layout to provide visual interest.

▶ Start by building the basic table structure, including all the cells and rows of the table. As you customize the table, you can remove extraneous cells.

The basic structure is a three-row by four-column table as shown in Figure E-12. Notice the use of row and cell placeholders such as R1C1, which stands for Row One, Cell One. These placeholders are visible in the browser and provide reference points that are helpful as you build a table. The following code shows the basic table syntax:

```
<TABLE BORDER>
<TR><TD>R1C1</TD><TD>R1C2</TD><TD>R1C3</TD><TD>R1C4</TD> </TR>
<TR><TD>R2C1</TD><TD>R2C2</TD><TD>R2C3</TD><TD>R2C4</TD> </TR>
<TR><TD>R3C1</TD><TD>R3C2</TD><TD>R3C3</TD><TD>R3C4</TD> </TR>
</TABLE>
```

▶ Making the borders visible with the BORDER attribute provides another visual reference to the structure of the table. When you complete your design, you can turn borders off by removing the BORDER attribute from the <TABLE> element.

▶ One of the design characteristics of the template is a fixed width that is not dependent on the user's browser size or screen resolution. You learned about the difference between relative and fixed-width tables. To accomplish this characteristic, use a pixel value in the global WIDTH attribute. Figure E-13 shows the result of setting the width to 590 pixels. The following code shows the WIDTH attribute:

```
<TABLE BORDER WIDTH=590>
<TR><TD>R1C1</TD><TD>R1C2</TD><TD>R1C3</TD><TD>R1C4</TD> </TR>
<TR><TD>R2C1</TD><TD>R2C2</TD><TD>R2C3</TD><TD>R2C4</TD> </TR>
<TR><TD>R3C1</TD><TD>R3C2</TD><TD>R3C3</TD><TD>R3C4</TD> </TR>
</TABLE>
```

FIGURE E-11: Sketch of visualized layout

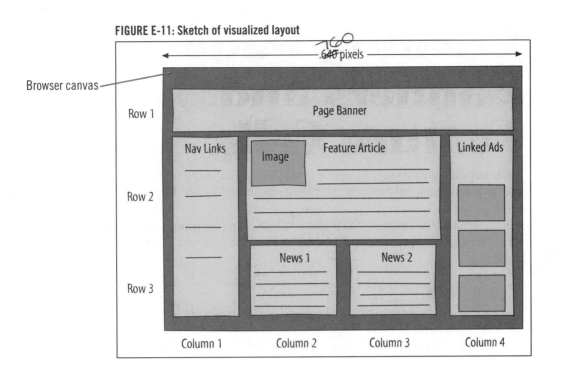

FIGURE E-12: Basic three-row by four-column table

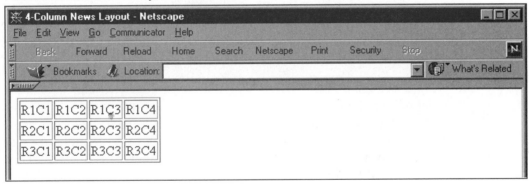

FIGURE E-13: Width set to 590 pixels

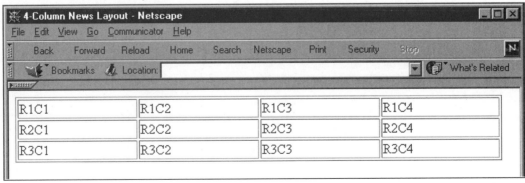

Creating Page Banners and Feature Cells

A **banner** on a Web page is a graphic or text image that either announces the name of the Web site or sponsoring company or is an advertisement on the page. Banners have a prominent placement on the page. According to the design sketch you set up for the template, the page banner will span the top of the page. The **feature cell** contains the prominent article or most important information on the page. It should be the focus of the page and, therefore, in the visual center of the page.

Details

► Creating the Page Banner Cell

In Figure E-14, the page banner cell is R1C1, which now contains the text "Page Banner." This cell spans the four columns of the table using the COLSPAN attribute. To create the column span successfully, you must remove all but one cell in the first row of the table. Also shown are the results of the column span. The first table row now contains only one cell with COLSPAN=4. The ALIGN attribute horizontally centers the text. The HEIGHT attribute sets the height of the cell to 50 pixels. The following code shows the COLSPAN attribute:

```
<TABLE BORDER WIDTH=590>
<!-- Row 1 Contains Page Banner -->
<TR><TD COLSPAN=4 ALIGN=CENTER HEIGHT=50>Page Banner</TD></TR>
<TR><TD>R2C1</TD><TD>R2C2</TD><TD>R2C3</TD><TD>R2C4</TD></TR>
<TR><TD>R3C1</TD><TD>R3C2</TD><TD>R3C3</TD><TD>R3C4</TD></TR>
</TABLE>
```

► Creating the Feature Cell

Figure E-15 shows that the feature cell in the layout is R2C2 and that it spans two columns. This column span requires the removal of one cell in row two to make room for the span. The code shows the removal of cell R2C3 to accommodate the column span. The HEIGHT attribute sets the vertical height for the feature cell to 200 pixels. The code shows the COLSPAN attribute in the feature cell:

```
<TABLE BORDER WIDTH=590>
<!-- Row 1 Contains Page Banner -->
<TR><TD COLSPAN=4 ALIGN=CENTER HEIGHT=50>Page Banner</TD></TR>
<!-- Row 2 Contains Feature Article -->
<TR><TD>R2C1</TD><TD COLSPAN=2
HEIGHT=200>Feature</TD><TD>R2C4</TD></TR>
<TR><TD>R3C1</TD><TD>R3C2</TD><TD>R3C3</TD><TD>R3C4</TD></TR>
</TABLE>
```

FIGURE E-14: Page banner cell

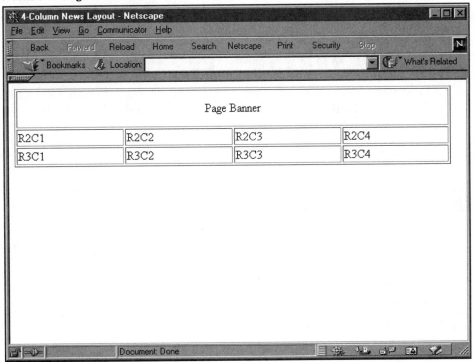

FIGURE E-15: Feature cell

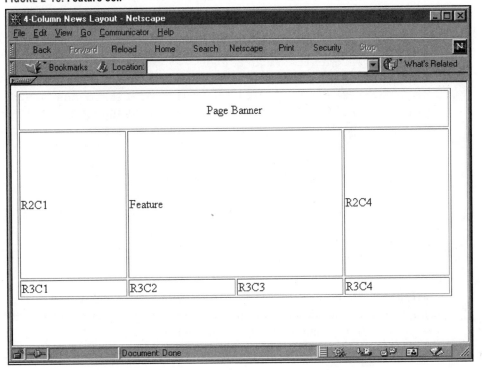

Working with Columns and Cells

The template design shown in Figure E-16 includes navigation links (Nav Links) on the left side of the page and linked advertisements (Linked Ads) on the right side. The design clearly distinguishes between links within the Web site and links to other advertisers.

Details

▶ Creating the Link Columns

The Nav Links and Linked Ads columns in the layout reside in cells R2C1 and R2C4, respectively. These cells span rows two and three of the table. The row spans require the removal of cells R3C1 and R3C4, illustrated in Figure E-16. Notice that the column widths have shifted because of the removal of cells.

▶ Setting the Column Widths

You can set column widths using the WIDTH attribute at the cell level. Column widths must be set in only one cell per column. Also, set the column widths in only one row of the table. In the example template, no rows contain a cell in each column of the table. The best way to set the widths for the columns is to add a fourth row to the table. This row acts as a width control row. These cells contain the WIDTH attributes and no content. Figure E-16 shows the template with the addition of a fourth row to control the column widths. Notice that the new row, which contains no content, appears as a few pixels of additional space at the bottom of the table. With the table borders turned off, the control row appears as white space at the bottom of the page. The following code shows the addition of the control row:

```
<TABLE BORDER WIDTH=590>
<!-- Row 1 Contains Page Banner -->
<TR><TD COLSPAN=4 ALIGN=CENTER HEIGHT=50>Page Banner</TD></TR>
<!-- Row 2 Contains Nav Links, Feature, Linked Ads -->
<TR><TD ROWSPAN=2>Nav Links</TD><TD COLSPAN=2 HEIGHT=200>
Feature</TD><TD ROWSPAN=2>Linked Ads</TD></TR>
<!-- Row 3 Contains News 1, News 2 -->
<TR><TD WIDTH=25%>News Column 1</TD>
<TD WIDTH=25%>News Column 2</TD></TR>
<!-- Row 4 Contains Width Controls -->
<TR><TD WIDTH=25%></TD><TD WIDTH=25%></TD><TD WIDTH=25%>
</TD><TD WIDTH=25%></TD><TR>
</TABLE>
```

▶ Setting Precise Widths Using Images

You can define column widths precisely if you use a graphic within the cell. Because the browser cannot wrap or truncate a graphic, the cell always will be at least as wide as the graphic. Some designers use transparent pixel GIFs to size their columns.

▶ Vertically Aligning Cells

To prepare the table for content, add the VALIGN=TOP attribute to all of the <TR> elements in the template. Adding this attribute forces the content to flow down from the top of the cell, rather than starting at the default vertical alignment setting, which is MIDDLE. Add this code to every <TR> element in the table. The code for a single row element is: <TR VALIGN=TOP>

tip

You can set widths at the cell level to either a pixel or percentage amount. Test carefully to make sure that the layout is browser compatible, as column widths can be troublesome.

X

FIGURE E-16: Link columns and a column width control row

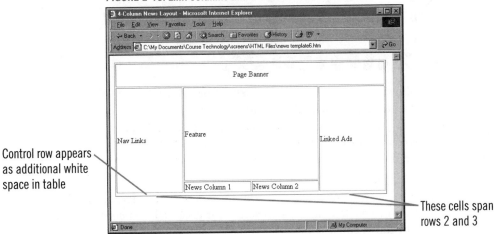

Control row appears as additional white space in table

These cells span rows 2 and 3

FIGURE E-17: Testing content in Netscape Navigator 4.x

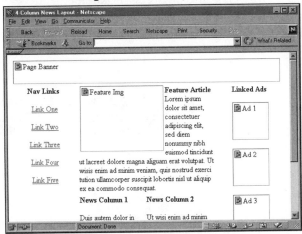

FIGURE E-18: Testing content in Internet Explorer 5.0

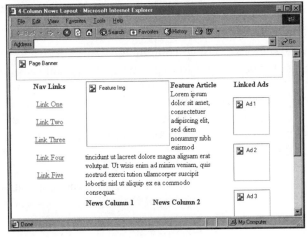

Design Matters

Testing the Template

To verify that your template works properly, populate it with test content. Figure E-17 shows the template with links, image spaces, and body copy in Netscape Navigator 4.x. The table borders are turned off. Notice how the content flows down the page as a result of the fixed table width. Test your template in multiple browsers. Figure E-18 shows the same template in Internet Explorer 5.0. The template displays properly in both browsers. The complete code for the template is in the end of unit material for this unit.

Web Design

Reviewing Template Examples

The following templates cover a variety of page layout needs. You may choose to stack different templates on top of each other for more complex layouts. Remember that in these examples, the HEIGHT attribute gives the blank tables some vertical height. Normally you would remove this attribute and let the content determine the height of the table.

▶ **Two-Column Template**

Figure E-19 shows a typical two-column template. The left cell is for navigation, the right cell for content. This template is well suited for lengthier text content. You can adjust the width of the right cell to constrain the text width.

```
<TABLE WIDTH=590 HEIGHT=250 BORDER>
<TR><TD WIDTH=100>Column 1</TD>
<TD>Column 2</TD></TR>
</TABLE>
```

FIGURE E-19: Two-column template

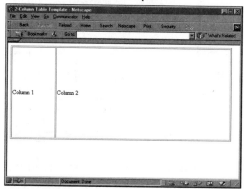

▶ **Two-Column with Banner Template**

Figure E-20 shows a basic two-column template with an additional column span in the first row. You can use the banner row for logos, navigation graphics, or banner ads.

```
<TABLE WIDTH=590 BORDER>
<TR><TD COLSPAN=2 HEIGHT=50>Banner</TD></TR>
<TR><TD HEIGHT=250 WIDTH=20%>Column 1</TD><TD>Column 2</TD></TR>
</TABLE>
```

FIGURE E-20: Two-column with banner template

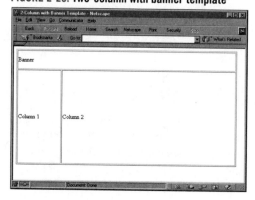

► Three-Column Template

Figure E-21 shows a three-column template. Use a three-column template to contain plain text or a variety of mixed content.

```
<TABLE WIDTH=590 HEIGHT=300 BORDER>
<TR>
<TD WIDTH=33%>Column 1</TD>
<TD WIDTH=33%>Column 2</TD>
<TD WIDTH=33%>Column 3</TD>
</TR>
</TABLE>
```

FIGURE E-21: Three-column template

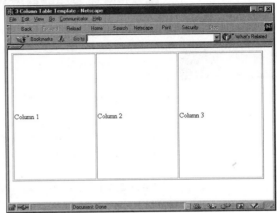

► Three-Column with Banner Template

Figure E-22 shows the addition of a banner to the three-column layout. This layout works well as a top-level page of a section or an entire Web site. The columnar structure lends itself to scanning rather than reading.

```
<TABLE WIDTH=590 BORDER>
<TR>
<TD HEIGHT=50 COLSPAN=3>Banner</TD>
</TR>
<TR>
<TD HEIGHT=250 WIDTH=33%>Column 1</TD>
<TD WIDTH=33%>Column 2</TD>
<TD WIDTH=33%>Column 3</TD>
</TR>
</TABLE>
```

FIGURE E-22: Three-column with banner template

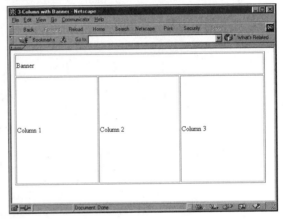

► Three-Column Main Template

Figure E-23 shows the three-column main template with a dominant center column that attracts the user's eye. This template is effective as a top-level or section-level page of a Web site.

```
<TABLE WIDTH=590 BORDER>
<TR>
<TD HEIGHT=300 WIDTH=15%>Column 1</TD>
<TD WIDTH=70%>Column 2</TD>
<TD WIDTH=15%>Column 3</TD>
</TR>
</TABLE>
```

FIGURE E-23: Three-column main template

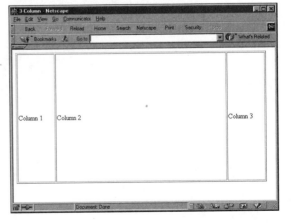

Reviewing More Template Examples

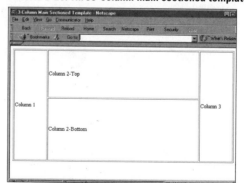

The following templates cover additional page layout options. Remember that the HEIGHT attribute used in these examples gives the blank tables some vertical height. When creating your own pages, you would remove this attribute and let the content determine the height of the table.

▶ **Sectioned Template**

Figure E-24 shows the center and right columns divided into four content areas. Use this template when you want to provide the user a choice between a variety of topics or sections. You can place navigation information in the left column. You most likely would use this template as a top-level page.

```
<TABLE WIDTH=590 HEIGHT=300 BORDER>
<TR>
<TD ROWSPAN=2 WIDTH=20%>Column 1</TD>
<TD >Column 2-Top</TD>
<TD>Column 3-Top</TD>
</TR>
<TR>
<TD>Column 2-Bottom</TD>
<TD>Column 3-Bottom</TD>
</TR>
</TABLE>
```

FIGURE E-24: Three-column sectioned template

▶ **Three-Column Main Sectioned Template**

Figure E-25 shows the center column divided into two content areas. Another variety of a top-level page, this one lets you break up the primary area of the screen into two sections. Left and right columns can be used for navigation or associated links.

```
<TABLE WIDTH=590 HEIGHT=300 BORDER>
<TR>
<TD HEIGHT=300 WIDTH=15% ROWSPAN=2>Column 1</TD>
<TD WIDTH=70%>Column 2-Top</TD>
<TD WIDTH=15% ROWSPAN=2>Column 3</TD>
</TR>
<TR>
<TD>Column 2-Bottom</TD>
</TR>
</TABLE>
```

FIGURE E-25: Three-column main sectioned template

Practice

► Concepts Review

Fill in the blank with the best answer.

1. Three print-based design structures that Web designers can duplicate with tables are *grid-based layouts*, *gutters* ~~*<table>*~~, *columns* ~~*<tr>*~~, and ~~*<td>*~~.

2. The three basic table elements are ~~*<caption>*~~, *<td>*, and *<table>*.

3. The ~~*<tr>*~~ *align* attribute can be used with the <CAPTION> element to place the caption above the table.

4. The three levels of a table structure are *global*, *row level*, and *cell level*.

5. Use the *cellspacing* attribute to adjust spacing *between* table cells and use the *cellpadding* attribute to adjust spacing *within* table cells.

6. *Cell-level* attributes take precedence over row-level attributes.

7. The *BG color* attribute lets you color the background of a cell.

8. ~~*<table*~~ *width="75%">* is the code for a table that fills 75% of the browser window.

9. If you have extra character *spaces* in the code for a table, extra white space appears within the table.

10. Using the <DIV> element with the ALIGN=CENTER attribute is the best way to *center* a table.

11. The basic table structure consists of a *3 rows* by *4 columns* table.

12. The _____ contains the prominent article or most important information on the page.

13. When setting column widths in a table, set the widths in only one row of the table and choose a row that contains one cell for every column in the table. True/False? _____

14. The *valign* attribute lets you align content to the top of a cell.

15. The _____ template is best suited for lengthier text content and offers you the opportunity to use the top row for logos, navigation graphics, or banner ads.

► Explore Further...

1. What are the benefits of stacking tables?
   - simplify table design (smaller is easier to work with)
   - display in same order they appear in code. (user can start reading as next one downloads)

2. What is the difference between removing the BORDER attribute and setting BORDER=0?
   By setting Border=0 allows you to join contents of adjacent cells.

3. What is the major disadvantage of relative width tables?
   design is not fixed; depends on browser.

4. Write the code to remove the default spacing from a table.
   <table border="0" cellpadding="0" cellspacing="0">

Web Design

5. Why would you want to remove the default spacing from a table?

removing default spacing joins the contents of adjacent cells.

6. Describe two ways that multiple tables can affect the way your pages download.

1. tbls appear in order they appear in code

2. easier to build complex tbls by breaking them down to simpler comp.

▶ Independent Challenges

1. As you spend more time browsing the Web for various reasons, you will begin to notice patterns in the way certain sites are designed. These sites use page templates.

a. Log on to the Internet and find Web sites that you think use page templates. Print two pages that share a similar design and, therefore, similar template.

b. Create a sketch of a page from the Web site that depicts your idea of the page template.

c. Examine the code to see how the template actually was built. In Navigator, this requires that you click View on the menu bar, then click Page Source. In Internet Explorer, click View on the menu bar, then click Source.

d. Use your word-processing program to write a brief essay that compares and contrasts your method with the designer's method of building the template.

e. Type **Your Name** at the bottom of the document, save the document, print a copy, and then close it.

2. In this unit, you have learned about template design by following the progress of a single design. The best way to appreciate the design process is by coding a template yourself. Also, building a mock-up of a finished page using your own content can be a great way to become more familiar with templates.

a. Using a simple text editor, code the template example from this unit. See below for the basic code that you can use for coding the template.

b. Build a mock-up of a finished page using content that you design yourself. Be sure your name is included somewhere on the page. When you are done, test the page in multiple browsers and note any differences in the way the content is displayed.

```
<TABLE  WIDTH=590>
<!-- Row 1 Contains Page Banner -->
<TR>
<TD COLSPAN=4 HEIGHT=50><IMG WIDTH=580 HEIGHT=50 ALT="Page Banner"></TD>
</TR>
<!-- Row 2 Contains Nav Links, Feature Article,
Linked Ads -->
<TR VALIGN=TOP>
<TD ROWSPAN=2 ALIGN=CENTER>
<B>Nav Links</B>
<P><A HREF="dummy link">Link One</A></P>
<P><A HREF="dummy link">Link Two</A></P>
<P><A HREF="dummy link">Link Three</A></P>
<P><A HREF="dummy link">Link Four</A></P>
<P><A HREF="dummy link">Link Five</A></P>
</TD>
<TD COLSPAN=2 HEIGHT=200 VALIGN=TOP>
<IMG WIDTH="180" HEIGHT="140" ALIGN=LEFT ALT="Feature
Img">
```

```
<B>Feature Article</B><BR>Lorem ipsum dolor sit amet,
consectetuer adipiscing elit, sed diem nonummy nibh
euismod tincidunt ut lacreet dolore magna aliguam erat
volutpat. Ut wisis enim ad minim veniam, quis nostrud
exerci tution ullamcorper suscipit lobortis nisl ut
aliquip ex eacommodo consequat.
</TD>
<TD ROWSPAN=2 ALIGN=CENTER><B>Linked Ads</B>
<P><IMG  WIDTH=80 HEIGHT=80 ALT="Ad 1"></P>
<P><IMG  WIDTH=80 HEIGHT=80 ALT="Ad 2"></P>
<P><IMG  WIDTH=80 HEIGHT=80 ALT="Ad 3"></P>
</TD>
</TR>
<!-- Row 3 Contains News 1, News 2 -->
<TR VALIGN=TOP>
<TD><P><B>News Column 1</B></P>Duis autem dolor in
hendrerit in vulputate velit esse molestie consequat, vel
illum dolore eu feugiat nulla facilisis at vero eros et
accumsan et iusto odio dignissim qui blandit praesent
luptatum
</TD>
<TD><P><B>News Column 2</B></P>Ut wisi enim ad minim
veniam, quis nostrud exerci taion ullamcorper suscipit
lobortis nisl ut aliquip ex en commodo consequat.
</TD>
</TR>
<!-- Row 4 Contains Width Controls -->
<TR><TD WIDTH=150></TD><TD WIDTH=150></TD><TD
WIDTH=150></TD><TD WIDTH=150></TD></TR>
</TABLE>
```

3. As you visit various sites, you should be more aware of those that use tables to organize the information on the page. Using what you know about the various table attributes available, you should be able to identify the design choices that were made by the site designers . There are many ways in which tables are used in sites. The assignment below identifies five possibilities; select and complete three of them.

a. Log on to the Internet and find examples of Web sites that use fixed tables. Print out one page from a site, and then use your word processor to write a short essay that describes why you think the designers chose a fixed layout for the content. Type **Your Name** at the bottom of the document, save the document, print a copy, and then close it.

b. Find examples of Web sites that use relative tables. Print out the page from one site, and then use your word processor to write a short essay that describes why you think the designers chose a relative layout for the content. Type **Your Name** at the bottom of the document, save the document, print a copy, and then close it.

c. Find examples of Web sites that fill the screen at 640 × 480 resolution without showing a horizontal scroll bar. Print out the page from one site, and then use your word processor to write a short essay that describes why you think the designers chose to use this resolution and explain how effective it is.

d. Find examples of Web sites that are built on a three-column layout. Print out the page from one site, and then use your word processor to write a short essay that describes why you think the designers chose to use this layout.

e. Find examples of Web sites that contain a banner cell that spans the layout. Print out the page from one site, and then use your word processor to write a short essay that describes how effective the banner is on the page.

Web Design

You will continue to work on the site you began in Unit A and continued through the previous units. You will recall that to complete the ongoing case study for this book, you must create a complete, stand-alone Web site. The site must contain from six to ten pages and display at least three levels of information. By this point, you will have selected your own content and started to organize your site. You should have created a visual diagram that indicates the main page, section pages, and content pages, as well as indicates the links between the pages.

a. Design the page templates for the different information levels of your Web site. Create sketches for each template, and describe why the templates fit your content.

You will find all of the page templates shown in this unit on the Student Online Companion site at *www.course.com/illustrated/designingsites*.

b. Use these templates as a starting point for your Web pages. Adapt the page templates to meet your own needs, or build your page templates from scratch.

c. Test the page templates with content in different browsers to make sure that they display properly.

d. Once your templates test properly, start to build the files for your Web site by copying the templates to individual files and naming them to match your flowchart from Unit C.

▶ Visual Workshop

1. In this Visual Workshop, the image shown in Figure E-26 is from a site that uses tables effectively to organize information. Identify the elements and write the code that you think was used to create the tables. Write a brief essay explaining how effective the table is in this application. Be sure to include details of the table construction.

FIGURE E-26

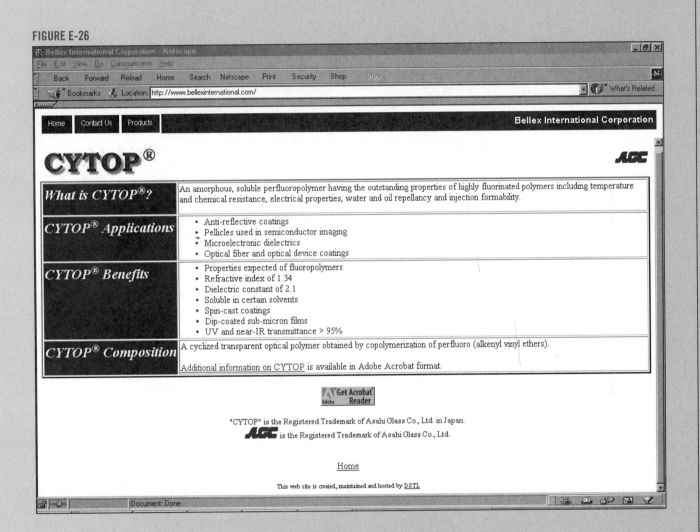

Web Design

► Visual Workshop

2. In this Visual Workshop, the image shown in Figure E-27 is from a site that uses tables effectively to organize information. Identify the elements and write the code that you think was used to create the tables. Write a brief essay explaining how effective the table is in this application. Be sure to include details of the table construction.

FIGURE E-27

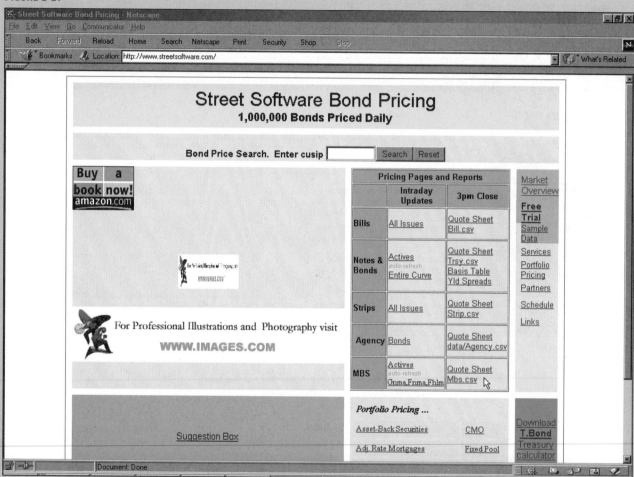

Understanding
Web Typography

Web Design

Objectives

- ► **Explore type design principles**
- ► **Control typography with <FONT>**
- ► **Control typography with CSS**
- ► **Work with style sheets**
- ► **Understand CSS font properties**
- ► **Specify font values**
- ► **Specify block-level space values**
- ► **Style with CSS**

Type can be used to create a strong recurring theme throughout a well-designed Web site. Web site visitors respond instinctively to words set in type. The consistent use of type provides valuable information cues to the reader, and recent innovations provide powerful tools for working with type. Until recently, Web typography meant having to use too many <FONT> tags and lots of text as graphics. Today, CSS offers a potent style language, allowing you to manipulate a variety of text properties to achieve professional, effective results, all without resorting to graphics that add download time.

Exploring Type Design Principles

Type is a flexible medium that can express emotion, tone, and structure based on the choices you make. A **typeface** is a design for a set of characters. Typefaces often come as a family of typefaces, with individual typefaces for italic, bold, and other formatting in the main design. You designate a specific typeface, formatting, and size when designing type for your Web site. You have to be careful not to use too many typefaces and sizes. As you work with type, consider choosing fewer fonts and sizes, using available fonts, designing for legibility, and avoiding using text as graphics.

Details

▶ Designing for the Web actually restricts your type choices because you must stick with fonts that your users have installed on their computers. If you specify a font that is not available, the browser substitutes the default font.

▶ In strict typography terms, a typeface is the name of the type, such as Times New Roman or Futura Condensed. A font is the typeface in a particular size, such as Times Roman 24 point. For the most part, in HTML the two terms are interchangeable.

▶ Your pages look cleaner when you choose fewer fonts and sizes of type. The size and face of the type you use on your pages determine the legibility of your text. Decide on a font for each different level of topic importance, such as page headings, section headings, and body text. Communicate the hierarchy of information with changes in the size, weight, or color of the typeface. For example, a page heading should have a larger, bolder type, whereas a section heading should appear in the same typeface, only lighter or smaller.

▶ Pick a few sizes and weights in a type family. For example, you might choose three sizes, such as 24 point for headings, 18 point for subheadings, and 12 point for body text. You can vary these styles by changing the weight; for example, 12-point bold type can be used for topic headings within text. Consistently apply the same fonts and the same combination of styles throughout your Web site. Avoid making random changes in your use of type conventions because consistency develops a strong visual identity on your pages, as is demonstrated in Figure F-1.

▶ To control how text appears on your pages more effectively, think in terms of font families, such as serif and sans-serif typefaces depicted in Figure F-2, rather than specific styles. Because of the variable nature of fonts installed on different computers, you never can be sure the user will see the exact font you have specified. You can, however, specify font substitution attributes (described later in this unit) that let you specify a variety of fonts within a font family, such as the common sans-serif fonts Arial or Helvetica.

▶ The user's browser and operating system determine how a font is displayed or if it is displayed at all. If you design your pages using a font that your user does not have installed, the browser defaults to Times on a Macintosh computer or Times New Roman on a PC. Be aware that even the most widely available fonts appear in different sizes on different operating systems.

▶ Times (or Times New Roman) is available on PC, Macintosh, and Unix operating systems. It is the default browser font. Courier is the default monospace font. Arial or Helvetica are the default sans-serif fonts. Arial and Verdana come with Internet Explorer 4.0 and up, so many Macintosh and PC users have these fonts installed. Some Macintosh users only have Helvetica, so it is a good idea to specify this font as an alternate choice when you are using sans-serif fonts.

▶ Figures F-3 and F-4 show the same paragraph in Times and Arial at the default browser size. Because its x height (the height of the letter x in the font) is smaller than that of other fonts, Times at the default size can be hard to read, even though it is a serif typeface. Some find Arial more legible online.

▶ Remember that the computer screen has a lower resolution than the printed page. Fonts that are legible on paper can be more difficult to read on screen. Keep fonts big enough to be legible and avoid specialty fonts that degrade when viewed online.

tip

Provide enough contrast between your text color and the background color. Darker text on a light background is easiest to read. Also, adding more white space to the page around your blocks of text and between the lines makes reading easier.

FIGURE F-1: Same font for headlines and navigation in different sizes

Instantly familiar banner —

Typeface for headings —

Browser's default typeface for body text —

FIGURE F-2: Serif and sans-serif typefaces

A **serif** is a fine line that finishes off the main strokes of a letter —

Serif   Sans-Serif

FIGURE F-3: Paragraph in Times at the default browser size

The font determines where the text wraps at the end of each line —

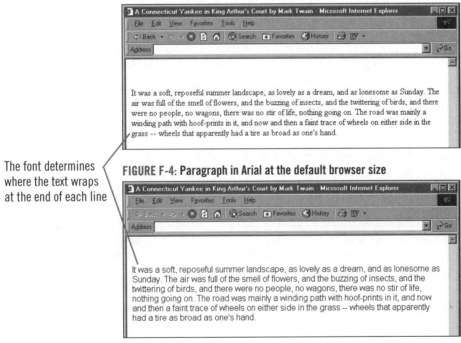

FIGURE F-4: Paragraph in Arial at the default browser size

Web Design

Avoid Using Text as Graphics

If you must use a specific font, create text as a graphic. Using Adobe Photoshop or another graphics program, create text and save it as either a GIF or JPG file. This technique allows you to add drop shadows and other effects to your text. However, because you also are adding "download overhead" with every additional graphic, save text graphics for important purposes, such as the main logo for your page or for reusable navigation graphics. Remember that including text as graphics means users cannot search for that text. Whenever possible, use HTML-styled text on your pages.

Controlling Typography with \<FONT\>

Until the addition of the \<FONT\> element in HTML 3.2, an HTML author could do little to control type display on a Web page. This is because HTML is intended to express document structure only, not document style. The \<FONT\> element, although simplistic in its control over text display, allows HTML authors to choose the color and size of their type.

Details

▶ In the HTML 3.2 specification, the W3C cautioned that the \<FONT\> element may not be included in future versions of HTML. With HTML 4.0, the \<FONT\> element has been deprecated in favor of CSS. To ensure forward compatibility with all browsers, move to CSS and limit or replace the \<FONT\> element in your code. Currently, however, the \<FONT\> element still is widely used on the Web and supported by browsers. You can use it to set font size and color and to specify font substitution.

▶ Use the SIZE attribute to set the font size. You can use absolute sizing to specify the exact size for the font. The range of sizes is one to seven, with three being the default. Size one is the smallest and size seven is the largest. The sizes are relative to the default browser size. The following code sets the font size to six:

```
<FONT SIZE=6>Some text</FONT>
```

You also can set sizes relative to the default base font using the plus (+) or minus (–) signs. Setting SIZE=+2 results in a font two sizes larger than the default (size three). The following code sets the size to six. This SIZE attribute expresses default size three plus three:

```
<FONT SIZE=+3>Some text</FONT>
```

▶ To control which fonts browsers use, you can include a list of alternate fonts, forcing the browser to look for matching fonts installed on the user's machine. Specify alternate fonts in the \<FONT\> element by listing a string of fonts within quotes in the FACE attribute. For example, the following code tells the browser to display the text in Arial. If Arial is not available, the browser attempts to use Helvetica. If neither is available, the text appears in the browser default font, usually Times New Roman.

```
<FONT SIZE=6 FACE="ARIAL, HELVETICA">some text</FONT>
```

▶ You can set font color with the COLOR attribute, using either a color name or hexadecimal color code.

```
<FONT SIZE=6 FACE="ARIAL, HELVETICA" COLOR=RED>some text</FONT>
```

Figure F-5 shows how the \<FONT\> element formats the type size, face, and color on the Web page. The highlighted code shows the syntax of the \<FONT\> element for that code.

tip

You can download a package of Web fonts from Microsoft at *www.microsoft.com/ typography/fontpack/ default.htm*. The core fonts package includes Arial, Verdana, and a number of other fonts designed specifically for the Web.

FIGURE F-5: Text formatted with the <FONT> element

```
<HTML>
<HEAD>
<TITLE> A Connecticut Yankee in King Arthur's Court by Mark Twain
</TITLE>
</HEAD>
  <BODY>
<DIV ALIGN=RIGHT>
from <I>A Connecticut Yankee in King Arthur's Court</I> by Mark
Twain</DIV>
<HR>
<FONT SIZE=5 COLOR=GRAY>Chapter 1</FONT> <BR>
<FONT SIZE=6>The Tale of the Lost Land: Camelot</FONT>
<FONT FACE=ARIAL>
<P>
"CAMELOT — Camelot," said I to myself. "I don't seem to remember
hearing of it before. Name of the asylum, likely."
</P>
```

Controlling Typography with CSS

This lesson acquaints you with the CSS properties that affect how type appears in the browser. This is not meant to be a complete CSS lesson but rather a typography-oriented look at the benefits of its use. CSS is based on rules that select an HTML element and declare style characteristics for the element. You can state sets of rules, known as **style sheets**, in the head section of an HTML document or include them in a separate document.

Details

▶ CSS offers much greater control over type characteristics than does the <FONT> element. You can use standard type conventions, such as using point or pixel sizes, setting line height, and specifying indents and alignment. You gain more control with much less code. For example, suppose that you want every <H1> element on your Web site to be green and centered. Using the <FONT> element, you need the following code for every instance of the <H1> element:

```
<H1 ALIGN=CENTER><FONT COLOR=GREEN>The Heading</FONT></H1>
```

With CSS, you can express this style information once as a rule in a style sheet that affects every <H1> element on any page that uses CSS.

```
H1 {COLOR:GREEN; TEXT-ALIGN:CENTER}
```

▶ Style sheet rules are easy to interpret. The style sheet in Figure F-6 shows a simple style rule for the <P> element that sets all <P> elements in the document to blue 24-point text. Note that the style rules are contained in the <STYLE> element in the document's <HEAD> section.

▶ Style rules are composed of two parts: a selector and a declaration. The **selector** determines the element to which the rule is applied. The **declaration** details the exact property values. Figure F-7 is an example of a simple rule showing the two parts. This rule forces the browser to display all <H1> headings in red. The declaration contains a property and a value. The **property** is a quality or characteristic. The precise specification of the property is contained in the **value**. CSS includes over 50 properties, each with a specific number of values.

▶ You must include all CSS rules within a <STYLE> element or define them using a STYLE attribute. The <STYLE> element always is contained in the <HEAD> section as shown in Figure F-8. The rule must be added to an entire HTML document. Alternatively, you can define the style for a single <H1> element using the STYLE attribute.

```
<H1 STYLE="COLOR: BLUE">Some Text</H1>
```

You generally would use the STYLE attribute to override a style that was set at a higher level in the document.

▶ An **external style sheet** is a text document with a .css extension that contains the style rules. Use external style sheets to set rules when working with a number of HTML documents. Placing style sheets in an external document lets you specify rules for different HTML documents. This is an easy and powerful way to use style sheets. Figure F-9 shows an example of a simple external style sheet named style1.css. Notice that the CSS comment line begins with the characters "/*" and ends with the characters "*/". The style sheet file contains no HTML code, only CSS style rules.

▶ To link to this external style sheet, add the <LINK> element within the head section of any HTML file as shown in the code in Figure F-10. The file containing this code displays with the characteristics specified by the style sheet. All pages that are linked to this style sheet display the style rules. The advantage of the external style sheet is that you only have to change the style rules in one document to affect all the pages on a Web site.

FIGURE F-6: A simple rule

```
<HEAD>
<TITLE>Sample Document</TITLE>
<STYLE>
P {COLOR: BLUE; FONT-SIZE: 24pt}
</STYLE>
</HEAD>
```

FIGURE F-7: Style rules and declaration syntax

```
Selector ──── H1 {COLOR: RED} ──── Value
                 │        │
              Property  Declaration
```

FIGURE F-8: A CSS rule in a <Style> element

The TYPE attribute to the <STYLE> element defines the style language as CSS

```
<HEAD>
<TITLE>Sample Document</TITLE> <STYLE TYPE="text/css">
H1 {COLOR: RED}
</STYLE>
</HEAD>
```

FIGURE F-9: Simple external style sheet

```
/* Stylesheet #1 */
BODY {COLOR: RED}
H1 {COLOR: GREEN}
H2 {COLOR: GREEN; BORDER: SOLID BLUE}
```

FIGURE F-10: Code to link to external style sheet

```
<HEAD>
<TITLE>Sample Document</TITLE>
<LINK HREF="style1.css" REL="stylesheet">
</HEAD>
```

The HREF attribute specifies the URL of the style sheet and all relative file location rules apply

The REL attribute specifies the relationship between the linked and current documents

Solving Problems with Style Sheets

The main problem with style sheets is browser support. Currently, Internet Explorer 5.0 is the leader in style sheet support but still does not support the specification completely. Netscape Navigator 4.x is far behind in CSS support, but Netscape 6 has full support for XML and CSS level 1 (among others). Strange results appear when browsers cannot interpret the rules properly. Finally, older browsers will not be able to interpret your CSS rules at all. Test carefully to make sure you can live with the results if your rules are ignored.

Working with Style Sheets

You must apply the style rules you build to the elements in the document. The power in CSS comes from the different methods of selecting elements. You can choose from a variety of selection methods, including selecting multiple elements, selecting by context, and selecting with the CLASS attribute. More complex selection involves the creation of artificial divisions, using two elements designed expressly for CSS: <DIV> block division and the <SPAN> inline division.

Details

▶ Using multiple selectors lets you use less code to accomplish the same results. For example, to make both <H1> and <H2> headings green, you could use one rule expressed in two lines, or these two rules can be expressed in a single rule statement using multiple selectors for the same property, as shown in Figure F-11.

▶ A context-based selector lets you specify the exact context in which a style is applied. The following rule specifies that <I> elements appear blue only within <H1> elements:

```
<STYLE TYPE="text/css">
H1 I {COLOR: BLUE}
</STYLE>
```

▶ The CLASS attribute lets you write rules and then apply them to groups of elements that you have classified. Basically, the CLASS attribute lets you define your own tags and then apply them anywhere you want. To create a class, first declare it within the <STYLE> element. Figure F-12 shows an example of a rule with a class selector. The selected paragraph will display the style properties of the quote class.

▶ The use of the <DIV> block division and the <SPAN> inline division elements, in combination with the CLASS attribute, effectively allows you to create entirely new HTML elements that are specific to your working environment. You then can use these techniques in external style sheets to apply your style properties across multiple documents in a Web site or other HTML-based applications.

▶ The <DIV> element lets you specify logical divisions within a document that have their own names and style properties. <DIV> is a block-level element that contains a leading and trailing carriage return. You can use the <DIV> element with the CLASS attribute to create customized block-level elements. To create a division, first declare it within the <STYLE> element. Figure F-13 specifies a division named "INTRO" as the selector for the rule. Next, specify the <DIV> element in the document, and then use the CLASS attribute to specify the exact type of division.

▶ The <SPAN> element lets you specify inline elements within a document that have their own name and style properties. Place inline elements within a line of text, like the <B> or <I> elements. You can use the <SPAN> element with the CLASS attribute to create customized inline elements and apply styles more accurately.

To create a span, first declare it within the <STYLE> element. Figure F-14 specifies a <SPAN> element named "LOGO" as the selector for the rule. Next, specify the <SPAN> element in the document, and then use the CLASS attribute to specify the exact type of <SPAN> element.

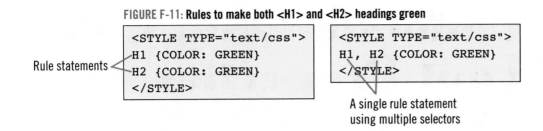

FIGURE F-11: **Rules to make both <H1> and <H2> headings green**

```
<STYLE TYPE="text/css">
H1 {COLOR: GREEN}
H2 {COLOR: GREEN}
</STYLE>
```

Rule statements

```
<STYLE TYPE="text/css">
H1, H2 {COLOR: GREEN}
</STYLE>
```

A single rule statement
using multiple selectors

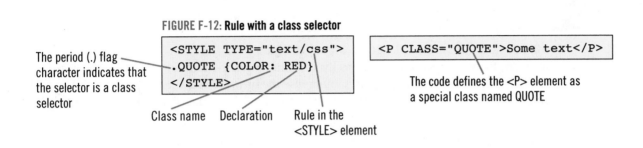

FIGURE F-12: **Rule with a class selector**

The period (.) flag
character indicates that
the selector is a class
selector

```
<STYLE TYPE="text/css">
.QUOTE {COLOR: RED}
</STYLE>
```

Class name   Declaration   Rule in the
                            <STYLE> element

```
<P CLASS="QUOTE">Some text</P>
```

The code defines the <P> element as
a special class named QUOTE

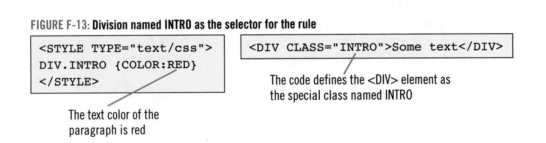

FIGURE F-13: **Division named INTRO as the selector for the rule**

```
<STYLE TYPE="text/css">
DIV.INTRO {COLOR:RED}
</STYLE>
```

The text color of the
paragraph is red

```
<DIV CLASS="INTRO">Some text</DIV>
```

The code defines the <DIV> element as
the special class named INTRO

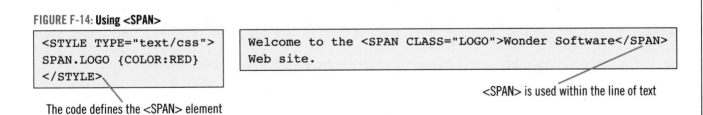

FIGURE F-14: **Using <SPAN>**

```
<STYLE TYPE="text/css">
SPAN.LOGO {COLOR:RED}
</STYLE>
```

The code defines the <SPAN> element
as a special class named LOGO

```
Welcome to the <SPAN CLASS="LOGO">Wonder Software</SPAN>
Web site.
```

<SPAN> is used within the line of text

Web Design

Understanding CSS Font Properties

CSS lets you control over 50 style properties. The font properties you will work with most often include font families and alternates, font size, font weight, line height, letter spacing, text indent, and color. This lesson discusses all of these font properties.

Details

▶ **Selecting a Specific Font Family and Alternates**

The font family property lets you specify any font or generic font family. The users must have the font installed on their computers, otherwise the browser uses the default font. Figure F-15 shows the rule that specifies Arial as the font for the <P> element and the code that tells the browser to use Arial, but if Arial is not present, use Helvetica.

You can specify a list of alternate fonts by using commas as separators. The browser attempts to load each successive font in the list. If no fonts match, the browser uses its default font. You can add a generic name for greater portability across browsers and operating systems. You can use the following generic names for font families: serif, sans-serif, and monospace. If you do not specify any font family, the browser displays the default font.

▶ **Specifying Font Size**

CSS offers a variety of measurement units. For example, to specify font size, you can use any of the measurement units shown in Table F-1. Figure F-16 shows the results of the style rule that sets the <BLOCKQUOTE> element to 18-point Arial. Remember, you have to separate multiple property statements with semicolons.

> **tip**
>
> To specify a size for the body text, use BODY as the selector.

▶ **Specifying Font Weight**

CSS allows either a numerical or descriptive value for font weight. Commonly used descriptive values include Normal, Bold, Bolder, and Lighter.

Test values other than bold. Not all weights are available for all typefaces. Experiment to determine what works.

▶ **Specifying Line Height**

CSS allows you to specify either a percentage or absolute value for the line height, commonly called leading. The percentage is based on the font size. Setting the value to 150% with a 10-point font size results in a line height of 15 points. For absolute values, use any of the standard CSS measurement units.

Figure F-17 shows the text with font weight and adjustment in line height.

Specifies Arial

```
<STYLE TYPE="text/css">
P {FONT-FAMILY: ARIAL}
</STYLE>
```

```
<STYLE TYPE="text/css">
P {FONT-FAMILY: ARIAL, HELVETICA}
</STYLE>
```

If Arial is not present, use Helvetica

```
<STYLE TYPE="text/css">
P {FONT-FAMILY: ARIAL, HELVETICA, SANS-SERIF}
</STYLE>
```

Tells the browser to use a sans-serif font if Arial or Helvetica are not available

FIGURE F-16: **Specifying font size**

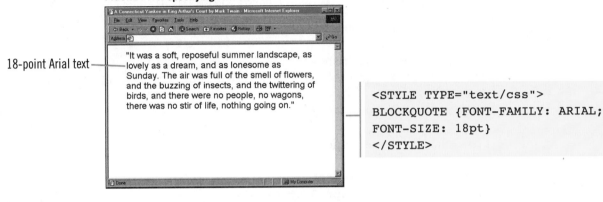

18-point Arial text

```
<STYLE TYPE="text/css">
BLOCKQUOTE {FONT-FAMILY: ARIAL;
FONT-SIZE: 18pt}
</STYLE>
```

FIGURE F-17: **Specifying font weight and line height**

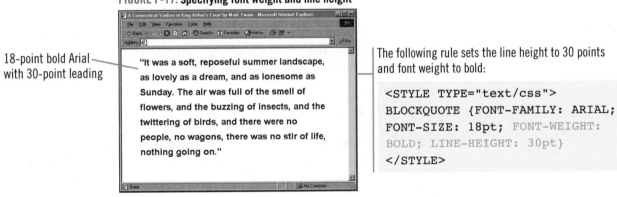

18-point bold Arial with 30-point leading

The following rule sets the line height to 30 points and font weight to bold:

```
<STYLE TYPE="text/css">
BLOCKQUOTE {FONT-FAMILY: ARIAL;
FONT-SIZE: 18pt; FONT-WEIGHT:
BOLD; LINE-HEIGHT: 30pt}
</STYLE>
```

TABLE F-1: **CSS measurement units**

unit	code abbreviation	description
Centimeter	cm	Standard metric centimeter
Em	em	The width of the capital M in the current font, usually the same as the font size
Ex	ex	The height of the letter x in the current font
Inch	in	Standard U.S. inch
Millimeter	mm	Standard metric millimeter
Relative		A font size relative to the base font size; for example, 150% equals one and one-half the base font size
Pica	pc	Standard publishing unit equal to 12 points
Pixel	px	The size of a pixel on the current screen
Point	point	Standard publishing unit, with 72 points in an inch

Web Design

UNDERSTANDING WEB TYPOGRAPHY

Specifying Font Values

The additional font properties of letter spacing, text indent, and color add variety and can be used to enhance your text in the Web site.

▶ **Using Font Property Shortcuts**

The font property is a shortcut that lets you specify the most common font properties in a single statement. You must use the following syntax in the exact order, and always include a font size: Selector {FONT: FONT-WEIGHT FONT-SIZE/LINE-HEIGHT FONT-FAMILY}

You can abbreviate this rule:

```
<STYLE TYPE="text/css">
BODY {FONT-WEIGHT: BOLD; FONT-SIZE: 18pt; LINE-HEIGHT: 30pt; FONT-
FAMILY: ARIAL}
</STYLE>
```

to the following shorter version:

```
<STYLE TYPE="text/css">
BODY {FONT: BOLD 18pt/30pt ARIAL}
</STYLE>
```

▶ **Specifying Letter Spacing**

Kerning is the printer's term for adjusting the white space between letters. To adjust kerning, use the letter-spacing property. Use any of the CSS measurement units for the value. The rule shown in Figure F-18 sets the letter spacing to 2 points.

▶ **Specifying Text Indents**

Use the text indent property to set the amount of indentation for the first line of text in an element, such as a paragraph. Use any of the CSS measurement units for the value. Figure F-19 shows the result of the text indent property set at an indent of 18 points. You can create a hanging indent by using a negative value in the text indent property. For example, the following code creates a paragraph with a 12-point hanging indent:

```
<STYLE TYPE="text/css">
P {TEXT-INDENT: -12pt}
</STYLE>
```

▶ **Specifying Color**

The COLOR attribute sets the color of the text in an element. You also can use the COLOR attribute to set the color of borders. You can use any one of the 16 predefined colors or specify a hexadecimal value. The following rule sets the text color to blue:

```
<STYLE TYPE="text/css">
H1 {COLOR: BLUE}
</STYLE>
```

▶ **Specifying Text Background Color**

You can set the background color—the color behind the text—for any element. Figure F-20 shows an <H2> element with this style. The result of this rule is white text on a blue background.

FIGURE F-18: 2 points of letter spacing

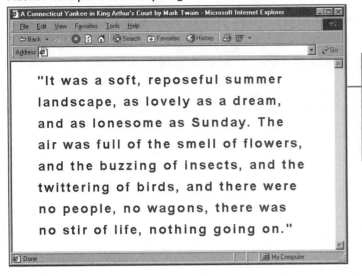

"It was a soft, reposeful summer landscape, as lovely as a dream, and as lonesome as Sunday. The air was full of the smell of flowers, and the buzzing of insects, and the twittering of birds, and there were no people, no wagons, there was no stir of life, nothing going on."

```
<STYLE TYPE="text/css">
BLOCKQUOTE {FONT-FAMILY: ARIAL;
FONT-SIZE: 18pt;
FONT-WEIGHT: BOLD; LINE-HEIGHT:
30 pt; LETTER-SPACING: 2pt}
</STYLE>
```

FIGURE F-19: 18-point text indent

```
<STYLE TYPE="text/css">
BLOCKQUOTE {FONT-FAMILY: ARIAL;
FONT-SIZE: 18pt;
FONT-WEIGHT: BOLD; LINE-HEIGHT:
30 pt; LETTER-SPACING: 2pt;
TEXT-INDENT: 18pt}
</STYLE>
```

"It was a soft, reposeful summer landscape, as lovely as a dream, and as lonesome as Sunday. The air was full of the smell of flowers, and the buzzing of insects, and the twittering of birds, and there were no people, no wagons, there was no stir of life, nothing going on."

FIGURE F-20: Specifying color

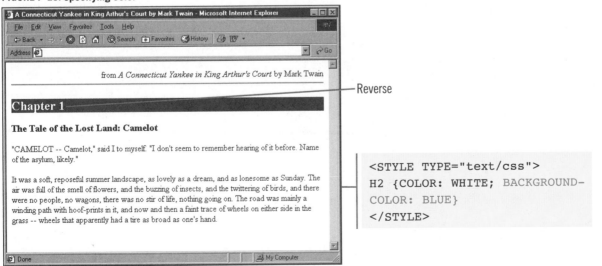

Reverse

```
<STYLE TYPE="text/css">
H2 {COLOR: WHITE; BACKGROUND-
COLOR: BLUE}
</STYLE>
```

Specifying Block-Level Space Values

CSS allows you to specify property values for the space around block-level elements. You can set the following three properties: padding (the area between the text and border), border (the area separating the padding and margin), and margin (the area outside the border). Figure F-21 shows these three areas around a block-level text element.

Details

▶ Specifying Text Padding

You can specify the padding amount with any CSS measurement unit. Use the PADDING attribute to set the padding on all four sides, or set individual margins with the following settings: PADDING-TOP, PADDING-BOTTOM, PADDING-LEFT, and PADDING-RIGHT. The following rule sets the left and right padding to 24 points:

```
<STYLE TYPE="text/css">
P {PADDING-LEFT: 24pt; PADDING-RIGHT: 24pt}
</STYLE>
```

▶ Specifying Text Margins

You can specify the margin amount with any CSS measurement unit. Use the MARGIN attribute to set the text margin on all four sides, or set individual margins with the following settings: MARGIN-TOP, MARGIN-BOTTOM, MARGIN-LEFT, and MARGIN-RIGHT. The following rule sets the margin to 30 pixels:

```
<STYLE TYPE="text/css">
P {MARGIN: 30px}
</STYLE>
```

▶ Specifying Text Borders

CSS offers a wide variety of border options including width, style, and color. You can use the BORDER shortcut property to specify multiple border properties at one time. Use the following syntax: {BORDER: BORDER-STYLE BORDER-WIDTH BORDER-COLOR}

For example, the following code sets a solid, 2-point red border around the text:

```
<STYLE TYPE="text/css">
{BORDER: SOLID 2pt RED}
</STYLE>
```

FIGURE F-21: **White space around block-level elements**

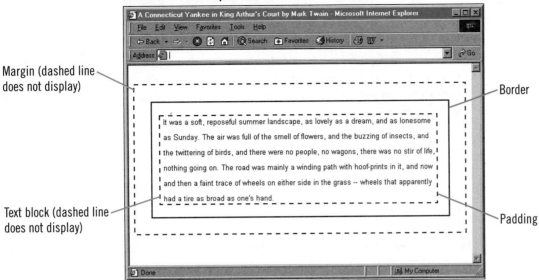

Margin (dashed line does not display)

Border

Text block (dashed line does not display)

Padding

Coding Easy-to-Read Rules

To the browser, it does not matter how you space and indent your style rules, as long as the syntax is correct. Many HTML authors indent their style rules to make them easier to read and maintain. Figure F-22 compares how it is possible to express a single-line style rule in a much neater fashion and, as a result, how the same rule is easier to read using indenting and alignment.

FIGURE F-22: **Coding styles compared**

```
<STYLE TYPE="text/css">
P         {
          FONT-FAMILY: ARIAL, HELVETICA, SANS-SERIF;
          FONT-SIZE: 10pt;
          LINE-HEIGHT: 20pt;
          MARGIN-LEFT: 20px;
          MARGIN-RIGHT: 20px
          }
</STYLE>
```

Using indenting and alignment

```
<STYLE TYPE="text/css">
P {FONT-FAMILY: ARIAL, HELVETICA, SANS-SERIF;
FONT-SIZE: 10pt; LINE-HEIGHT: 20pt;
MARGIN-LEFT: 20px;
MARGIN-RIGHT: 20px}
</STYLE>
```

Single-line style rule

Web Design

Styling with CSS

In this lesson, you will see how to set up a style sheet for a document using a variety of font properties. For example, if your job is to develop an online library of public domain texts, you would want to set up a style sheet that you could apply to all the documents in the collection. In the example shown in Figure F-23, the public domain content is the first chapter from Mark Twain's *A Connecticut Yankee in King Arthur's Court.*

Details

▶ To set up a style sheet, start by determining the logical divisions for the document. Each division has its own unique type characteristics that can be stated as style rules. Figure F-23 shows the document divisions you could use for this type of document.

Using style sheets, you can create a different set of style rules for each division—standard paragraph, book title, credit, chapter number, and chapter title. For this example, you can build the style sheet internally in the <STYLE> section. Later, you can move the rules to an external style sheet for use with multiple documents.

▶ You can set up the style for the most basic content division—the standard paragraph. Select the <P> element and state the style rules. Place all style rules within the <STYLE> element in the document's <HEAD> section. Figure F-23 shows the results of the style changes to the <P> element.

▶ To style the chapter number, set up a class name for the chapter number. Call this class "CHAPNUMBER." Here are the style characteristics for the class: default browser font, white text on a gray background, 24-point bold text with 36-point leading, and 20-pixel left margin. Specify the class name and state the rule. Figure F-24 shows the code for the rule and the results of the new style. It reflects changing the element that contains the chapter number to apply the new style. The code had looked like this:

```
<H2>Chapter 1</H2>
```

The new code replaced the <H2> with <DIV> and specified the CLASS attribute value as "CHAPNUMBER."

▶ To style the chapter title, call the chapter title class "CHAPTITLE." Specify the class name and state the rule, and then apply the style in the code. The style characteristics are default browser font, 18-point bold text with 30-point leading, 2 points of spacing between each letter, and 20-pixel left margin. Figure F-24 shows the code and results of the new style.

▶ To style the credit and book title, finish the document style sheet by setting up classes for the credit and book title. The credit is a block element and, therefore, a <DIV>. The style requirements are default font, 10-point type on 20-point leading, right-aligned, black bottom border rule, and 20-pixel left margin. State the style rule for class CREDIT. The book title is contained within a line of text. Use the inline <SPAN> element to apply a style to the book title. First, set up the style rule, which makes the text italic. Figure F-25 shows the results of the final style changes—the styled document.

FIGURE F-23: Standard paragraph style and logical document divisions

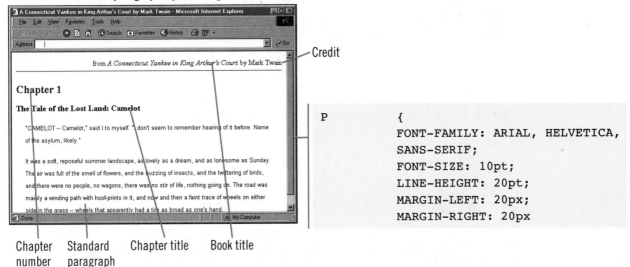

Credit

Chapter
number

Standard
paragraph

Chapter title

Book title

```
P                {
                 FONT-FAMILY: ARIAL, HELVETICA,
                 SANS-SERIF;
                 FONT-SIZE: 10pt;
                 LINE-HEIGHT: 20pt;
                 MARGIN-LEFT: 20px;
                 MARGIN-RIGHT: 20px
```

FIGURE F-24: Chapter number and title style

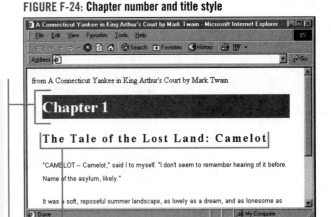

```
.CHAPNUMBER
        {
        FONT-SIZE: 24pt;
        LINE-HEIGHT: 36pt;
        FONT-WEIGHT: BOLD
        MARGIN-LEFT: 20px;
        BACKGROUND-COLOR: GRAY;
        COLOR: WHITE;
        }
<DIV CLASS="CHAPNUMBER">Chapter 1</DIV>
```

```
.CHAPTITLE
        {
        FONT-SIZE: 18pt;
        LINE-HEIGHT: 30pt;
        FONT-WEIGHT: BOLD;
        LETTER-SPACING: 2pt;
        MARGIN-LEFT: 20px;
        }
<DIV CLASS="CHAPTITLE">The Tale of the
Lost Land: Camelot</DIV>
```

FIGURE F-25: Credit and book title style

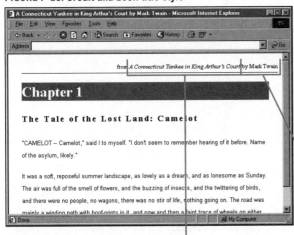

```
SPAN.BOOKTITLE {FONT-STYLE: ITALIC}
Then apply the class using <SPAN>:
<DIV CLASS="CREDIT">from <SPAN
CLASS="BOOKTITLE">A Connecticut Yankee
in King Arthur's Court</SPAN> by Mark
Twain</DIV>
```

```
DIV.CREDIT {
        TEXT-ALIGN: RIGHT;
        FONT-SIZE: 10pt;
        BORDER-BOTTOM: SOLID 1px BLACK;
        LINE-HEIGHT: 20pt;
        MARGIN-LEFT: 20px;
        }
Apply the style:
<DIV CLASS="CREDIT">by Mark Twain</DIV>
```

Practice

► Concepts Review

Fill in the blank with the best answer.

1. _Times_ is the default browser font.
2. _Face_, _size_, and _color_ are three attributes you can use with the <FONT> element.
3. The two ways to set size with the <FONT> element are _absolute_ and _relative_. sizing.
4. _____ and _____ are the two parts of a style rule.
5. _____ and _____ are the two parts of a property declaration.
6. Use the _____ attribute to override a style for a specific element.
7. The common filename extension for style sheets is _____.
8. _____ and _____ are two elements designed for use with style sheets.

9. P {FONT-SIZE: 14pt; LINE-HEIGHT: 20pt} is a rule specifying that <P> elements appear as _____ text with _____ leading.
10. P I {COLOR: RED} is a rule specifying that <I> elements display _____ only when they appear within <P> elements.
11. H1 {COLOR: WHITE; BACKGROUND-COLOR: BLACK} is a style rule to create a _____ on _____ reverse <H1> heading.
12. P {TEXT-INDENT: -24pt; MARGIN-LEFT: 30px; MARGIN-RIGHT: 30px} is a style rule for a <P> element with a 24-point _____ and a 30-pixel margin on the left and right sides.
13. To set up a style sheet, start by setting up logical _____ for the document.

▶ Explore Further...

1. What are two drawbacks to graphics-based text?

   1. download time is increased.

   2. graphic-based text is not searchable.

2. What does the browser do if you specify a font that is not stored on a user's computer?

   It displays the default font for the user's browser

3. Why would you want to limit use of the <FONT> element and what should you do instead?

   is depreciated in HTML 4.0 you should use CSS.

4. Why is FACE="ARIAL, HELVETICA" a common font substitution string?

5. Name three ways to select elements.

6. Describe the three white space areas you can affect with style rules.

7. Write a rule defining a division named NOTE. Specify 12-point bold Arial text on a yellow background.

Web Design

► Independent Challenges

1. Your experience in reading about and coding HTML files should be such that, minimally, you can create simple HTML documents to display Web pages through your browser. This unit taught you the benefits of using CSS to enhance your Web pages and create continuity though a Web site.

a. Open an HTML document that has blocks of text that you have created in one of your classes. If you do not have a simple HTML document to use, you will find the example file from this chapter on the Web Design Illustrated Student Online Companion Web site. You can find this Web site at *www.course.com/illustrated/designingsites*. Download and open the file twain.htm in your browser, and then save the file to your hard drive.

b. Convert the existing HTML document to use CSS.

c. Build styles using the existing standard HTML elements in the file.

d. Decide on logical divisions for the document. Give the divisions class names.

e. Write style rules for the division.

f. Apply the styles to the divisions using <DIV> or <SPAN>.

g. Make changes in the file to create continuity and thus craft the best page you can.

h. Remove the files and place them in an external style sheet.

i. Link the HTML file to the style sheet. Test to make sure the file displays properly.

j. Test your work. If possible, test the work in multiple browsers (both Internet Explorer and Netscape Navigator) to verify that all styles are portable. You can download older versions of browsers from *www.browsers.com*.

2. If you have worked extensively with word processors, desktop publishing programs, or even simple card-making programs, you are familiar with the vast array of fonts that are available to you through computers. You see what typography can do for a message when you look at advertising whether it is print media or television. The Web also offers the same variety of typefaces for delivering messages. If you cannot find a site that you feel is suitable for each part of the assignment below, go to the Student Online Companion site at *www.course.com/illustrated/designingsites* for suggested sites.

a. Browse the Web for examples of good typography. Print the Web pages you have selected and then use your word processor to write a short design critique of why the type works effectively on the Web sites you find. Type **Your Name** at the bottom of the document, save the document, print a copy, and then close it.

b. Browse the Web for examples of sites that use typography in a confusing or poor manner. Print the Web pages and then use your word processor to write a short design critique of why the type is confusing or misleading to the user. Type **Your Name** at the bottom of the document, save the document, print a copy, and then close it.

c. Create a simple HTML document to mock up a page for testing body text fonts. Try four different styles of fonts at different resolutions to determine which is the most readable. Test your work on a variety of subjects (friends, family, coworkers) to see if they agree with your choices.

d. Type **Your Name** at the bottom of the document, print each of the pages, explain why you chose the typography you did for each, and then close the document.

e. Test the finished file's compatibility by viewing it in multiple browsers (both Internet Explorer and Netscape Navigator) to verify that all fonts are portable.

f. Save the HTML file as a sample font file.

3. You have had the opportunity to see how fonts and font styles can work to enhance a Web page. Fonts can express moods, convey ideas, and generally help present the material on the site. You can see how changing fonts can change the whole look and feel of a Web site.

a. Browse the Web for examples of sites that use typography to evoke a particular feeling for that site.

b. Save the page to your hard disk. (*Hint*: Using the browser, you can find the Save Page command on the File menu.)

c. Print the Web page and then use your word processor to write a short design critique of how the type works to express the message on the Web site you find. Type **Your Name** at the bottom of the document, save the document, print a copy, and then close it.

d. Open the HTML file you saved and view the source code. Find the parts of the file that specify the font. Change the fonts to a new font. View the page and print the page with the new font.

e. Use your word processor to write a short design critique of how the type changes the message on the Web site you found. Type **Your Name** at the bottom of the document, save the document, print a copy, and then close it.

You will continue to work on the Web site you have been developing through this book. You will recall that to complete the ongoing case study for this book, you must create a complete, stand-alone Web site. The site must contain from six to ten pages and display at least three levels of information. By this point, you should have selected your own content and started to organize your site. You should have created a visual diagram that indicates the main page, section pages, and content pages as well as indicating the links between the pages and have created navigational graphics.

a. Use CSS for the case study project. Design the type hierarchy for the information levels in your Web site.

b. Create a type specification page that shows examples of the various typefaces and sizes and where each of them will be used.

c. Determine the body copy typeface and size for your Web site.

d. Mock up a couple of test pages with some content. Test for legibility of your text. Try different leading, padding, and margins to see how this affects the clarity of the text.

e. Once you have decided on your typefaces, start to add actual content to the different pages of the Web site using the styles you have developed to display the text.

▶ Visual Workshop

1. In this Visual Workshop, the image shown in Figure F-26 is from the *www.whitehouse.gov* Web site. It shows text that is formatted using various typefaces. There are margins and color as well as document divisions. Using what you learned in this unit, write a brief essay describing how block-level elements such as divisions, margins, and padding are used to make this page effective.

FIGURE F-26

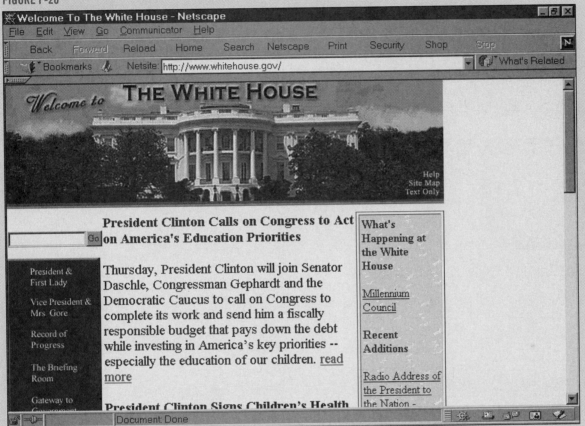

Web Design

▶ Visual Workshop

2. In this Visual Workshop, the image shown in Figure F-27 is from the *http://www.school.discovery.com/* Web site. It shows text that is formatted using various typefaces. There are margins and color as well as document divisions. Using what you learned in this unit, write a brief essay describing what you see in the image and how it might be coded using style rules and CSS.

FIGURE F-27

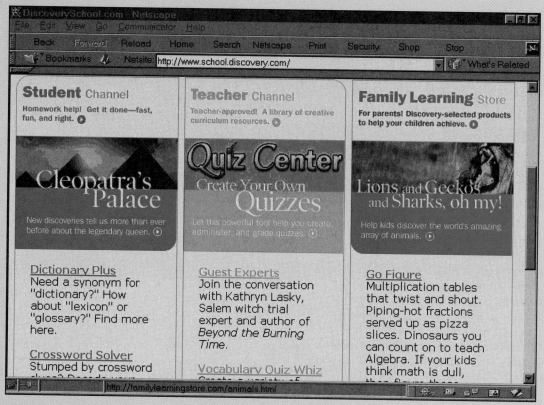

Using
Graphics and Color

Objectives

► **Understand file format basics**
► **Understand color basics**
► **Choose a graphics tool**
► **Use the <IMG> element**
► **Specify image width and height**
► **Understand alignment and white space**
► **Use transparent spacer GIFs and single-pixel rules**
► **Work with background images**
► **Work with colors**

Using graphics and text together is the characteristic that makes the Web so attractive and popular, but it also can be the undoing of many Web sites. Use graphics wisely, and you can create an engaging Web site. If you use too many images or graphics that are too large or complex, your user will have to endure long download times, and they may not wait. Also, the incorrect use of color in many Web sites creates unreadable text or navigation confusion for the user. Use color judiciously to communicate and guide the reader or to create branded areas of your site. Test your color choices carefully to make sure they appear properly across different browsers.

Understanding File Format Basics

You currently can use only three image file formats on the Web—GIF, JPG, and PNG. These formats all compress images to create smaller files. The higher the compression, the lower the image quality. Knowing which file format to use for which type of image is important. If you choose the wrong file type, your image will not compress or appear as you expect. Of the three Web-based image file formats, JPG supports 24-bit color, GIF supports 8-bit color, and PNG supports both 8-bit and 24-bit color. The file format's **color depth** controls the number of colors the image can display. The greater the bit depth, the greater the number of colors that can be displayed.

Details

▶ GIF

The **Graphics Interchange Format (GIF)** is designed for online delivery of graphics. GIF is the everyday file format for all types of simple colored graphics and line art. GIF uses a **lossless** compression technique, meaning that no color information is discarded when the image is compressed. The color depth of GIF is 8-bit, allowing a palette of no more than 256 colors. In fact, the fewer colors you use, the greater the compression. The GIF file format excels at compressing and displaying flat color areas, making it the logical choice for line art and color graphics. Because of its limited color depth, GIF is not the best file format for photographs.

▶ GIF's Transparency

This feature lets you seamlessly integrate graphics into your Web site. Choose one color in an image to appear as transparent in the browser. The background color or pattern will show through the areas that you have designated as transparent. Using transparent areas allows you to create graphics that appear to have an irregular outside shape rather than being bound by a rectangle. Figure G-1 shows the same shape with and without transparency.

▶ JPG

The **Joint Photographic Experts Group** (**JPG**, sometimes **JPEG**) format is best for photographs or continuous tone images. JPGs are 24-bit images that allow millions of colors; therefore, use JPG for all 24-bit full-color photographic images, as well as more complicated graphics that contain color gradients, shadows, and feathering. JPGs do not use a palette to display color. JPGs use a **lossy** compression routine specially designed for photographic images. When the image is compressed, some color information is discarded, resulting in a loss of quality from the original image. Because the display device is the low-resolution computer monitor, the loss of quality usually is not noticeable. The resulting faster download time compensates for the loss of image quality. Using imaging software, you can translate photographic images into the JPG format. When you create the JPG file, you also can balance manually the amount of compression versus the resulting image quality. Many photos can sustain quite a bit of compression while still maintaining image integrity.

▶ PNG

The **Portable Network Graphics (PNG)** format is designed specially for the Web. PNG has been available since 1995 but has been slow to gain popularity because of its lack of browser support. Now that more browsers support it, use PNG as a substitute for GIF. It is a royalty-free file format that is intended to replace GIF. This lossless format compresses 8-bit images to smaller file sizes than GIF. PNG also is intended to work as an image-printing format, so it supports 8-bit indexed-color, 16-bit grayscale, and 24-bit true color images. Even though PNG supports 24-bit color, its lossless compression routine does not compress as efficiently as JPG; do not use it for photos.

The W3C has created a draft specification for a Multiple-image Network Graphics format (MNG), which will support animation. PNG has built-in text capabilities for image indexing, allowing you to store a string of identifying text within the file itself. PNG supports transparency and interlacing but not animation.

tip

Whether you are creating GIFs or JPGs, remember always to save an original copy of your artwork or photo. Both file formats permanently degrade the quality of an image as a result of compression. Once you have converted to GIF or JPG, you cannot return to the original image quality.

FIGURE G-1: Transparent and nontransparent GIFs

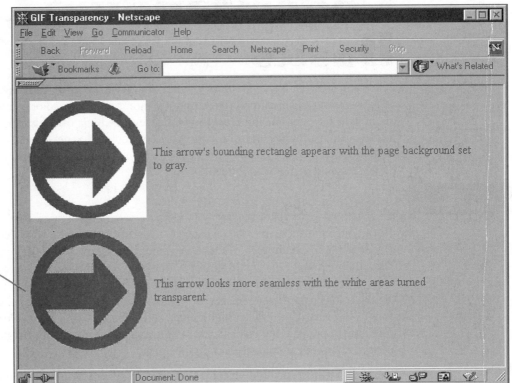

Create transparent areas using a graphics editor. All pixels of the transparent color in the image will let the background color show through.

FIGURE G-2: Individual frames of a GIF animation

Using Animated GIFs

The GIF format lets you store multiple images and timing information about the images in a single file with the .gif extension. You can build animations consisting of multiple static images that play continuously, creating the illusion of motion. When you create a GIF animation, you can determine the time between frames and the number of times the animation plays. With a little imagination, you can create all types of effects including text scrolls, color changes, animated icons, and slide shows. Figure G-2 shows a series of individual GIFs that can be combined to play as an animated GIF. You can create animated images with GIF animation software such as Adobe Photoshop and Illustrator, Paint Shop Pro, Macromedia Fireworks, Graphic Workshop Professional, and Ulead PhotoImpact. These tools streamline the process of setting the timing, color palette, and individual frame effects.

GIF animation is somewhat limited when compared with the results of other proprietary animation tools such as Macromedia Shockwave or Flash, which can play synchronized sounds and allow Web users to interact with the animation. Unlike most proprietary tools, you do not need any special plug-ins to view animated GIFs, and, if you limit color and motion when creating your animations, you can keep your file sizes small for faster downloads. Use restraint when adding animated GIFs to your pages because they can be repetitive and distract from the page content.

Understanding Color Basics

Before you create or gather graphics for your Web site, you need a basic understanding of how color works on computer monitors. Your computer monitor displays color by mixing the three basic colors of light—red, green, and blue. Each of these three basic colors is called a **color channel**. Your monitor can express a range of intensity for each color channel, from 0 (absence of color) to 255 (full intensity of color). Colors vary widely from one monitor to the next, based on both the user's preferences and brand of equipment.

Details

▶ The amount of data used to create color on a display is called the color depth. If your monitor can display 8 bits of data in each of the three color channels, it has a 24-bit color depth (8 × 3 = 24). These 24-bit images can contain almost 17 million different colors and are called **true color images**. Both JPG and PNG support 24-bit color. If your users have 24-bit color displays, they can appreciate the full color depth of your images. But, many monitors cannot display 24-bit images. Some have only 16-bit color depth (called **high color**), and some have only 8-bit color depth. If your monitor does not support the full color depth of an image, the browser must resort to mixing colors that attempt to match the original colors in the image.

▶ The browser must mix its own colors when you display a 24-bit image on an 8-bit monitor or in a file format that does not support 24-bit color. Because the 8-bit monitor has only 256 colors to work with, the browser must try to approximate the missing colors by creating colors from those the browser already has. This type of color mixing, called **dithering**, occurs when the browser encounters a color that it does not support, such as when you try to turn a 24-bit photographic image into an 8-bit 256-color image. Dithered images often appear grainy and pixilated. The dithering will be most apparent in gradations, feathered edges, or shadows.

▶ Figure G-3 shows the same image in both JPG and GIF formats displayed at 8-bit 256 color. The JPG file on the left has a lot of dithering in the sky area of the photo where the browser was forced to mix colors to approximate the existing colors in the image. The GIF file on the right exhibits a different type of color matching called banding. Unlike dithering, **banding** is an effort to match the closest colors from the GIF's palette to the original colors in the photo. When you create a GIF, you can choose whether or not to use dithering. A nondithered image will be smaller than one that uses dithering, but banding may create an unacceptable image. JPGs, when viewed on an 8-bit or 16-bit display, will dither to the closest colors. Photos are best saved as JPGs, even when viewed at a lower color depth, because the dithering creates a more acceptable image than banding.

▶ One way to control the dithering process is to create images that use **nondithering colors**. The 216 nondithering colors that are shared by PCs and Macintoshes are called the **Web palette** or browser-safe colors. The nondithering palette only applies to GIF or 8-bit PNG, not 24-bit JPG. These colors display properly across both platforms without dithering. Most Web-capable graphics programs include the Web palette colors. If you do create graphics for the Web, to avoid trouble use the Web palette as your color palette for all flat-color areas of your graphics.

tip

Although your browser allows you to copy graphics, you should never use someone else's work without permission unless it is a public domain Web site and freely available for use, or you may find yourself in a cyber-lawsuit. New digital watermarking technology lets artists copyright their work with an invisible signature.

FIGURE G-3: 24-bit photographic image on an 8-bit display

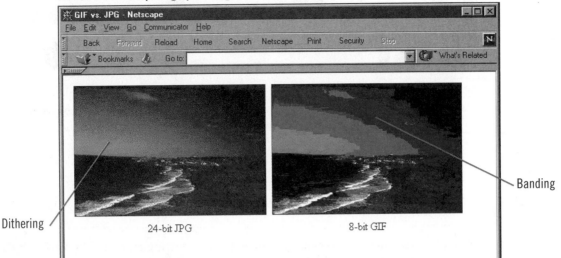

Dithering

24-bit JPG

8-bit GIF

Banding

Finding Images

You can acquire images from a variety of sources. One way is from a graphics professional you hire to create and prepare your images. If your budget does not allow for funding this service, consider one of the following resources:

- **Stock photo collections:**

Stock photo collections can cost from thousands of dollars for a few images to under $20 for thousands of images at your local computer discount store or mail-order retailer. These collections contain royalty-free images that you can use for any Web site. You can manipulate the graphics to add or delete text or images, change the color, or make any other modifications. Most stock photo collections include a built-in browsing program that lets you search for a particular image, and some also provide basic image-editing software.

- **Digital camera:**

A digital camera lets you take your own photos and use them on the Web. These cameras store photos in a JPG format, so you do not have to convert them. Most also provide image-cataloging software, and some include basic image-editing software.

- **Scanner:**

Good scanners are available for under $150. You can scan your own photos or images and save them as GIF, JPG, or PNG files for use on your Web site. Remember to set the scanner resolution to 72 dpi to match the computer display resolution.

- **Public domain Web sites:**

Many Web sites maintain catalogs of images online that are available for download. Some of these sites charge a small membership fee, so you can download as many images as you want. Other public domain Web sites are completely free of charge.

- **Create your own:**

If you need a basic image or if you have graphic-design skills, you can download a shareware graphics tool and learn to use it. Keep the type of image you create simple, such as text on colored backgrounds, and use fundamental shapes and lines. Look at examples of the graphics on other Web sites. Many are simple but effective and may provide a useful model for your own images.

- **Clip art:**

Clip art is a viable alternative for the Web, especially as more polished collections become available for sale on CD-ROM. Price generally corresponds to quality for clip art—if you pay $9.95 for 20,000 images, the quality of the images most likely will reflect the cost. You also can use a graphics program to customize clip art to meet your particular needs.

Web Design

Choosing a Graphics Tool

As a Web designer, you may be in the enviable position of having a complete staff of graphic-design professionals creating and preparing graphics for your site. Most Web designers, however, do not have this luxury. Whether you want to or not, you eventually must use a graphics tool.

Details

▶ Most of your graphics tasks will be simple, such as resizing an image or converting an image from one file to another. More complex tasks could include changing color depth or adding transparency to an image. These are tasks that anyone can learn to do, using any of the popular graphics software currently available.

▶ When it comes to creating images, you may want to enlist professional help. Your Web site will not benefit if you choose to create your own graphics and you are really not up to the task. Professional-quality graphics can greatly enhance the look of your Web site. Take an honest look at your skills, and remember that the best Web sites usually are the result of a collaboration of talents.

▶ You will use graphics software to create or manipulate graphics. Most Web designers use Adobe Photoshop. This is a full-featured product that takes time to master. Adobe Illustrator, a high-end drawing/painting tool, also is available. Other commercial tools you can consider include Ulead PhotoImpact and Macromedia Fireworks. Most are available as downloadable demos, so you can try before you buy. In general, look for a tool that meets your needs and will not take a long time to learn. Table G-1 lists Web sites for the graphic tools mentioned here. This list is not exhaustive, so you may have to try different tools to find the one that suits your needs.

▶ Although you also can choose from a variety of shareware graphics tools, such as LView Pro and Graphic Workshop Professional, you may prefer to use a commercial package. Some of the more established tools are Paint Shop Pro and Adobe Photoshop and Illustrator. These tools contain a full range of image-editing features. Like shareware, most graphics tools can be downloaded. Some programs allow you to work with the tools for a trial period before buying and registering.

TABLE G-1: Graphic tools Web sites

some tools you can use are:	you can find graphics tools at:
Adobe Photoshop and Illustrator	www.adobe.com
Graphic Workshop Professional	www.mindworkshop.com/alchemy/gwspro
LView Pro	www.lview.com
Macromedia Fireworks	www.macromedia.com
Paint Shop Pro	www.jasc.com
Ulead PhotoImpact	www.ulead.com

FIGURE G-4: Three passes complete this progressive JPG image

Using Interlacing and Progressive Displays

Interlacing and **progressive formats** are the gradual display of a graphic in a series of passes as the data arrives in the browser. Rather than wait for the complete image to see anything, each additional pass of data creates a clearer view of the image until the complete image is displayed. The only real advantage to displaying graphics in these methods is that users see a blurred view of the complete image, giving them something to look at while waiting for the entire graphic to download. It is an appealing way to deliver graphics at modem connection speeds; users with faster connections won't notice the difference. GIF and PNG files use an interlacing format, whereas JPG files use a progressive format. Figure G-4 shows three rendering passes to display a complete image. Most Web-capable graphics editors let you choose to save in an interlaced or progressive format when saving images. The disadvantage of choosing this display method is that older browsers may not display the graphic properly, and more processing power is needed on the user's machine to render the image.

Using the <IMG> Element

By definition, <IMG> is a replaced element, meaning that the browser replaces the <IMG> element with the image file referenced in the SRC attribute. <IMG> is an empty element, so never use a closing tag with it.

Details

▶ The browser treats the image as it treats a character; normal image alignment is to the baseline of the text, where the text sits on the line. Images that are within a line of text must have spaces on both sides, or the text will touch the image.

▶ The <IMG> element only needs the SRC attribute to display an image in the browser. For example, the code

```
<IMG SRC="logo.gif">
```

is a valid <IMG> element that displays a GIF file named "logo." The <IMG> element has a variety of attributes. Table G-2 lists the most commonly used attributes.

ALIGN, BORDER, VSPACE, and HSPACE have been deprecated in HTML 4.0 in favor of CSS, following a trend replacing IMG attributes with style sheets. Table G-3 shows the equivalent CSS properties that replace these attributes.

▶ Style properties usually are expressed as global rules that specify the characteristics for every occurrence of an element. The variety of uses for graphics on a Web page defies a homogenous rule. The style rule below makes all images left-aligned:

```
IMG {FLOAT:LEFT}
```

This rule may be too restrictive because every image in the document will be left-aligned. A good alternative is to express the style information using the STYLE attribute in the <IMG> element. For example, the following code shows two images, one left-aligned and one right-aligned:

```
<IMG SRC="logo.gif" STYLE="FLOAT:LEFT" WIDTH=40 HEIGHT=40
ALT="Company Logo">
```

```
<IMG SRC="product.gif" STYLE="FLOAT:RIGHT" WIDTH=80 HEIGHT=60
ALT="Our Product">
```

▶ Many of the standard CSS text properties can be used with the <IMG> element. This unit includes both standard HTML code and, wherever applicable, the equivalent CSS properties expressed using the STYLE attribute.

Specifying the ALT Attribute

There are many benefits to including ALT attribute text. The ALT attribute text is displayed if the image does not appear, providing a description of the image. In both Internet Explorer 4.0/5.0 and Netscape Navigator 4.0, the ALT attribute text also appears as a pop-up when the user places the cursor over the image, as illustrated in Figure G-5.

FIGURE G-5: Specifying the <ALT> attribute

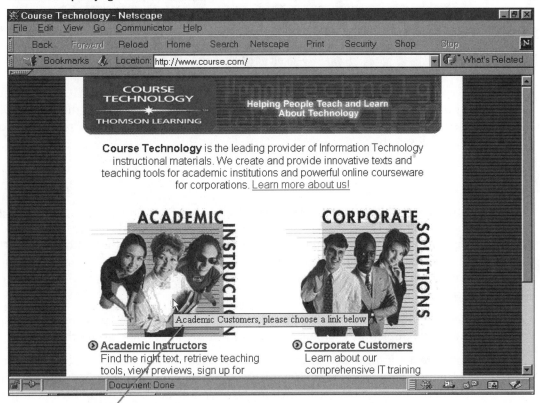

ALT popup

TABLE G-2: <IMG> element attributes

attribute	use
ALIGN	Specifies the position of the image in relation to the surrounding text
ALT	Displays an alternate string of text instead of an image if the user has a text-only browser or has graphics turned off; the Internet Explorer 4.0+ and Netscape Navigator 4.0 browsers display the ALT value as a pop-up window when a mouse points to the image
BORDER	Determines whether a border appears on the image; the border value must be stated in pixels; you can use this attribute to turn off the hypertext border if the image is a link
HEIGHT	Specifies the height of the image in pixels
HSPACE	Specifies the amount of horizontal white space on the left and right sides of the image, in pixels
SRC	The only required attribute, SRC specifies the URL of the graphic file you want to display; as with any URL, the path must be relative to the HTML file
VSPACE	Specifies the amount of vertical white space on the top and bottom sides of the image, in pixels
WIDTH	Specifies the width of the image in pixels

TABLE G-3: CSS properties that replace <IMG> element attributes

deprecated attribute	equivalent CSS property
ALIGN	FLOAT allows you to flow text around an image or other object; for example, IMG {FLOAT: LEFT}
BORDER	BORDER lets you set a border on an image or remove the border from a linked image
VSPACE and HSPACE	The PADDING or MARGIN properties set white space around an image; you can control individual sides of the image or apply white space around the entire image

Specifying Image Width and Height

Every <IMG> element on your Web site should contain WIDTH and HEIGHT attributes. These attributes provide important information to the browser by specifying the amount of space to reserve for the image. This information dramatically affects the way your pages download, especially at slower connection speeds.

Details

► If you have included the width and height, the browser knows how much space the image needs. The browser reserves the space on the page without waiting for the image to download and displays the rest of your text content. If the browser does not know the width and height values, it must download the image before displaying the rest of the page. This means the user will be looking at a blank page while waiting for the image to download. Figure G-6 shows the result of including the width and height.

The code indicates the browser should reserve a 305 × 185 pixel space for the trains.gif image and should display the alternate text "Trains Picture" if it cannot display the image.

► If you are not using a table format design, you should set the width and height to preserve the look of your layout, whether the images are displayed or not. In Figure G-7, the width and height have been omitted. Notice that when the browser does not know the width and height, the text wrapping and appearance of the page change dramatically when the image is not displayed.

► You can manipulate the width and height of the image using the WIDTH and HEIGHT attributes in the <IMG> element. Although it is tempting to use these attributes to change graphic size without opening a graphics program, it is not a good idea. If the original graphic's area is too large and you reduce the size using the WIDTH and HEIGHT attributes, you are not changing the file size of the image—only the area that the browser reserves for the graphic. The user still is downloading the original graphic file. Also, if you do not maintain the ratio of width to height, you distort the image. The ability to manipulate image size using the WIDTH and HEIGHT attributes comes in handy only in certain circumstances. When creating a layout mock up, you can test image sizes by manipulating the code. Figure G-8 shows an image in its actual size, the size after changing the width and height values in proportion to one another, and the distorted size caused by incorrect width and height values.

► One way to keep file sizes small is to size graphics appropriately. Nothing is worse than opening a new Web page and waiting to download a large 600 × 400 pixel image. One of the easiest ways to make your graphics download quickly is to keep their dimensions small and appropriate to the size of the page. You can think of image size in relation to the number of columns in your layout. Size your graphics to occupy one or two columns of the page.

Removing the Hypertext Border from an Image

When you create a hypertext image, the browser's default behavior is to display the hypertext border around the image, as shown in Figure G-9. The code for the second globe that has the hypertext border turned off is given in both standard HTML and CSS. This border appears blue when new and purple after you click the image. In a well-designed site, this border is unnecessary because users often use their mouse to point to each image to see if the hypertext cursor appears. Also, the color of the border does not always complement your graphic. To remove the hypertext border, add the BORDER=0 attribute to your <IMG> tag.

FIGURE G-6: Code for the image showing the WIDTH and HEIGHT attributes

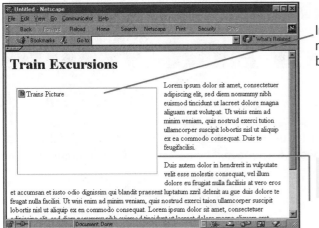

Image size is reserved in browser

```
<IMG SRC="trains.gif" WIDTH=305
HEIGHT=185 ALT="Trains Picture">
```

FIGURE G-7: Browser unable to reserve image size

Browser does not know width and height of image

FIGURE G-8: Manipulating images with WIDTH and HEIGHT attributes

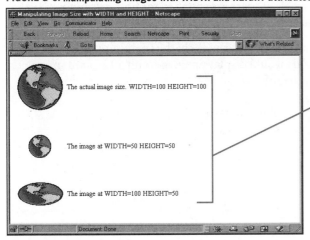

```
<!-Globe 1->
<IMG SRC="globel.gif" WIDTH=100 HEIGHT=100
ALT="Globe"> <!-Globe 2->
<IMG SRC="globel.gif" WIDTH=50 HEIGHT=50
ALT="Globe"> <!-Globe 3->
<IMG SRC="globel.gif" WIDTH=100 HEIGHT=50
ALT="Globe">
```

FIGURE G-9: Removing hypertext border

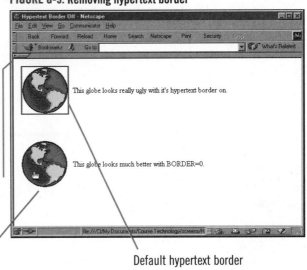

```
<!-Standard HTML->
<IMG SRC="globel.gif" WIDTH=100 ALT="GLOBE"
BORDER=0 ALIGN=MIDDLE>
<!-CSS->
<IMG SRC="globel.gif" WIDTH=100 ALT="GLOBE"
STYLE="BORDER:NONE" ALIGN=MIDDLE>
```

This hypertext border is off, yet image still is clickable

Default hypertext border

Understanding Alignment and White Space

You can align text along an image border using the ALIGN attribute. The default alignment of the text and image is bottom-aligned, which means the bottom of the text aligns with the bottom edge of the image.

Details

- ► You can change the alignment from the default BOTTOM by using either the TOP or MIDDLE values. Figure G-10 shows all three alignment values and the code for each.

- ► You also can use the ALIGN attribute to wrap text around images. Figure G-11 shows two images (the images are turned off); the first image is left-aligned and the second image is right-aligned. The code shows both <IMG> elements and the CSS equivalents.

- ► Add white space around your images to reduce clutter and improve readability. As shown in Figure G-12, the default spacing is very close to the image. To increase the white space around an image, you can add the VSPACE and HSPACE attributes to the <IMG> element and set the values to a pixel amount. In Figure G-13, 15 pixels of space are specified for both attributes. VSPACE affects both the top and bottom sides, whereas HSPACE affects both left and right sides.

- ► CSS offers more control over image white space. You can apply the margin properties to individual sides of an image. The following code would display an image with a 12-point margin on the right and bottom sides, floating to the left of text:

```
<IMG ALT="SAILBOAT" BORDER=0 STYLE="MARGIN-RIGHT:12pt;
MARGIN=BOTTOM:12pt; FLOAT:LEFT" SRC="SAIL.GIF">
```

FIGURE G-10: The three types of alignment and their CSS equivalents

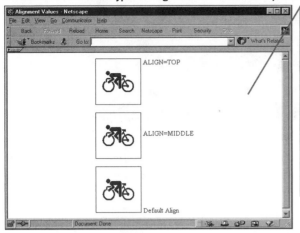

```
<!-Standard HTML->
<IMG SRC="cycle.gif" ALIGN=TOP BORDER=1>
<IMG SRC="cycle.gif" ALIGN=MIDDLE
BORDER=1>
<IMG SRC="cycle.gif" BORDER=1>
<!-CSS->
<IMG SRC="cycle.gif" STYLE="VERTICAL-
ALIGN:TOP" BORDER=1>
<IMG SRC="cycle.gif" STYLE="VERTICAL-
ALIGN:MIDDLE"BORDER=1>
<IMG SRC="cycle.gif" BORDER=1>
```

```
<!-Standard HTML->
<IMG SRC="planning.jpg" WIDTH=125 HEIGHT=184
ALT="125 x 184 image" ALIGN=LEFT>
<IMG SRC="planning.jpg" WIDTH=125 HEIGHT=184
ALT="125 x 184 image" ALIGN=RIGHT>
<!-CSS->
<IMG SRC="planning.jpg" WIDTH=125 HEIGHT=184
ALT="125 x 184 image" STYLE="FLOAT:LEFT">
<IMG SRC="planning.jpg" WIDTH=125 HEIGHT=184
ALT="125 x 184 image" STYLE="FLOAT:RIGHT">
```

FIGURE G-11: Text wrapping

ALIGN=LEFT   ALIGN=RIGHT

FIGURE G-12: Default image spacing

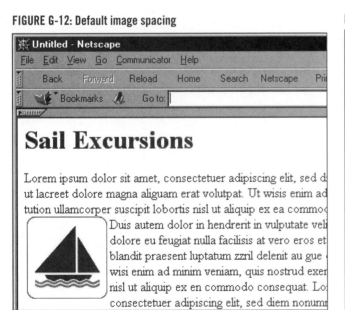

FIGURE G-13: Adding white space around an image

```
<IMG ALIGN=LEFT ALT="SAILBOAT" BORDER=0
HSPACE=15 VSPACE=15 SRC="SAIL.GIF">
```

Using Transparent Spacer GIFs and Single-Pixel Rules

When you create a GIF or PNG, you can choose one color to be transparent. A **transparent spacer GIF**, on the other hand, is a single-pixel graphic of just one color that is specified as transparent. This is a single-pixel transparent block. You can use the transparent spacer GIF to solve spacing problems that cannot be solved with standard HTML.

Details

▶ The transparent spacer GIF is occasionally the only way to accomplish a desired result. For example, you might use a transparent spacer GIF to enforce column widths in tables or indent or align text in a nonstandard way. As CSS support becomes commonplace, you should be able to forgo transparent spacer GIFs altogether.

▶ A commonly used technique in Web design is to use the WIDTH and HEIGHT attributes to change the transparent spacer GIF to any size. One HTML editing tool, NetObjects Fusion, uses transparent spacer GIFs as an integral part in the way it builds Web pages. You can reuse the same transparent spacer GIF over and over on your Web site, and it only has to download once to the user's cache.

Figure G-14 shows an example of a three-column table with exact column widths specified by the transparent spacer GIFs at the top of each column. The code is for the bottom table showing the transparent spacer GIFs with the borders turned off.

▶ Single-pixel lines or rules work exactly like transparent spacer GIFs, except they are a single color rather than transparent. You can change a single-pixel rule to any size by using the WIDTH and HEIGHT attributes. This creates reusable graphics of horizontal or vertical lines of varying thickness that you can use to enhance your Web page layout. Figure G-15 shows the same single-pixel black graphic stretched to different shapes and sizes by changes in the WIDTH and HEIGHT attributes in the <IMG> element. The code is given for the three rules; notice that each SRC attribute references the same graphic.

FIGURE G-14: Transparent spacer GIFs

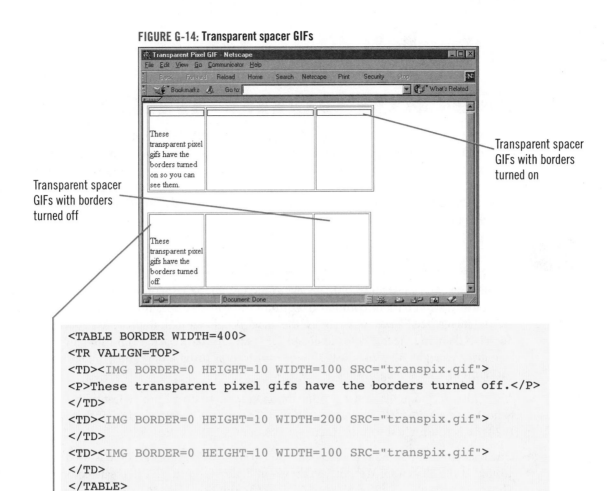

Transparent spacer GIFs with borders turned on

Transparent spacer GIFs with borders turned off

```
<TABLE BORDER WIDTH=400>
<TR VALIGN=TOP>
<TD><IMG BORDER=0 HEIGHT=10 WIDTH=100 SRC="transpix.gif">
<P>These transparent pixel gifs have the borders turned off.</P>
</TD>
<TD><IMG BORDER=0 HEIGHT=10 WIDTH=200 SRC="transpix.gif">
</TD>
<TD><IMG BORDER=0 HEIGHT=10 WIDTH=100 SRC="transpix.gif">
</TD>
</TABLE>
```

FIGURE G-15: Single-pixel rules

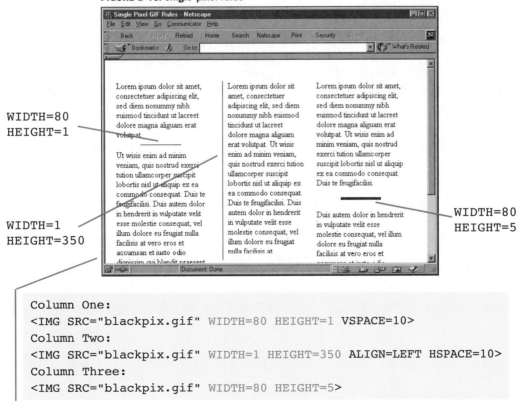

WIDTH=80
HEIGHT=1

WIDTH=1
HEIGHT=350

WIDTH=80
HEIGHT=5

```
Column One:
<IMG SRC="blackpix.gif" WIDTH=80 HEIGHT=1 VSPACE=10>
Column Two:
<IMG SRC="blackpix.gif" WIDTH=1 HEIGHT=350 ALIGN=LEFT HSPACE=10>
Column Three:
<IMG SRC="blackpix.gif" WIDTH=80 HEIGHT=5>
```

Working with Background Images

You can add the BACKGROUND attribute to the <BODY> element to tile images across the background of a Web page. Any image can be used as a background graphic, though many are not appropriate for the task. The Web provides many images that you can use to create seamless backgrounds that do not interfere with your text. Use background images creatively to provide an identifying theme for your site, to frame your content at different screen resolutions, or to provide a light, textured background.

Details

► In too many Web sites, complicated background graphics distract the user. If your site includes a lot of text, avoid dark or complex backgrounds. Most text does not read well against a background image (see Figure G-16) unless the image is light enough to provide a good contrast for the text. Changing the text color to create light text on a dark background sometimes improves legibility by heightening contrast. However, instead of using a dark, busy image to tile a page background, choose a light, simple image.

► A common technique is to use a thin ribbon graphic that will not repeat within the browser window at even the highest screen resolution. This means creating a graphic that is longer than 1024 pixels (the highest common screen resolution is 1024 × 768 pixels).

► One background graphic is a 1075 × 5 pixel graphic. When this graphic is used as the background at the Shareware Web site, as shown in Figure G-17, it tiles to create columns of color. This page is displayed at an 800 × 600 screen resolution. The color columns created by the background graphic frame the content areas of the page.

► CSS allows you more control over background image tiling than standard HTML. To apply a background image that tiles indefinitely across the page, use the <BODY> element as the selector with the BACKGROUND property as follows:

```
BODY {BACKGROUND: URL(texture4.jpg)}
```

Note the URL syntax in the rule. The path and filename are contained within parentheses. The default for CSS background graphics is the same as using the BACKGROUND attribute.

► The CSS BACKGROUND-REPEAT property allows you to create a single column or row of the image, rather than tiling the image completely across the page. Figure G-18 shows the background image repeated on the *y*-axis. You also can tile across the *x*-axis.

Here is the rule for repeating the graphic on the *x*-axis:

```
BODY {BACKGROUND: URL(texture4.jpg); BACKGROUND-REPEAT: REPEAT-X}
```

► You also can use the BACKGROUND-POSITION property to change the position of the background graphic. For example, you can create a right-aligned repeat on the *y*-axis using the following rule for right-aligning the background:

```
BODY {BACKGROUND: URL(texture4.jpg); BACKGROUND-REPEAT: REPEAT-Y
BACKGROUND-POSITION RIGHT}
```

FIGURE G-16: Poor choice for a background

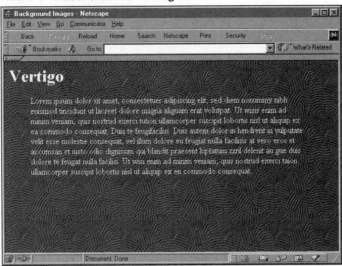

FIGURE G-17: Background graphic as component of page

Yellow navigation column

Yellow background fills screen at resolutions over 640 × 480

FIGURE G-18: Background graphic repeated on *y*-axis

Graphic image

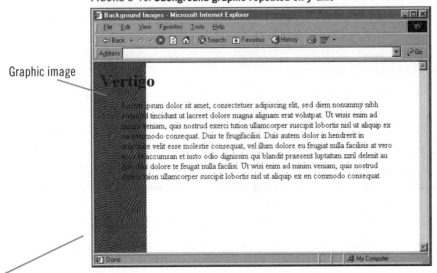

Rule for repeating the graphic on the *y*-axis:

```
BODY {BACKGROUND: URL(texture4.jpg); BACKGROUND-REPEAT: REPEAT-Y}
```

Working with Colors

HTML uses hexadecimal numbers to express RGB color values. **Hexadecimal numbers** are a base-16 numbering system, so the numbers run from 0 through 9 and then A through F. When compared with a standard base-10 numbering system, hexadecimal looks strange because it includes letters in the numbering scheme. The Student Online Companion for this book has an online color chart you can use. Some HTML reference books have a printed color chart of hexadecimal colors, but, in general, you always should use an online color resource for checking color values to get a much more realistic view of the actual color.

Details

▶ Hexadecimal color values are six-digit numbers; the first two define the red value, the second two define the green, and the third two define the blue. You can use these values in a variety of elements with either the BGCOLOR attribute or the COLOR attribute to define color in your Web pages. CSS also accepts hexadecimal color values. Hexadecimal values should always be contained in quotes and preceded by a number sign as shown: <BODY BGCOLOR="#FFFFFF">

▶ Although you can use color names for many hexadecimal colors, some browsers do not support color names. You are better off using hexadecimal values rather than color names. Table G-4 lists the 16 basic color names that are recognized by most browsers and stated in the W3C HTML 4.0 specification. To use these universal color names, state the color in the attribute value, as shown in the following example: <BODY BGCOLOR="YELLOW">

▶ You can use hexadecimal color to specify a background color for your pages. Use the BGCOLOR attribute in the <BODY> element, or with CSS use the BACKGROUND-COLOR property with BODY as the selector. The <BODY BGCOLOR="#FFFFFF"> code sets the background color to white using HTML. The BODY {BACKGROUND-COLOR: #FFFFFF} selector sets the background color to white using CSS.

▶ You can work with three layers when designing your pages. The foreground layer contains your content (text and images). The middle layer displays the image specified in the BACKGROUND attribute. The specified image tiles repeatedly. With CSS you have more control over the tiling of the image. Finally, the background layer displays the BGCOLOR value.

▶ You can use background color in tables for different purposes, all by using the BGCOLOR attribute. The table <TABLE>, table row <TR>, table header <TH>, and table data <TD> elements all accept the BGCOLOR attribute.

▶ You can set a background color for an entire table by adding the BGCOLOR attribute to the beginning <TABLE> tag. The following is an example of a <TABLE> tag: <TABLE CELLPADDING=5 BORDER BGCOLOR="#FFF8DC" WIDTH=300>. The page shown in Figure G-19 uses this technique.

▶ By using the BGCOLOR attribute to set the background color, you can create reverse text in table cells. Figure G-20 shows the first row in the table with the BGCOLOR attribute set to red, blue, and green, respectively in each cell, and the text color set to white. In this example, the <FONT> element is setting the text color.

▶ By combining the BGCOLOR attribute with a table that has default spacing turned off, you can create continuous seamless areas of color as shown in Figure G-21. Remove the default table spacing by setting the attribute values as shown in the following <TABLE> tag: <TABLE BORDER=0, CELLPADDING=0, CELLSPACING=0>

▶ You can change your hypertext link colors using hexadecimal values or standard color names. Table G-5 lists the three attributes that all reside within the <BODY> element. An example of the syntax is: <BODY LINK=#CC3399" VLINK=#9900FF">

tip

Browser-safe hexadecimal colors always are made up of the following two-digit color values: 00, 33, 66, 99, CC, and FF. Therefore, 0066FF is a browser-safe color, but 0F66FF is not.

tip

Changing link colors is acceptable as long as you maintain color consistency and preserve the contrast between the new and visited link colors to provide a recognizable difference to the user.

FIGURE G-19: Table background color

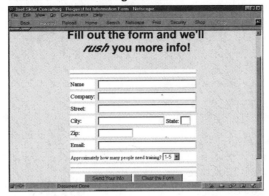

FIGURE G-20: Table cell reverse

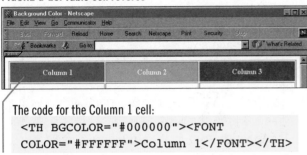

The code for the Column 1 cell:

```
<TH BGCOLOR="#000000"><FONT
COLOR="#FFFFFF">Column 1</FONT></TH>
```

FIGURE G-21: Continuous color areas

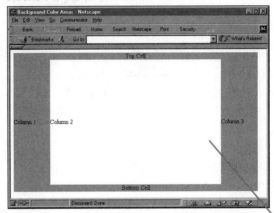

```
<TABLE WIDTH=600 BORDER=0 CELLPADDING=0 CELLSPACING=0>
<TR><TD COLSPAN=3 BGCOLOR="#CCCCCC" ALIGN=CENTER>Top Cell</TD></TR>
<TR><TD HEIGHT=300 WIDTH=15% BGCOLOR="#C0C0C0">Column 1</TD>
<TD WIDTH=70%>Column 2</TD> <TD WIDTH=15% BGCOLOR="#C0C0C0">Column
3</TD></TR> <TR><TD COLSPAN=3 BGCOLOR="#C0C0C0" ALIGN=CENTER>Bottom
Cell</TD></TR>
</TABLE>
```

TABLE G-4: Color names recognized by most browsers (highlighted colors are browser safe)

color name	hex	color name	hex	color name	hex	color name	hex
Aqua	00FFFF	Gray	808080	Navy	000080	Silver	C0C0C0
Black	000000	Green	008000	Olive	808000	Teal	008080
Blue	0000FF	Lime	00FF00	Purple	800080	White	FFFFFF
Fuschia	FF00FF	Maroon	800000	Red	FF0000	Yellow	FFFF00

TABLE G-5: Attributes to change link colors

attribute	description	default color
LINK	The unvisited link color	Blue
ALINK	The active link color; this is the color that displays when the user points to a link and holds down the mouse button	Red
VLINK	The visited link color	Purple

Practice

► Concepts Review

Fill in the blank with the best answer.

1. _GIF_, _JPG_, and _PNG_ are the three image file formats you can use on a Web site.
2. The _JPG_ and _PNG_ file formats support 24-bit color.
3. The amount of colors that can be used in an image is the color's _depth_ control.
4. GIF supports _256_ colors.
5. The _GIF_ and _PNG_ file formats support transparency.
6. An _animated GIF_ is a series of images that create the illusion of motion on a Web page using techniques not unlike cell animation.
7. _____ and _____ are the gradual display of a graphic in a series of passes as the data arrives in the browser.
8. 24-bit images can contain almost 17 million different colors and are called _____.

9. _____ occurs when the browser encounters a color it does not support.
10. It is not a good idea to change a graphic size using the _width height_ attributes in the <IMG> element.
11. The _____ properties set white space around an image.
12. Use the _GIF_ image format for a two-color company logo.
13. Use the _JPG_ image format for a photograph.
14. Use the _JPG_ image format for text with a gradient drop shadow.
15. The _border=0_ is the attribute and value for removing the hypertext border for an <IMG> element.
16. A _____ is a single-pixel graphic of just one color that is specified to be transparent.
17. You work with _____ layers when designing pages.
18. The _<table>_ and _<tr>_ are two of the table elements that accept the BGCOLOR attribute.

► Explore Further...

1. Explain the difference between lossy image compression and lossless file compression.

_____

_____

2. Describe the options available for acquiring images for your site.
   scanning, digital camera, stock photos

_____

3. Explain what happens when you display a 24-bit image on an 8-bit monitor.
   colors the browser can't match are dithered or banded

_____

4. List the three attributes you should always include in the <IMG> tag and then explain why you should include them.
   1. SRC
   2. Width & Height
   3. Alt

► Independent Challenges

1. The Web site for this book includes images that you can download and use to develop your own sites. You will create one HTML file that includes all the elements detailed in this Independent Challenge to build a simple page that contains text and multiple images.

   a. Create a new HTML file using a simple editor.

   b. Find an image of your own and insert it in the file, or download an image from the Student Online Companion site at *www.course.com/illustrated/designingsites.*

   c. Practice using the ALIGN attribute by adding text around the image.

   d. Copy the image and then change the ALIGN attribute and its values to view the way text wraps.

   e. Test the work in multiple browsers to verify that the text wraps consistently.

   f. Find another image of your own or download another image and add it to the Web site.

   g. Practice using the ALIGN attributes by adding text around the image. Change the HSPACE and VSPACE attributes to add white space around the image.

   h. Test the work in multiple browsers to verify that the text spacing is consistent.

   i. Find another image of your own or download another image. Add it to the HTML file you are working on. Do not include the WIDTH and HEIGHT attributes in the <IMG> tag.

   j. With the images turned off in your browser, view the page.

   k. Add the appropriate width and height information to the <IMG> tag for that image.

   l. Again, turn the images off in your browser and view the page. Note the differences between the two results and the way your layout is affected. Using your word processor, write a brief statement explaining the differences. Type **Your Name** at the bottom of the document, save the document, print a copy, and then close it.

   m. Save the HTML file as UnitGIndep1.htm, view the file in a browser, and then print the page.

2. The Web site for this book includes images that you can download and use to develop your own sites. Go to the Student Online Companion site at *www.course.com/illustrated/designingsites* and click the link for Unit G. You can use the images there, in addition to any you may have of your own, to build a simple layout. You will create one HTML file that includes all the elements detailed in this Independent Challenge.

   a. Download the transparent spacer GIF (transpix.gif) from the Student Online Companion site at *www.course.com/illustrated/designingsites.*

   b. Create a new HTML file using a simple editor.

   c. Test the capabilities of the transparent spacer GIF. Change the WIDTH and HEIGHT attributes to manipulate the size of the image and its spacing on the page.

   d. Download one of the single-color pixel graphics from the Student Online Companion site (bluepix.gif, redpix.gif, blackpix.gif, or graypix.gif) and add it to the file to build a simple layout.

   e. Test the capabilities of the single-pixel GIFs. Change the WIDTH and HEIGHT attributes to manipulate the size of the image and its use on the page.

   f. Create a table in the file. Experiment with background color in tables. Use the BGCOLOR attribute at different levels of a sample table to add color. Test the result in both Internet Explorer and Netscape Navigator. Note the ways that both browsers handle table color.

   g. Save the file as UnitGIndep2.htm, view the file in a browser, and then the print the page.

3. The visual experience you have surfing the Web is filled with images and color. Although design is often a very subjective decision, you have learned that there are suitable ways to use color and images to convey messages.

   a. Browse the Web for sites that make effective use of background images. Choose a Web site, print a page from the site, and then use your word processor to write a short design description of how the background images enhance the site. Type **Your Name** at the bottom of the document, save the document, print a copy, and then close it.

   b. Browse the Web for sites that make effective use of color. Pick a site that has a definite color scheme, print a page from the site, and then use your word processor to write a short design critique that explains how the use of color enhances the site. Type **Your Name** at the bottom of the document, save the document, print a copy, and then close it.

You will continue to develop the Web site you have been working on throughout this book. For this Independent Challenge, you will focus on the graphics in the site.

   a. Gather or create the boilerplate graphics to use on the different pages of your site. These include any banner, navigation, section, or identifying graphics. Add these graphics to the test pages of your site.

   b. Test the images in multiple browsers to make sure they display properly.

   c. Determine the color choices for your Web site. Pick the colors you will use for text, background color in tables, and page backgrounds. If you will be using single-color graphics, such as lines or bullets, create them now.

d. Establish graphics standards for your Web site, including but not limited to the following:

   • Determine if you will use a standard amount of white space around each graphic

   • Determine exactly which <IMG> attributes should be included in all <IMG> tags

   • Formulate a standard for all ALT attributes

   • Formulate a lowest common denominator set of image standards for your site; this will be used as the base-level display standard for testing your graphics

   • Write a short standards document that can be provided to anyone contributing to the site

► Visual Workshop

1. In this Visual Workshop, the image in Figure G-22 shows several graphics techniques that you learned about in this unit. Write a brief essay explaining three techniques you can see in this image.

FIGURE G-22

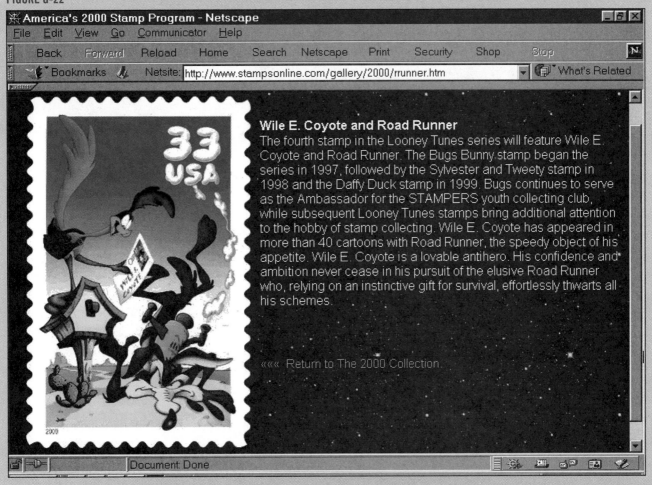

Web Design

▶ Visual Workshop

2. For this Visual Workshop, review the image shown in Figure G-23. Several graphics techniques are used on this page. Write a brief essay explaining what you see. Then, describe how you might change the design to improve the graphics on the page. If you think the graphic design is well done, explain your position.

FIGURE G-23

Understanding
HTML Frames

Objectives

- ► **Understand frames**
- ► **Work with frame syntax**
- ► **Restrict resizing and control scroll bars**
- ► **Control borders and margins**
- ► **Target in framesets**
- ► **Use special target names**
- ► **Plan for screen resolution**
- ► **Mix fixed and variable frames**

The HTML **frame** elements let you partition the canvas area of the browser into multiple windows called frames. Each frame can display a separate, independent HTML document. The use of frames has become a subject of controversy on the Web. In some cases, framed Web sites are poorly designed. They detract from the user's experience with heavy download times and confusing navigation. The judicious use of frames, however, can enhance your Web site, allowing you to consistently display navigation information and content concurrently. Frames can be the right solution for working out specific information problems or for providing large collections of content. This unit explains how to work with frames to display your information effectively.

Understanding Frames

HTML frames were introduced by Netscape for the 2.0 release of its browser and are now part of the HTML 4.0 specification. Frames now are supported in a wide variety of browsers. Controversial since their inception, frames can polarize Web designers—some lauding the benefits, others characterizing them as unnecessary. As you will see, frames can work well if you use them correctly. Far too many Web sites use frames just because they can, with no real benefit to the user.

► Frames allow you to divide the browser window into independent windows, each displaying a separate HTML document. Figure H-1 shows an example of a framed set of pages, called a **frameset**, that contains three independent frames. You can quickly identify a page that uses frames if you click a link in one section and it remains stationary while another section of the page changes in response to the link.

► Frames offer a number of benefits, including the ability to allow users to scroll independently in one frame without affecting the contents of an adjoining frame. Even though each of these frames displays a separate HTML file, they can be designed to work together to benefit the user. Figure H-2 shows a frameset that displays a table of contents in one frame, search tools in another, and content in a third. The table of contents and search tool are always visible to the user. This is an ideal way to present large collections of information that are hard to navigate using the traditional single-page browser display.

► Frames present a variety of drawbacks. Although Internet Explorer 5.0 solves this problem, most browsers do not let the user bookmark individual pages from a Web site. Because the pages are all referenced from a single HTML frames file, the user cannot return to an exact page within a site, only to the main framed page. In addition, because the browser is loading more than one document, the initial download time can be higher for a framed set of documents than for a single HTML document.

► Below is a list of design and planning tips that you need to consider before committing your content to a frame-based organization:

• Navigation:

Create clear navigation choices. Users can become confused if you build complicated framed document sets without enough navigation choices to let them jump to the page of their choice. The Back button in the browser only lets users load the previous page displayed within the frame, which may not be what they expect.

• Visual appeal:

Limit the number of frames to avoid breaking the browser window into too many sections. Frames work best when you keep them simple. Two or three frames per frameset should be enough to accommodate your information needs. Too many frames within the browser window, each with its own scroll bars, clutter the screen. This design can confuse the user, making it difficult to find information.

• Search engines:

Avoid using a framed document as the top-level page for your Web site. Provide a standard HTML page as your top-level page and use the framed content at a lower level of the Web site. Because the content is contained in the HTML files displayed in the frames, not in the frameset code, search engines that read the content of a page for indexing will find no information on a framed page. You also can use the <NOFRAMES> element to provide content for search engines.

• User preferences:

Make sure that your pages can stand alone if for some reason a user chooses to display a page on its own outside of the frameset. You may want to add a simple text-based navigation bar on each page that is not viewable within the framed document but can be used to navigate your Web site if a user breaks out of the frameset. You can give the user a choice to navigate your Web site either with or without frames by adding links on the main page to framed and unframed versions of your Web site.

FIGURE H-1: Three independent frames

Frame #1

Frame #2

Frame #3

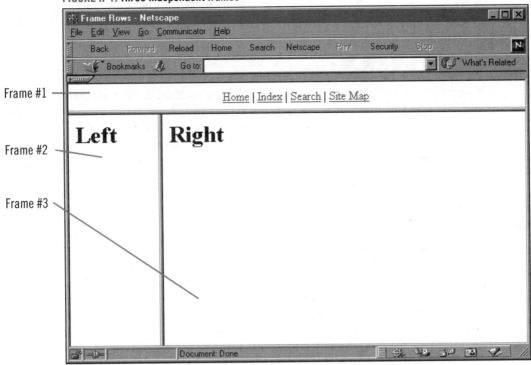

FIGURE H-2: Frames can aid navigation

Search and Contents frames display consistently

Scroll to read article

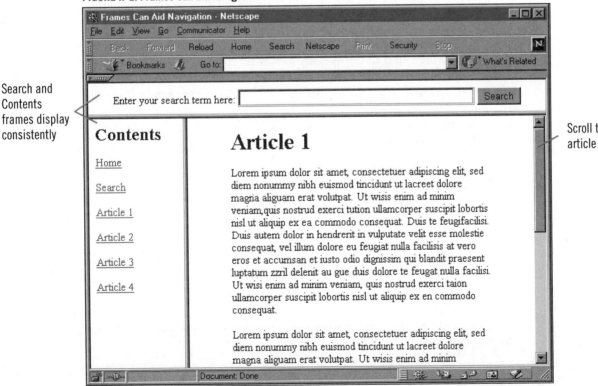

Unit H

Web Design

Working with Frame Syntax

A **frameset document** is an HTML document that instructs the browser to arrange specific HTML files and divide up the page. Frameset documents themselves have no actual content; therefore, they have no <BODY> element. You can combine frameset rows and columns to create the structure you need to display the content in your Web pages. To create this frameset, first create the individual HTML files and then create the master HTML frameset document file containing the frame code that holds the documents together.

Details

▶ The <FRAMESET> element is the container for the frameset code. The COLS and ROWS attributes let you specify the characteristics of the frameset. You can specify a frameset as either COLS or ROWS, but not both. The width (specific to columns) and height (specific to rows) can be expressed as either a percentage value or pixel count in the COLS and ROWS attributes. As with tables, percentage widths build frames that are relative to the browser window size. Absolute pixel widths are fixed regardless of the browser size. Figure H-3 shows an example of a simple frameset document that divides the browser canvas into two equal rows.

▶ The <FRAME> element determines the contents of each frame. Row framesets fill top to bottom. The first <FRAME> element tells the browser the file to display in the top row, and the second <FRAME> element points to the file for the bottom row.

<FRAME> is an empty element. The SRC attribute provides the location of the file that displays within the frame. Other attributes to the <FRAME> tag let you name the frame for targeting, specify if frames have a scroll bar, and apply an option to allow the user to resize the frame.

▶ In Figure H-4, the frameset is divided into two-column frames. In this frameset, the left column is fixed at 150 pixels wide. The right column defaults to fill the remainder of the browser window. In the code, note the syntax in the opening <FRAMESET> tag. The COLS attribute determines the width of the columns. The first value sets the left column to 150 pixels. The asterisk (*) character tells the browser to fill the right column to the remainder of the browser window. Because the left column is set to a fixed width, it will remain unchanged regardless of the user's browser size or screen resolution. Also note that in column framesets, the frames fill left to right. The first <FRAME> element fills the left column, and the second fills the right column.

▶ Figure H-5 shows a rows frameset that contains a nested columns frameset in the second row. Nesting allows you to break the screen into both row and column frames. Notice that two closing </FRAMESET> tags are necessary to close both framesets.

Design Matters

Using the <NOFRAMES> Tag

The <NOFRAMES> tag lets you provide an alternate page for users who do not have a frames-compliant browser. Enclose the contents of a standard Web page, excluding the <HTML> tag, within the <NOFRAMES> tag. Even though most browsers can display frames, it still is a good idea to add <NOFRAMES> content to help search engines index your framed content. When encountering a framed set of pages, some search engines look for the <NOFRAMES> element for content information.

FIGURE H-3: Two-row frameset

Both rows fill 50% of the browser window

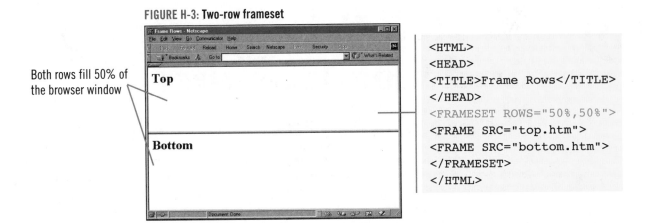

```
<HTML>
<HEAD>
<TITLE>Frame Rows</TITLE>
</HEAD>
<FRAMESET ROWS="50%,50%">
<FRAME SRC="top.htm">
<FRAME SRC="bottom.htm">
</FRAMESET>
</HTML>
```

FIGURE H-4: Two-column frameset

```
<HTML>
<HEAD>
<TITLE>Frame Columns</TITLE>
</HEAD>
<FRAMESET COLS="150,*">
<FRAME SRC="left.htm">
<FRAME SRC="right.htm">
</FRAMESET>
</HTML>
```

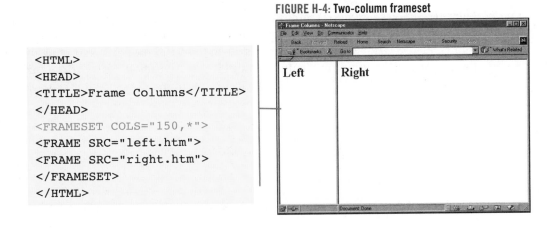

FIGURE H-5: Nested frameset

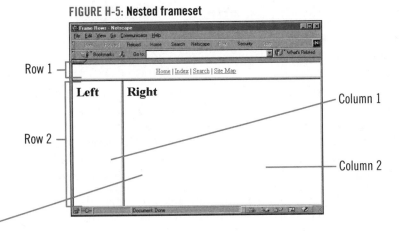

Row 1

Row 2

Column 1

Column 2

```
<HTML>
<HEAD>
<TITLE>Frame Rows</TITLE>
</HEAD>
<FRAMESET ROWS="40,*">
<FRAME SRC="topnav.htm"> <!- This is row 1 - >
<FRAMESET COLS="20%,80%"> <!- The nested frameset fills the 2nd row ->
<FRAME SRC="left.htm"> <!- This is column 1 - >
<FRAME SRC="right.htm"> <!- This is column 2 ->
</FRAMESET>
</FRAMESET>
</HTML>
```

Restricting Resizing and Controlling Scroll Bars

By default, the user has the option of resizing your frames by clicking and dragging the frame border. In most situations, you probably want to restrict resizing, so the user sees the frameset the way you intended. Similar to your ability to restrict resizing, you can control whether or not a frame displays scroll bars. Scroll bars let you navigate to portions of the page not visible on the screen.

Details

▶ Figure H-6 shows a frameset that the user has resized by clicking and dragging the frame border. Unless you have a specific reason, you probably want to restrict the user's ability to resize your frames. As you can see, the top row comes down too far in the page, restricting the content for the article and limiting the Contents available for navigation. To restrict resizing, add the NORESIZE attribute to the <SRC> elements in your frameset as shown in the code below.

```
<HTML>
<HEAD>
<TITLE>Restricting Resizing</TITLE>
</HEAD>
<FRAMESET ROWS="50,*">
<FRAME SRC="search.htm" NORESIZE>
    <FRAMESET COLS="135,*">
    <FRAME SRC="contents.htm" NORESIZE>
    <FRAME SRC="article1.htm" NORESIZE>
    </FRAMESET>
</FRAMESET>
</HTML>
```

▶ By default, scroll bars in frames are set to appear automatically if the content is not accessible within the frame window. In most cases, this is the best setting for scroll bars because you will not need to worry about them. No matter the user's browser size or screen resolution, if scroll bars are necessary, they will appear. Sometimes, however, you may want to control whether scroll bars display. Use the SCROLLING attribute in the <SRC> element to control scroll bars. The valid values are "YES," "NO," or "AUTO," which is the default setting.

▶ Figure H-7 shows a three-frame frameset. Notice that the top frame displays a scroll bar even though no additional content follows the search text box.

The browser displays a scroll bar because the height of the top frame is slightly smaller than the browser finds necessary to display the contents. One way to solve this problem is to change the height of the frame. Because this frame looks good at this height, the other option is to remove the scroll bar.

▶ Figure H-8 shows the result of adding the SCROLLING=NO attribute to the <SRC> element. The scroll bar no longer displays, which enhances the look of the frameset. Also, because a scroll bar indicates additional information, omitting the scroll bar reflects more accurately the content of this page.

FIGURE H-6: Resized frame

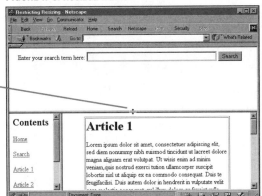

User resized the frame by clicking and dragging the border

FIGURE H-7: Unnecessary default scroll bar

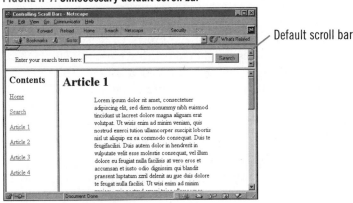

Default scroll bar

FIGURE H-8: Frame with no scroll bar

SCROLLING=NO removes the scroll bar

```
<HTML>
<HEAD>
<TITLE>Controlling Scroll
Bars</TITLE>
</HEAD>
<FRAMESET ROWS="50,*">
<FRAME SRC="search.htm" SCROLLING=NO>
<FRAMESET COLS="135,*">
<FRAME SRC="contents.htm">
<FRAME SRC="article1.htm">
</FRAMESET>
</FRAMESET>
</HTML>
```

Controlling Borders and Margins

As with tables, you can choose not to display frame borders or to remove the default border spacing between frames entirely. This technique lets you create seamless frames with no visible dividing line, unless a scroll bar pops up. You can also control the margins in frames as you design your pages.

Details

▶ Figure H-9 shows an example of a two-frame frameset with the frame borders turned off. Unfortunately, the two major browsers, Netscape Navigator and Internet Explorer, do not agree on the attributes you should use to achieve this effect. Netscape Navigator 4.0 requires FRAME-BORDER=NO and BORDER=0 attributes. Internet Explorer 5.0 can interpret correctly FRAMEBORDER=NO, but you need to set FRAMESPACING=0 to remove the default border spacing between frames. All of these attributes reside in the opening <FRAMESET> tag. To make sure that the frame border and spacing are turned off for both browsers, use the syntax for both browsers including both attributes to turn the borders off.

▶ Two frame attributes let you control the pixel width of both the vertical and horizontal margins in a frame. MARGINWIDTH lets you control the left and right margins, while MARGIN-HEIGHT affects the top and bottom margins. Setting these attributes to zero (0) lets you remove the margins entirely, allowing your content to touch the sides of the frame. You most likely would use these attributes in combination with the frame border attributes described above. Add the MARGINHEIGHT and MARGINWIDTH attributes to the <FRAME> element for the frame you want to affect.

▶ Figure H-10 shows a frameset with two different margin settings.

The left frame has both margin attributes set to zero (0). Even so, the top margin still includes some space because of built-in leading in the line of text. The left margin, however, has been completely removed. In the right column, both margins have been set to 30 pixels.

FIGURE H-9: Frame border turned off

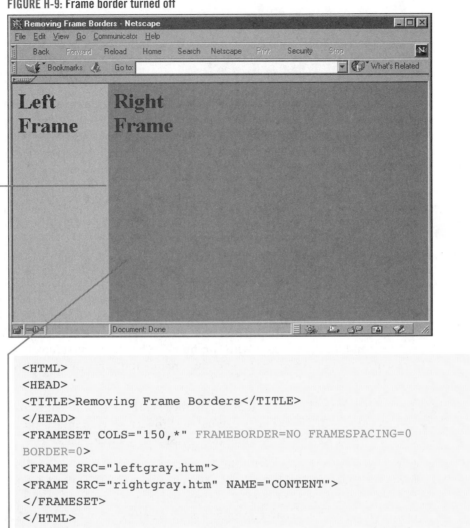

No border between frames

```
<HTML>
<HEAD>
<TITLE>Removing Frame Borders</TITLE>
</HEAD>
<FRAMESET COLS="150,*" FRAMEBORDER=NO FRAMESPACING=0
BORDER=0>
<FRAME SRC="leftgray.htm">
<FRAME SRC="rightgray.htm" NAME="CONTENT">
</FRAMESET>
</HTML>
```

FIGURE H-10: Frame borders and margins removed

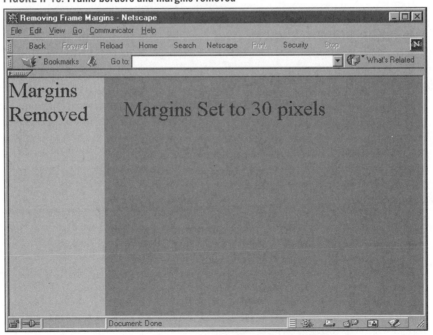

Web Design

Targeting in Framesets

The power of frames comes from the ability to have one frame display information consistently while the contents of a second frame might change based on the user's choice. By default, a link loads into the same frame from which it was selected. You can change this default behavior and target the destination of a link to another frame in the frameset. In this lesson you will learn how to target within the simple frameset. To target from one frame to another, you must name your frames using the NAME attribute in the FRAME element and then target links to display their content in the named frame.

Details

▶ Figure H-11 shows an example of targeting from one frame to another. The user clicks a link in the Links frame to display the requested article in the Articles frame. Typically, the Links frame would have a table of contents; it would remain available as the user read the selected articles.

▶ To name a frame, add the NAME attribute to the <FRAME> element. You do not have to name all of the frames within a frameset, only the frames you want to target. Figure H-12 shows a frameset and the HTML code with two frames. The NAME attribute in the second <FRAME> element names the right frame window "main." You now can target this window to display linked content.

▶ To target the named frame, you must edit the HTML document that contains the <A> elements and provide TARGET attributes that tell the browser which frame displays the content. You can use the TARGET attribute in either the <BASE> or <A> elements.

▶ In the example in Figure H-12, the HTML document that occupies the left frame window is named "navcol.htm." Adding the <BASE> element lets you set the default target frame for all of the links in the document. <BASE> is an empty tag that resides in the <HEAD> section of the document. The code in navcol.htm shows the <BASE> element. The <BASE> element contains the TARGET attribute set to "main." This establishes the default window target name for all of the links contained in the file. The following code will display any link that the user selects in the frame window named "main":

```
<HEAD>
<TITLE>Frame Links</TITLE>
<BASE TARGET="main">
</HEAD>
```

▶ You can override a default base target by using the TARGET attribute in the <A> element. This allows you to target a specific link to a destination different from the base target. You can target a different window within the frameset or can use one of the special targeting values in the next section. The following <A> element targets article1.htm to the frame named "frame2":

```
<A HREF="article1.htm" TARGET="frame2">Article 1</A>
```

FIGURE H-11: Targeting from one frame to another

Click a link in the Links frame…

…and the content is displayed in the Articles frame

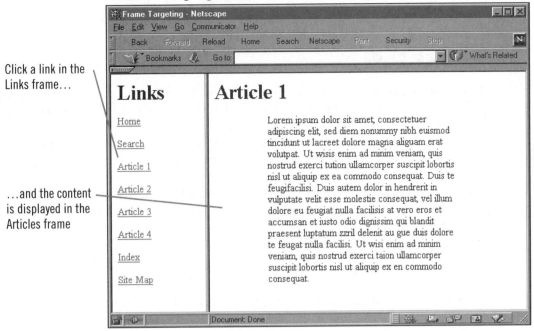

FIGURE H-12: Naming a frame for targeting

SRC="navcol.htm"

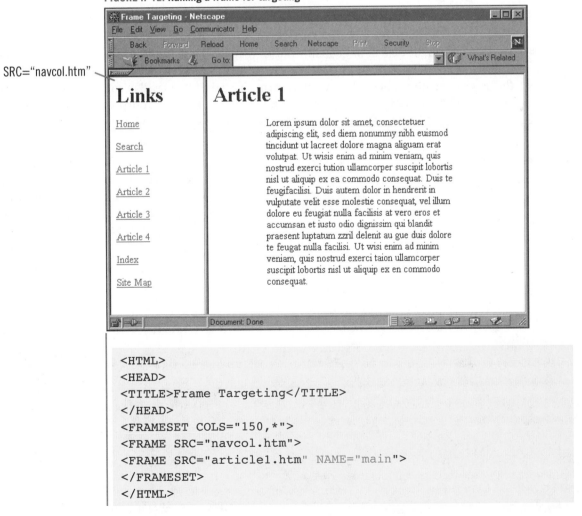

```
<HTML>
<HEAD>
<TITLE>Frame Targeting</TITLE>
</HEAD>
<FRAMESET COLS="150,*">
<FRAME SRC="navcol.htm">
<FRAME SRC="article1.htm" NAME="main">
</FRAMESET>
</HTML>
```

Using Special Target Names

Details

Special target names can help you in a variety of situations. For example, you can use special target names when you link to other sites from within a frameset. There are four special target names that you can use with the TARGET attribute in either the <BASE> or <A> elements. All of these special names begin with an underscore. The browser will ignore any other target name that begins with an underscore. Table H-1 lists the special names.

▶ Figure H-13 shows the Lotus Web site displayed in a frame. As you can see, loading the framed Lotus Web site within a frameset does not work well. The size of the frame is too small to display the Web site properly, causing multiple horizontal and vertical scroll bars. You can solve this problem by using special target names to break out of the frameset. There are two ways to handle this problem. You can use _blank to load the Lotus Web page in a new browser window or use _top to load the Lotus Web page to the top of the existing window.

▶ The _blank special target name lets you load the linked content into a new instance of Netscape Navigator. Figure H-14 shows how the _blank target name was used in the left navigation column for company links. The Lotus link is used as an example in the figure. Notice that the Back button is not available in the new browser window because this is the first page in the new window. Not being able to use Back can be disorienting to users who rely on it for navigation.

▶ The targeting information is in the file that contains the links, not the frameset file. In this example, the _blank target name resides in the <BASE> element, setting the default target for all of the links within the file.

▶ Using _blank as the default target name means that every link in this window will launch a new browser window. Before long (unless the user knows to close each window when done with it) the user's computer either will run out of memory or the screen will become cluttered by overlapping windows. For this reason, limit the use of _blank to special purposes, or do not use it at all. If you decide to use _blank, you can help the user by letting them know that clicking the link will open a new browser window.

▶ Using _top as a special target name displays the linked content in a nonframed window using the same instance of the browser. Figure H-15 shows how using this special target name works when used in the left navigation column for company links. The browser clears the frameset and loads the Lotus link in the same window. The Back button is available if the user wants to return to the previous page. Because the browser maintains only one open window, there is no additional memory overhead or confusion for the user.

TABLE H-1: Special target names

name	description
_self	This is the default behavior for links in a frameset. The linked content is loaded into the same window as the <A> element. You most likely would use this in the <A> element to override a base target.
_blank	This name opens a new browser window to display the linked content. This result can cause navigation confusion for the users, who may not realize that they are looking at a new instance of the browser.
_parent	This name lets you break out of a child frameset and display the link in the parent frameset one level up in the frameset hierarchy. This name only is useful when you have a link in a frameset that displays an embedded frameset. In most cases, using embedded framesets is poor navigation design that will confuse your user.
_top	The most useful of all the special names, _top lets you remove frames and display the linked content in a new browser window.

FIGURE H-13: Framed Lotus Web site displayed within a frameset

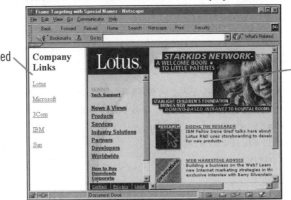

Links in this frame are targeted to the right frame

The Lotus Web site squeezed into the right frame

FIGURE H-14: Using _blank

The Back button is not available in the new window

Clicking the Lotus link opens a new window

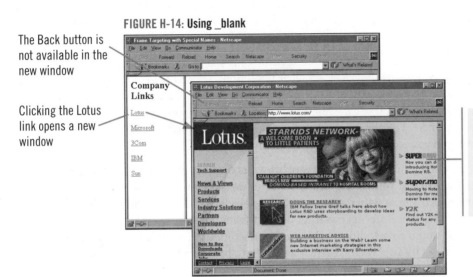

```
<HTML>
<HEAD>
<TITLE></TITLE>
<BASE TARGET="_blank">
</HEAD>
<BODY>
```

FIGURE H-15: Using _top

The Back button is available to return to the previous page

Clicking the Lotus link clears the frameset and loads the Lotus Web site

Web Design

Planning for Screen Resolution

The variable nature of the World Wide Web affects your framed pages. If you are planning on building a framed site, you must prepare your content for display within a frameset. Frameset display is affected by the base screen resolution you use to code your framed pages. You must decide on the lowest common denominator screen resolution that will display the frameset effectively.

Details

▶ Frame scroll bars and borders add to the screen space requirements of frames. Many Web sites that use frames build them for a base resolution of 800 × 600, forcing some users to change their screen resolutions to view the content. Even if you decide to code for a higher resolution, you always should test at a 640 × 480 resolution because some users will view your Web site at this resolution.

▶ Users with older monitors view pages at the lower resolutions, whereas users with newer monitors and computers may be viewing the pages at higher resolutions, such as 1024 × 768 or even 1600 × 1280. Although a frame may fill half the lower resolution screen, users at higher resolutions will have a lot of empty space on the screen. If you are not using a fixed width, and you are using Windows 95 or higher, you can test at different resolutions to the maximum resolution your system will support by changing the resolution on your computer through the Control Panel.

▶ Because small differences between the way browsers display frames can affect their look significantly, you have to test your work in different browsers. Figures H-16 and H-17 show the Anne Frank House Web site at 640 × 480 in Netscape Navigator 4.0 and Internet Explorer 5.0. The additional scroll bars in Internet Explorer distract from the seamless nature of the frameset. The HTML author would have to tinker with the frameset measurement values and scroll bar settings to get the frameset to display consistently across both browsers.

FIGURE H-16: Site in Navigator 4.0 at 640 × 480 resolution

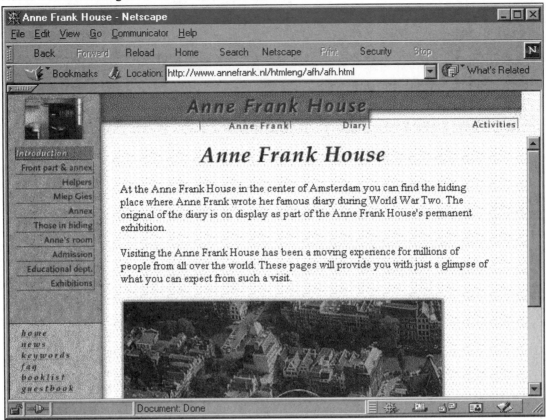

FIGURE H-17: Site in Internet Explorer 5.0 at 640 × 480 resolution

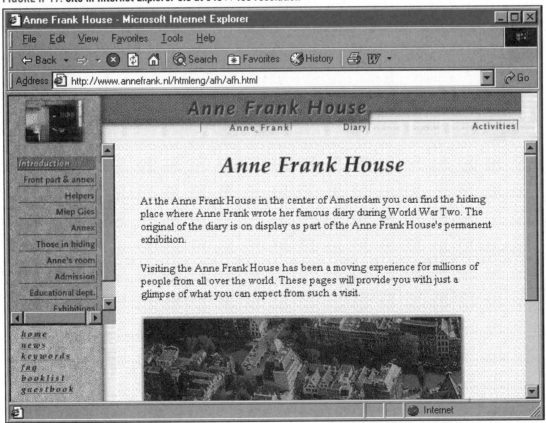

Web Design

Mixing Fixed and Variable Frames

You must build your pages to fit within the frames in which they will display. You also will need to accommodate different screen resolutions that can affect the size of the frame within the frameset. As with tables, decide whether you will use fixed or relative framesets. You also can choose to mix these two measurement types within a single frameset, which can be the best way to handle multiple screen resolutions.

Details

▶ Figure H-18 shows a frameset at 640 × 480 resolution that mixes a fixed frame and a variable frame to accommodate different resolutions. The code for the left column is fixed at 125 pixels. The asterisk (*) wildcard character sets the right column to a variable width that changes, based on the browser size.

▶ Tables in each HTML file keep the content aligned within the frameset. In Figure H-18, the table borders are turned on so you can see them. The table in the left frame has a fixed width of 75 pixels. The difference between the frame width of 125 and the table width of 75 is taken up by the scroll bar and frame margins. This frame and content will display consistently regardless of the screen resolution. The code for the table in the left frame content, leftfxd.htm, is

```
<HEAD>
<TITLE>Left Fixed Column</TITLE>
<BASE TARGET="main">
</HEAD>
<BODY>
<TABLE WIDTH=75 BORDER>
<TR>
<TD>
<H1>Links</H1>
<A HREF="index.htm">Home</A>
```

▶ The right frame is a variable width; therefore, the content within the right frame is contained in a centered table set to an 80% width. The 80% width allows for white space on both sides of the text. The code for the right frame content, article1.htm, is <TABLE WIDTH=80% BORDER>

▶ The same frameset at an 800 × 600 resolution is shown in Figure H-19. The left frame is fixed at 125 pixels. The only difference is that the scroll bar no longer appears in the left frame because of the increased resolution, giving the browser a larger canvas size. The right column still has centered content with white space on both sides of the text. Because the table in the right frame is variable, it adjusts to the new screen resolution.

▶ If you are building a row frameset, you can use this same fixed and variable coding method. Set one row to a fixed width, and let the second row default to the remainder of the browser canvas, as shown in Figure H-20. The top row is 80 pixels high. The second row fills the browser window regardless of screen resolution.

▶ A final example of the fixed/variable method is a common three-row frameset. In this set, the top and bottom rows contain navigation, whereas the middle row contains content. The top and bottom rows are fixed, and the middle row is variable, as shown in Figure H-21.

FIGURE H-18: Frameset at 640 × 480 resolution

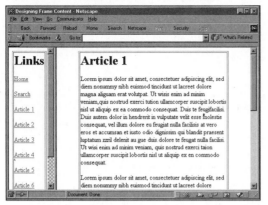

```
<HTML>
<HEAD>
<TITLE>Designing Frame Content</TITLE>
</HEAD>
<FRAMESET COLS="125,*">
<FRAME SRC="leftfxd.htm">
<FRAME SRC="article1.htm" name="main">
</FRAMESET>
</HTML>
```

FIGURE H-19: Frameset at 800 × 600 resolution

Frame width is fixed at 125 pixels

Table is centered; relative width of 80% adjusts to screen size

White space expands to accommodate larger browser size

Scroll bar no longer appears

FIGURE H-20: Fixed top row, variable second row

```
<HTML>
<HEAD>
<TITLE>Fixed/Variable
Rows</TITLE>
</HEAD>
<FRAMESET ROWS="80,*">
<FRAME SRC="topfxd.htm">
<FRAME SRC="btvarble.htm" >
</FRAMESET>
</HTML>
```

FIGURE H-21: Three-row frameset with variable middle row

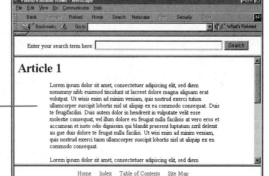

```
<HTML>
<HEAD>
<TITLE>Fixed/Variable Rows</TITLE>
</HEAD>
<FRAMESET ROWS="50,*,35">
<FRAME SRC="search.htm" SCROLLING=NO>
<FRAME SRC="article.htm" NAME="MAIN">
<FRAME SRC="botmcnt.htm" SCROLLING=NO>
</FRAMESET>
</HEAD>
```

Web Design

Practice

► Concepts Review

Fill in the blank with the best answer.

1. Framesets _____ initial download time because the browser is loading more than one document at a time.

2. _____ have problems with framesets because there is no actual content in the frameset code.

3. The two attributes you use to structure the look of a frameset are _____ and _____.

4. The purpose of the _____ element is to provide alternate content for browsers that cannot display frames.

5. The _____ attribute allows the HTML author to restrict the user's ability to resize frames.

6. The default setting for the SCROLLING attribute is _____.

7. The _____ attribute lets you control the pixel of the vertical leading.

8. The _____ element lets you set a default target for all links in a document.

9. The four special target names are _____, _____, _____, and _____.

10. Target names are case sensitive. True/False? _____

11. The special target name _____ is the default behavior for links in a frameset.

12. The _____ special target name launches a separate instance of the browser every time a user clicks a link.

13. You should opt for the _____ screen resolution to display your frameset effectively.

14. Use _____ to keep the content aligned within the frameset to control the display of content within a frameset.

15. Use a combination of fixed and variable size _____ within the frameset to accommodate frameset display at varying screen resolutions.

► Explore Further...

1. Describe the main benefits of frames.

_____

_____

2. How does the order of the <FRAME> element within the <FRAMESET> affect the display of the frameset?

_____

_____

3. List the correct attributes to the <FRAMESET> element that will remove the frame borders in both Netscape Navigator and Internet Explorer.

_____

_____

4. What are the two tasks you must perform to add targeting to a frameset?

_____

_____

5. What additional browser elements can affect the display of your frameset?

_____

_____

▶ Independent Challenges

1. The Web has many sites that benefit from using frames. As you browse around the Web, you can identify those sites and make use of frames to move through the site and get the information that you need.

a. Go to the Web and find a site that uses frames. If you have problems finding a site, go to the Student Online Companion site at *www.course.com/illustrated/designingsites* and click the links for the suggested sites.

b. Navigate the site you select and judge the effectiveness of the navigation and content presentation.

c. Test the site at different resolutions.

d. Test the site in at least two different browsers.

e. Using your word processor, write a short summary of your findings. Type **Your Name** at the bottom of the document, save the document, print a copy, and then close it.

2. The Web has many sites that use frames that may or may not have benefited from the their inclusion. Your experience on the Web will teach you to identify which framed sites work better than others.

a. Go to the Web and find a mainstream Web site that you think would benefit from frames. If you have problems finding a site, go to the Student Online Companion site at *www.course.com/illustrated/designingsites* and click the links for the suggested sites.

b. Using your word processor, write a short essay explaining how this site might be better if frames were used. Write a design critique and suggest ways that the Web site could be redesigned using frames. Be sure to identify the site and include an image of the site with your findings. Type **Your Name** at the bottom of the document, and save the document.

c. Test the Web site in at least two different browsers. Are there differences in the navigation between the browsers?

d. Navigate the Web site and judge the effectiveness of the navigation and content presentation. Using your word processor, continue the essay explaining how this site displays in the different browsers. Be sure to identify the site and include an image of the site with your findings. Save the document, print a copy, and then close it.

3. The unit reviewed the basic construction principles for creating frames. Code was given for creating frames. You should be able to create basic framed pages for sample sites.

- **a.** Visit the Student Online Companion Web Site at *www.course.com/illustrated/designingsites* and download two of the sample frame content files.
- **b.** Build a two-column frameset that contains a fixed left navigation frame and a variable right content frame.
- **c.** Target all of the links in the left frame to the right content frame.
- **d.** Restrict the user's ability to resize the frames.
- **e.** Save the files with your name in the filename.
- **f.** Visit the Student Online Companion Web site and download one of the sample frame content files from those that are available.
- **g.** Build a simple two-row or two-column frameset, and save the file using a filename with your name in it. Add links to your navigation frame that point to live Web sites.
- **h.** Use _top as a special target name to display the linked content in a nonframed window.
- **i.** Add a special target name that will load the linked Web sites into a new browser window.
- **j.** Test the links and view the browser's behavior. Print the files, and then save and close the files.

At this point, the Web site you have been working on through the course of this book should be fairly well formed. You will use what you learned in this unit to determine whether frames will enhance the effectiveness of your Web site and the presentation of your content.

a. Using your word processor, write a design summary that states how your Web site would benefit from the use of frames, and include a sketch of the structure and navigation of your proposed framed Web site.

b. Discuss targeting behavior and how you would handle links to sites outside of your own.

c. Discuss whether you would have a framed page or standard HTML page for the top-level page of your Web site.

d. If you determine that your Web site would benefit from frames, build a test frameset. Include some sample content pages. Code your frameset to work at both 640×480 and 800×600 resolutions.

e. Test your frameset at different resolutions and in different browsers. If the testing shows positive results, adopt the frameset for your completed Web site.

f. Type **Your Name** at the bottom of the design document, save the document, print a copy, and then close it.

► Visual Workshop

1. For this Visual Workshop, the image in Figure H-22 shows the Web site found at *www.roches.com* and displayed at 800 × 600 resolution in Netscape Navigator 4.7; it includes frames. Based on what you learned about frames, write a brief essay describing what techniques might have been used to create this page. Explain how frames are used to present relevant information to the user. What could you do to improve the use of frames at this resolution? Write a sample code for this frameset to reflect the improvements.

FIGURE H-22

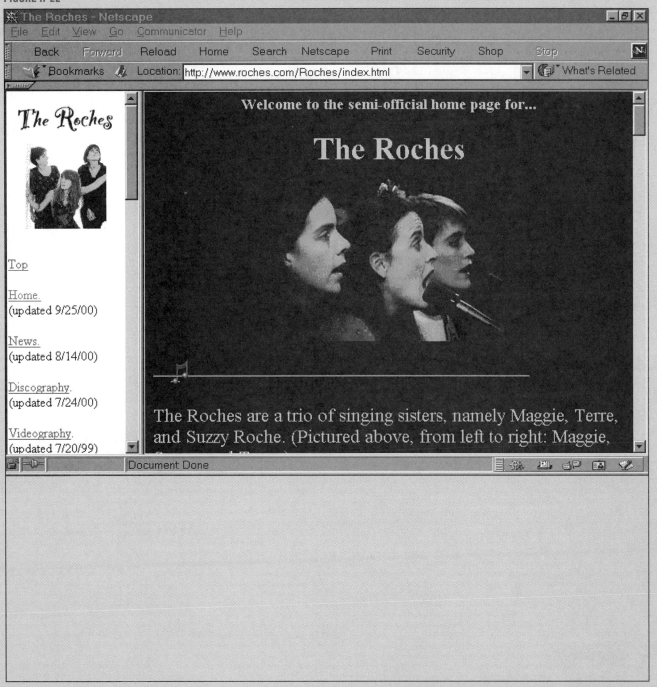

Web Design

► **Visual Workshop**

2. For this Visual Workshop, the image in Figure H-23 shows the Web site found at *www.lotus.com/home.nsf/welcome/events*. Explain how frames are used to display relevant information to the user in this site. Write sample code for the possible frameset.

FIGURE H-23

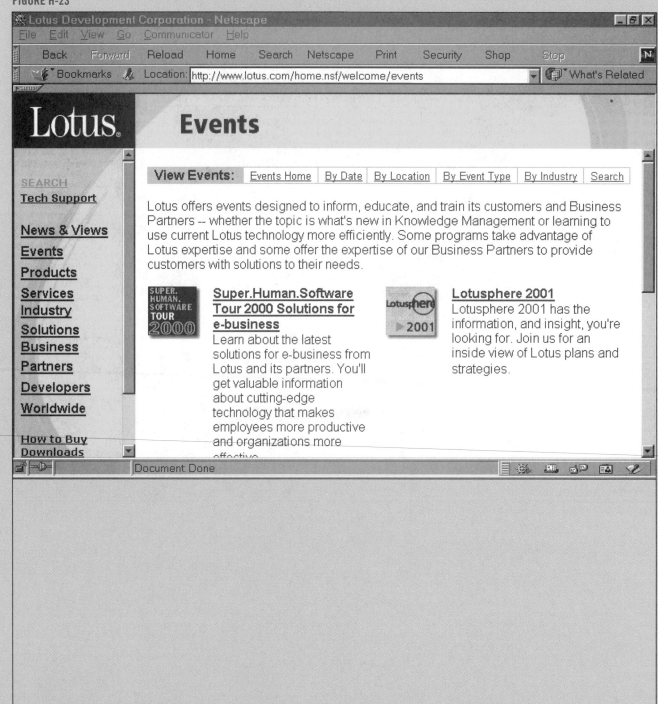

┌ Web Design ┐

Publishing
and Maintaining Your Web Site

Objectives

- ► **Choose an ISP**
- ► **Use the file transfer protocol to upload files**
- ► **Test your Web site**
- ► **Conduct user testing**
- ► **Refine and update your content**
- ► **Work with search engines**

You have done all the hard work, and now it is time to publish your Web site. Your first important decision to make is your choice of an Internet Service Provider (ISP) to host your Web site. You also need to know how to transfer your files to the Web server from the computer you used to develop your Web pages. After the Web site is established, you should test it with a variety of users and update or refine it as needed. Finally, you should make sure your Web site gets noticed. This appendix describes the details of publishing and maintaining a Web site.

Web Design

Details

Choosing an ISP

One of the most important choices you will make is that of your Web-hosting service or ISP. An **Internet Service Provider (ISP)** is the company that hosts your Web pages on a Web server, making them available to anyone who knows your URL. Shopping for an ISP can be a confusing experience because no two are exactly alike. Do some research to compare features and learn about offerings from various ISP vendors.

► Web Server Requirements

To make your Web site live (i.e., available to users on the Web), you transfer your Web site files to a Web server. A **Web server** is a computer connected to the Internet and running server software. The software lets the computer use the Hypertext Transfer Protocol to serve HTML files to Web browser clients. Unless your company or organization has a Web server, you must use the services of a Web-hosting provider. After you choose a server to host your files, you will need to select file transfer software and upload the Web site files from your development machine to the Web server.

Web-hosting services provide Web server space only and are more capable of hosting a complex commercial site. ISPs provide dial-up access, and most offer Web server space as part of the access package. Small Web sites (around 15–20 pages of content) do not need much more than 1–2 MB of server space to hold all of the HTML pages and graphics. Your ISP should provide at least 10 MB of space so your Web page has room to grow. Larger or more complex sites need more server space, especially if you have downloadable files, archives, lots of graphic content, or databases.

► Tips for America Online (AOL) Users

As an AOL subscriber, you are allowed 10 MB of Web server space, but you cannot have your own domain name. You also may experience slower connections to the Web because so many AOL subscribers are connected during peak times. If you are spending a lot of time on the Web, subscribe to a regular dial-up account from an ISP and then access AOL using your Internet connection. AOL currently charges less for users that "BYOA" (bring your own access) because they are not using the AOL network to access the Internet.

► Easy Dial-Up

Choose an ISP that allows you to connect to their network by placing a local phone call. Make sure that your provider has enough Points of Presence to make dialing easy. **Points of Presence (POPs)** are dial-up access points to your service provider's network. Your service provider should have at least one POP available so you can dial a local number to access the network. Major ISPs, such as AT&T, have POPs throughout the United States. A local ISP will cover only the area that includes their subscriber base. Try to match the size of your ISP to the size of your company—a local company does not need the services of a national ISP.

You should not receive a busy signal when you dial up to get Internet access. Unfortunately, you probably will not find out about access problems until after you have become a customer. Do not hesitate to change ISPs if you are not satisfied with ease of access.

► Free Utility Software

Your ISP should provide you with a **File Transfer Protocol (FTP)**, a standard communications application for transferring files over the Internet. Some ISPs provide HTML editors and other software as well. Some of this software may be shareware, so, if you decide to keep it, remember to register with the author.

► Accessible Technical Support

Technical support is not necessarily a feature, but it is an absolute necessity. Make sure that your ISP has competent, accessible customer service. When you are checking into ISPs, call and talk with someone in customer service. Tell them how experienced you are with computers, and let them know what you hope to accomplish (such as set up a Web site, transfer files, etc.). Time how long they keep you on hold when you are waiting to speak with customer service. Local ISPs may not have a large staff, but they also have fewer subscribers. National ISPs have so much volume that they may keep you on hold for an unacceptable length of time.

► Additional E-mail Addresses

All access accounts come with at least one e-mail address, called a **Post Office Protocol 3 (POP3)** account. If you are part of a group, you may want an account that has more than one mailbox so that each person receives his or her own e-mail.

► Personal and Commercial Accounts

Personal ISP accounts generally are less expensive than a business account. You have less disk space, fewer features, and a more complex URL, such as *www.webserver.com/users/yourname/*. Once you buy a domain name, your ISP usually upgrades you to a commercial account. Commercial accounts pay more for their services, so make sure you receive more, such as some of the features listed below.

► Domain Names

If you want to see if a domain name is available or to register your own domain name, visit Network Solutions (*www.networksolutions.com*). Network Solutions is the company responsible for registering *.com*, *.net*, and *.org* domain names. The site contains a simple form that lets you enter a domain name to see if it is already registered. If the domain name is available, you can register online. Domain names currently must be renewed every two years.

For an additional fee, your ISP often can register your Web site and provide Network Solutions with all the details, such as the server's primary and secondary Internet Protocol (IP) addresses. If you prefer, you can save the cost of doing this by filling out the online forms yourself, but you still need to contact your ISP to get the IP addresses.

► SQL Database Support

If you are planning on any type of electronic commerce or customized data presentation, you need database support. **Structured Query Language (SQL)** is a standard programming language for getting information from a database as well as updating and maintaining the database. Databases that understand SQL are the most common and most powerful databases.

► SSL Support

The **Secure Socket Layer (SSL)** is an Internet communications protocol that allows encrypted transmission of data between the user and the server. SSL is necessary if you are planning to set up an electronic commerce site or transmit other sensitive data. Encrypting the data ensures the information cannot be read if the transmission is intercepted.

► Multimedia Capabilities

Multimedia capabilities include support for RealNetworks technology (*www.real.com*), which is the current standard for streaming multimedia on the Web. If you have ever used the RealPlayer plug-in on the Web to view real-time audio or video, you have used this technology. **Streaming** is a server-based technology that transmits audio or video content in a continuous stream to the user, allowing the content to be played while it is downloading, rather than waiting to download a complete file. The success of these technologies depends on the speed and quality of the user's connection to the Internet.

► CGI Script Capabilities

The **Common Gateway Interface (CGI)** is the communications bridge between the Internet and the server. The **Hypertext Transfer Protocol (HTTP)** is the set of rules for exchanging files on the Web. Using programs called scripts, CGI can collect data sent by a user via HTTP and transfer it to a variety of data-processing programs, including spreadsheets, databases, or other software running on the server. The data-processing software then can work with the data and send a response back to CGI, and then onto the user.

The program that transfers the data is called a **CGI script**. You can write CGI scripts in a variety of programming languages. If you are not already familiar with writing CGI scripts, enlist the assistance of a programmer, unless you want to master programming skills in addition to your HTML skills. The information the CGI script processes is collected from the user with an HTML form. You have probably used a form, created with the HTML <FORM> elements, to submit data over the Internet, such as survey information or address and credit card information when purchasing an item. The information in this form could be sent through a CGI script to a database on the server that contains customer contacts. The HTML forms interface is easy to create. You need only the cooperation of a programmer to make your forms work for you.

Web Design

Using the File Transfer Protocol to Upload Files

To publish your pages on the Web, you must send your HTML code, images, and other files to the Web server. To do this, you need File Transfer Protocol (FTP) software, often called an **FTP client**.

Details

▶ Find the Right FTP Client

Some HTML-authoring software, such as Microsoft FrontPage 2000 and Macromedia Dreamweaver, include built-in software packages that let you upload files to your Web server if your ISP supports these features. You also can choose from many shareware FTP programs to upload your files. Visit your favorite shareware site, such as CNET Shareware.com, and search for FTP clients. Most FTP clients work on the same principles.

▶ Get the FTP Address

When you have decided which FTP software to use, contact your ISP's customer service department and ask for the correct FTP address for the Web server. You also need your account name and password, which in most cases will automatically point your FTP program to the proper directory on the server.

▶ Upload the Files

To upload your files, start your FTP program and connect to your Web server using the FTP information provided by your service provider. Your password allows you write access to your directory on the Web server. Figure AP-1 shows a screen with the FTP connection settings for a particular Web server. The FTP client is from the WS_FTP32 application developed by Ipswitch Software.

Once the FTP client connects to the Web server, you have the option of choosing the files you want to transfer. The FTP client usually displays directories on both local and remote computers. Figure AP-2 shows the FTP client with both local and remote system information.

Select the files that you want to upload in your local directory listing and transfer them to the Web server. You also can transfer files from the Web server to your computer. The first time you go live with your Web site, you must transfer all the files. Later you will need to upload only the files that you have updated. Once the files have reached the Web server, they are available for access immediately on the Web.

▶ Back Up Your Files

Always keep a backup of your Web site files in case you have any problems during FTP transmissions or if you accidentally delete or overwrite existing files. Of course, if you ever accidentally delete or overwrite files on your local computer, you always can use your Web site files as a backup.

FIGURE AP-1: FTP connection settings

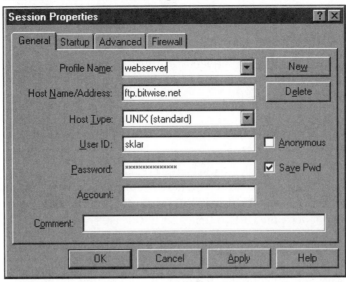

Local directory

Local file
listing

FIGURE AP-2: FTP dialog box showing remote and local machines

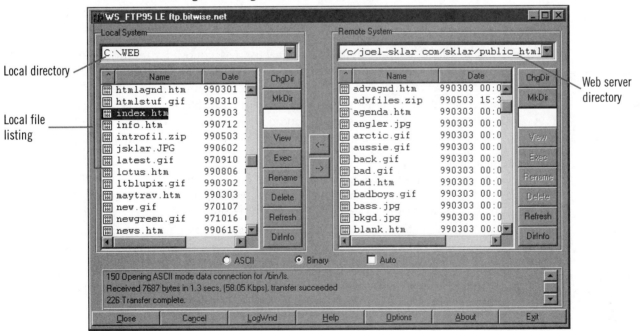

Web server
directory

Web Design

Testing Your Web Site

After you find an ISP and publish your Web site to the World Wide Web, it is time to test your Web site in the real-life Internet environment. Even though you tested throughout the development of your Web site, you need to continue testing after you post your files live on the Web.

Details

► **Establish a Testing Area**

If possible, load your files to the Web server and test them before making your URL available for users to access the Web site. If you have enough server space, you may want to establish a testing area on the Web site. You can do this by creating a subdirectory in your public HTML directory. Do not publicize the URL so that your testing area can remain private.

► **Maintain Directory Structure**

Make sure that you maintain the exact directory structure on the Web server that you used on your development computer to ensure that all relative file paths are correct.

► **Testing Considerations: Cache**

If you are testing from the same machine on which you developed the Web site, make sure to clear your cache. When you clear the cache, the browser has to retrieve all of the Web site's files from the server, recreating the experience of a first-time visitor to your Web site.

► **Testing Considerations: Environments**

Always test in as many different environments as possible. Remember to test for the following Web design variables:

- Multiple browsers:
  Test in as many browsers as you can to make sure your work is portable and displays consistently.

- Multiple operating systems:
  If you have a PC as a development machine, use a Macintosh for testing and vice-versa. You even can run different versions of UNIX on a PC, if necessary. Because computer chip development moves at lightning pace, machines become outdated quickly. You can find discounted and used machines that often are Internet capable. Remember, these machines will not be used to develop Web sites, so you do not need the latest or most powerful hardware. All the machine needs is an updated modem for you to conduct essential testing.

- Connection speeds:
  Do not rely on the same connection speed when testing your Web site as you did for development, especially if you work in a corporate environment where the connection to the Internet usually is faster than the average user's. Go to a friend's house, library, or Internet café and access your Web site from there. Test for download times at different connection speeds.

- Display types:
  Test at different screen resolutions and color-depth settings to make sure your colors display consistently. Make sure to test different color depths—8-bit 256 color, 16-bit high color, and 24-bit true color.

► **Testing Considerations: Links**

Click through all the links on your Web site, making sure every one takes the user to the intended destination. Any pages that link outside of your Web site need to be tested on a regular basis to make sure that the destination site has not moved, shut down, or posted content different from what you expect.

tip

According to Wired News (*www.wirednews.com*), 33% of Web users will leave a Web site if a page takes longer than 8 seconds to load. Make sure your pages download quickly.

Conducting User Testing

User testing can be as simple as asking a few colleagues to look at your Web site or as complex as conducting extensive formalized testing. Some companies invest in special user testing labs with videotaping and one-way mirrors to record user behavior, or software that can track a user's mouse movements and eye coordination as they look at your Web site. Even if you do not need this level of complexity, you should perform some type of user assessment of your work. The goal of user testing is to determine if your Web site is easy to navigate and provides easy access to content. The following are some considerations to make when planning for user testing of your site.

► Vary Your Subjects

Draw your test subjects from a variety of backgrounds, if possible. Gather test subjects that are representative of your target audience. Find users with varying computing skills and familiarity with the information. Avoid using friends as test users, as they only may compliment your work. You might choose to let users look at the Web site on their own time, but you can learn a lot by watching users interact with your Web site. Make sure to let them navigate and use the Web site without any outside help from you. Just stand back and watch.

► Formalize Your Testing

Formalize your testing by creating replicable methods of testing your Web site. Prepare a series of questions that users answer after viewing the Web site. Give them a specific task to complete or have them find a particular piece of information. Let them rate the ease of completing such tasks. Compare the results from different users to find any problem areas in navigation. Administer the same testing methods to a variety of users, and watch for trends and consistencies. This lets you compare results or focus on a particular feature of the Web site.

► Develop a Feedback Form

Develop a feedback form that users can fill out after they have tested the Web site. Include a set of criteria and let them rate the Web site on a progressive scale, or ask them a series of open-ended questions. You also may want to provide the feedback form online, letting users offer feedback directly from the Web site. Here are some sample questions you might ask:

- Did you find the information you needed?
- Was it easy or difficult to access the information you needed?
- Was the Web site visually attractive?
- Was the content easy to read?
- Was the Web site easy to navigate?
- Did you think the information was presented correctly?
- Did the information have enough depth?
- What area of the Web site did you like the best? Why?
- What area of the Web site did you like the least? Why?
- Would you recommend the Web site to others?

► Use What You Learn

Refine your content and presentation based on your user's feedback. When you are evaluating user feedback, look for trends rather than individual aberrations, such as one person's vehement dislike of your color scheme. Pay particular attention to the ease of access to your information. Users should be able to find what they want quickly.

Refining and Updating Your Content

If you have a commercial site, ask your system administrator to set up a program that analyzes your visitors and their preferences when they visit. This type of reporting program, available on most Web servers, reads the communication logs created by the server and extracts information in a report format. These statistical reports vary from program to program, but they can tell you how often users visit, which pages they request the most, and how your Web site traffic varies from month to month. There are many companies on the Web that specialize in Web site tracking and monitoring.

Details

► Plan for Ongoing Maintenance of Your Web Site

This is an area often neglected in the initial design and budgeting for a Web site, but it is vital to the success of the Web site. Plan to add new links, information, and featured content continually. The Web is a live, immediate medium, and you want your Web site to reflect that immediacy by keeping it fresh. Test your links to other Web sites regularly to make sure they are active. You will annoy your users if you send them to linked content that no longer exists. Figure AP-3 shows an example of the message a user receives after clicking a link that is not active. When you update your pages, let users know by including update information on your top-level page or on any page that promises up-to-date information. Figure AP-4 shows an older revision date. The content on this site is stable so frequent updates are not as necessary.

► Plan for Major Web Site Design Changes

Some Web sites reorganize their look on a yearly basis. You can perform ongoing testing and improvement of your test site while you still maintain your live Web site. Pay attention to the trends in the industry by visiting many other Web sites. Consider new technologies as they become available and when the bandwidth or browser variables allow you to incorporate them.

► Attract Notice to your Web Site

After you set up your live Web site, it is time to attract visitors. With the millions of pages on the Web, it can be difficult to get your Web site noticed. It is likely that you are trying to attract specific users to your site—people who use your product or who are interested in the same information. Within this narrow audience, publicize your URL as much as possible, in every collateral medium that you can, including business cards, letterheads, catalogs, mailings, and other media. Give users a reason to visit and to come back to your Web site by giving them something they cannot get in any other medium, such as up-to-the-minute pricing or technical information.

FIGURE AP-3: Clicking a link that is no longer active

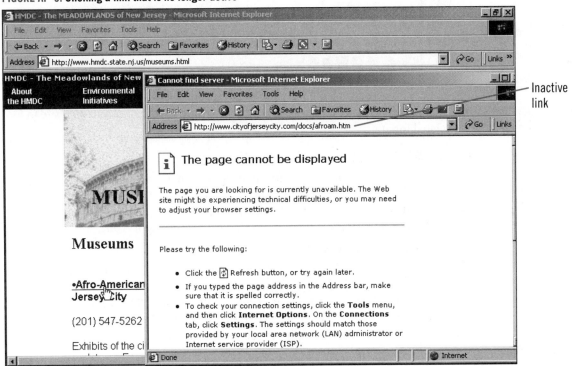

Inactive
link

FIGURE AP-4: Posting revision dates

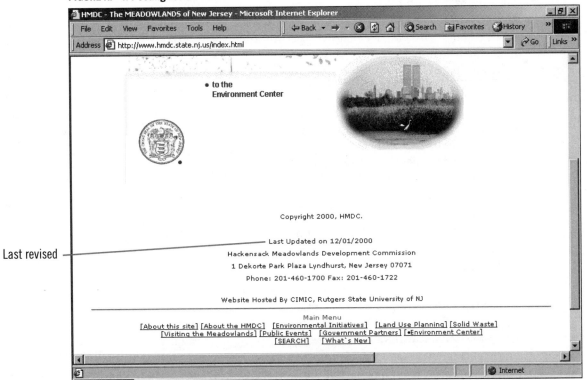

Last revised

Web Design

Working With Search Engines

Consider how visitors will find your Web site, other than by knowing your URL. Many who are interested in a specific topic or information will use a search engine Web site to look for sites on a related topic.

▶ **Use Search Engines**

Search engine Web sites use software programs that search out and index other Web sites in a catalog. Not all search engines are alike, so the way they search and catalog differs greatly. You can enhance your Web site to take advantage of search engine behavior. For more information on search engine details, visit the Web site *www.searchenginewatch.com.*

▶ **Submit URLs to Search Engines**

One way to have search engines list your URL is to visit each of the popular search engine sites and submit your URL. The site's search engine will search your Web site and index the information. Periodically return to the search engine site and search for your Web site name or pertinent search terms. Some search engines are much faster at this process than others, so you may have to resubmit your URL if you do not see your page listed.

▶ **Use Meaningful Titles**

All the pages of your Web site need pertinent information in the <TITLE> element. Some search engines read only the contents of the <TITLE> for Web site information. Also, the contents of the <TITLE> show up in the user's bookmarks or favorites list. Make sure to use meaningful titles that provide information to the user and accurately reflect your site.

▶ **Use <META> Elements**

You can use the <META> elements on your Web site to raise your Web site listing with certain search engines. The <META> tags will get you results with AltaVista, Excite, and HotBot, but other search engines ignore them completely.

▶ **Understand <META> Element Syntax**

The <META> element is an empty element that resides in the <HEAD> section of the HTML document. <META> allows you to specify information about a document that is invisible to the user. Certain programs, such as search engines, can use this information for document cataloging. <META> uses both NAME and CONTENT attributes, among others. The NAME attribute lets you specify a document property, such as "description" or "keywords." The CONTENT attribute contains the property's value. Table AP-1 lists the most commonly used NAME attribute values.

The code in Figure AP-5 shows an example of the <META> elements in use. Notice that the code uses one <META> element for each NAME and CONTENT attribute pair. The description property contains a short description of the Web site. The keywords property contains a list of potential search terms that the user might request.

▶ **Be Careful With Frames**

Avoid using a frameset at the top level of your Web site if at all possible. Because frameset files contain no content, they lack the information that many search engines look for. If you need to use frames at the top level of your Web site, make sure to use both <META> tags and information in the <NOFRAMES> element. Many search engines read the contents of <NOFRAMES> if they encounter a frameset. Figure AP-6 shows a frameset with appropriate <META> and <NOFRAMES> content. Notice that the <NOFRAMES> code includes a link to a nonframed version of the Web site.

▶ **Use <ALT> Text With Images**

Always add ALT information to all of the graphics on your page. Some search engines read the contents of the ALT attribute, which is especially useful if you start your page with a graphic.

```
<HTML>
<HEAD>
<META NAME="description" CONTENT="Joel Sklar Consulting - Specializing in Course
Development and Delivery on Web-related topics">
<META NAME="keywords" CONTENT="Joel, Joel Sklar, Sklar, HTML, XML, Web, Course
Design, Course Development, Technical Training, HTML Links, XML Links, CSS,
Cascading Style Sheets, HTML Resources, XML Resources">
</HEAD>
```

FIGURE AP-6: Frameset with appropriate <META> and <NOFRAMES> content

```
<HTML>
<HEAD>
<TITLE> Joel Sklar Consulting - Main Page</TITLE>
<META name="description" content="Joel Sklar Consulting - Specializing in Course
Development and Delivery on Web-related topics">
 <META name="keywords" content="Joel, Joel Sklar, Sklar, HTML, XML, Web, Course
Design, Course Development, Technical Training, HTML Links, XML Links, CSS,
Cascading Style Sheets, HTML Resources, XML Resources">
</HEAD>
<FRAMESET COLS="150,*">
<FRAME SRC="NAVCOL.HTM">
<FRAME SRC="ARTICLE1.HTM" NAME="CONTENT">
<NO FRAMES>
<BODY>
The Joel Sklar Consulting Web site is a resource for HTML authors and students.
<P>
You can view a <A HREF="index2.htm">non-framed</A> version of the site.
</P>
</BODY>
</NOFRAMES>
</FRAMESET>
</HTML>
```

TABLE AP-1: <META> NAME Attribute Values

NAME attribute values	description
Author	The author of the page
Description	A short text-based description of the content of the Web site
Keywords	A comma-separated list of keywords that are potential search terms a user might use to find your site
Generator	The name and version generated by page-authoring programs

HTML

Reference

Objectives

- ► **Core attributes**
- ► **Alphabetical HTML reference**
- ► **Categorical HTML reference**
- ► **Numeric and character entities**

This appendix includes element descriptions, sorted both alphabetically and by category. The elements listed in this appendix are the ones you will use most often. Included is a list of the Core attributes that are allowed with the majority of HTML elements, and a complete list of character entities. For more detailed information, visit the World Wide Web Consortium Web site at *www.w3.org*.

Web Design

Core Attributes

The Core attributes are allowed within all of the elements listed in the element tables.

TABLE AP-2: HTML Core Attributes

attribute	definition
ID	Specifies a document-wide unique id for an element
CLASS	Specifies a class name for an element; the class name can be used to specify style sheet rules
STYLE	Specifies a style sheet rule for the element
TITLE	Specifies a title for the element; contents of the title is displayed in Internet Explorer 5.0 as a pop up; Netscape Navigator 4.x does not support this attribute

Alphabetical HTML Reference

TABLE AP-3: Common HTML Elements

element	description	attributes
<!--comment text-->	Allows you to insert a comment to your code. Browsers do not display comments in the Web page. Place the comment within the tag, for example: <!-- This is a comment -->	None
<A>	Allows you to create a clickable hypertext anchor in a document. The hypertext anchor can be text or an image.	Core attributes plus: HREF — the target destination of the hypertext link NAME — the name of a fragment of the document TARGET — the window or frame in which the linked document displays
<B>	Allows you to boldface text	Core attributes
<BASE>	Sets the base URL or target for a page; this is an empty element	Core attributes plus: HREF — the absolute or relative original URL for the current document TARGET — the default window or frame in which links contained in the document display
<BASEFONT> **Deprecated**	Allows you to set a default size for the body text in the document	COLOR — the default text color FACE — the default text face SIZE — the default text size for the document from 1 to 7; normal browser default is size 3
<BLOCKQUOTE>	Indents text on both the left and right margins	Core attributes
<BODY>	Identifies the body section of the Web page	Core attributes plus: ALINK — the color for the currently selected link; deprecated in HTML 4.0 BACKGROUND — points to the image file that is tiled across the background of the page; deprecated in HTML 4.0 BGCOLOR — the page background color; deprecated in HTML 4.0 LINK — the color for unvisited links; deprecated in HTML 4.0 TEXT — the default text color; deprecated in HTML 4.0 VLINK — the color for visited links; deprecated in HTML 4.0
** **	Inserts a line break, forcing text to the next line; this is an empty element	Core attributes plus: CLEAR — when used with a floating image, forces text to appear at the bottom of the image
<CAPTION>	Indicates that the text appears as the caption of a table	Core attributes plus: ALIGN — the alignment of the caption, either top or bottom; top is the default
<CENTER> **Deprecated**	Centers text or images horizontally on the page	None
<DIV>	Indicates a division within the document	Core attributes plus: ALIGN — the horizontal alignment of the contents of the division
<EM>	Emphasizes text, usually as italic; browser determines the text style	Core attributes

Web Design

TABLE AP-3: **Common HTML Elements (continued)**

element	description	attributes
<FONT> **Deprecated**	Allows you to specify the font size for any string of text; range of sizes is 1 to 7, with 3 being the default	SIZE — sets the font size COLOR — sets the text color FACE — sets the font typeface
<FRAME>	Defines specific information for each frame in the frameset	Core attributes plus: FRAMEBORDER — the width of the frame's border MARGINHEIGHT — the margin height in pixels MARGINWIDTH — the margin width in pixels NORESIZE — prevents the user from resizing the frame by dragging the frame border NAME — sets a targeting name for the frame SCROLLING — determines whether scroll bars appear SRC — specifies the sources HTML file for the frame's content
<FRAMESET>	Defines the column and row characteristics of the frames in the frameset	Core attributes plus: COLS — separates the frameset into columns ROWS — separates the frameset into rows Both of these attributes need percentage or pixel values to specify the frame width or height
<H1> - <H6>	Defines text as a heading level; <H1> is the top level heading, and the largest text	Core attributes plus: ALIGN — the alignment of the heading text
<HEAD>	Identifies the Head section of the Web page, which is reserved for information about the document, not document content	Three attributes that are not commonly used: PROFILE — specifies the location of one or more meta data profiles about the document LANG — specifies the base language for the document DIR — specifies the default text direction
<HR>	Inserts a horizontal rule on the page; this is an empty element	Core attributes plus: WIDTH — the length of the rule in pixels SIZE — the height of the rule in pixels ALIGN — horizontal rule alignment; default is center NOSHADE — turns off the default 3-D shading of the rule
<HTML>	Identifies the file as an HTML file	None
<I>	Italicizes text	Core attributes
<IMG>	Inserts an image into a Web page	Core attributes plus: WIDTH — specifies the width of the image in pixels HEIGHT— specifies the height of the image in pixels SRC — the URL that points to the image file; this attribute is required ALIGN — allows you to wrap text around the image; valid values are left, middle, and right ALT — allows you to specify an alternate string of text if the image cannot be displayed by the browser BORDER — the border for the image; set this attribute to zero (0) to remove a hypertext border on an anchor image HSPACE — the horizontal white space in pixels on the left and right sides of an image VSPACE — the vertical white space in pixels on the top and bottom of an image

element	description	attributes
<LI>	Marks an individual list item; this is an empty tag	Core attributes
<LINK>	Defines a relationship between the document and external resources, such as a style sheet	Core attributes plus: TYPE — the type of external resource HREF — the URL of the external resource
<META>	Used within the document HEAD to provide information	NAME — the meta information name, such as keyword or description CONTENT — the content of the named information type
<NOFRAME>	Contains content that is viewable by browsers that do not support frames	Core attributes
<OL>	Creates a numbered indented list	Core attributes
<P>	Marks the beginning of a new block of text	Core attributes plus: ALIGN — the horizontal alignment of the paragraph content
<PRE>	Preserves the formatting and spacing of text as typed in the source code; displays the text in a monospace font, different from the standard browser text	Core attributes
<SPAN>	Serves as an inline division, used to apply a style class or rule to text	Core attributes
<STRONG>	Emphasizes text, usually as bold; browser determines the text style	Core attributes
<STYLE>	Used within the HEAD section to contain CSS style rules	TYPE — specify the type of style language; for CSS, use text/CSS as the value
<SUB>	Subscripts text	Core attributes
<SUP>	Superscripts text	Core attributes
<TABLE>	Marks the beginning and end of a table	Core attributes plus: ALIGN — floats the table to the left or right of text; deprecated in HTML 4.0 BORDER — specifies whether a border is displayed for a table BGCOLOR — the background color of the table; deprecated in HTML 4.0 CELLPADDING — the amount of space in pixels between the border of the cell and the cell content on all four sides CELLSPACING — the amount of space in pixels between the table cells on all four sides HEIGHT — the height of the table; deprecated in HTML 4.0 WIDTH — the width of the table, either to a fixed pixel width, or percentage relative width
<TD>	Marks an individual table cell	Core attributes plus: ALIGN — the horizontal alignment for table cells within the table row VALIGN — the horizontal alignment for table cells within the row BGCOLOR — the background color of the table row; deprecated in HTML 4.0 ROWSPAN — the number of rows spanned by a cell COLSPAN — the number of columns spanned by a cell

Web Design

Web Design

TABLE AP-3: **Common HTML Elements (continued)**

element	description	attributes
<TH>	Forces the contents of a cell to display as bold and centered	Core attributes plus: ALIGN — the horizontal alignment for table cells within the table row VALIGN — the vertical alignment for table cells within the row BGCOLOR — the background color of the table row; deprecated in HTML 4.0 ROWSPAN — the number of rows spanned by a cell COLSPAN — the number of columns spanned by a cell
<TITLE>	Specifies the title of the Web page; title text appears in the browser title bar and as the bookmark or favorites text	Two attributes that are not commonly used: LANG — specifies the base language for the document DIR — specifies the default text direction
<TR>	Marks a row of cells in a table	Core attributes plus: ALIGN — the horizontal alignment for table cells within the table row VALIGN — the vertical alignment for table cells within the row BGCOLOR — the background color of the table row; deprecated in HTML 4.0
<TT>	Specifies monospace text, usually Courier	Core attributes
<U> **Deprecated**	Underlines text	Core attributes
<UL>	Creates a bulleted indented list	Core attributes

Categorical HTML Reference

The following is a quick reference for the HTML elements and attributes used in this book, listed by category.

TABLE AP-4: **HTML Global Structure Elements**

element	description	attributes
\<HTML\>	Identifies the file as an HTML file	None
\<HEAD\>	Identifies the Head section of the Web page, which is reserved for information about the document, not document content	Three attributes that are not commonly used: PROFILE — specifies the location of one or more meta data profiles about the document LANG — specifies the base language for the document DIR — specifies the default text direction
\<TITLE\>	Specifies the title of the Web page; title text appears in the browser title bar and as the bookmark or favorites text	Two attributes that are not commonly used: LANG — specifies the base language for the document DIR — specifies the default text direction
\<META\>	Used within the document Head to provide information	NAME — the meta information name, such as keywords or description CONTENT — the content of the named information type
\<BODY\>	Identifies the Body section of the Web page	Core attributes plus: ALINK — the color for the currently selected link; deprecated in HTML 4.0 BACKGROUND — points to the image file that is tiled across the background of the page; deprecated in HTML 4.0 BGCOLOR — the page background color; deprecated in HTML 4.0 LINK — the color for unvisited links; deprecated in HTML 4.0 TEXT — the default text color; deprecated in HTML 4.0 VLINK — the color for visited links; deprecated in HTML 4.0
\<DIV\>	Indicates a division within the document	Core attributes plus: ALIGN — the horizontal alignment of the contents of the division
\<SPAN\>	Serves as an inline division, used to apply a style class or rule to text	Core attributes
\<H1\> - \<H6\>	Defines text as a heading level; \<H1\> is the top level heading and the largest text	Core attributes plus: ALIGN — the alignment of the heading text

TABLE AP-5: HTML Text Elements

element	description	attributes
<BLOCKQUOTE>	Indents text on both the left and right margins	Core attributes
 	Inserts a line break, forcing text to the next line; this is an empty element	Core attributes plus: CLEAR — when used with a floating image, forces text to appear at the bottom of the image
<EM>	Emphasizes text, usually as italic; browser determines the text style	Core attributes
<P>	Marks the beginning of a new block of text	Core attributes plus: ALIGN — the horizontal alignment of the paragraph content
<PRE>	Preserves the formatting and spacing of text as typed in the source code; displays the text in a monospace font, different from the standard browser text	Core attributes
<STRONG>	Emphasizes text, usually as bold; browser determines the text style	Core attributes
<SUB>	Subscripts text	Core attributes
<SUP>	Superscripts text	Core attributes

TABLE AP-6: HTML List Elements

element	description	attributes
<LI>	Marks an individual list item; this is an empty tag	Core attributes
<OL>	Creates a numbered indented list	Core attributes
<UL>	Creates a bulleted indented list	Core attributes

TABLE AP-7: HTML Table Elements

element	description	attributes
<CAPTION>	Indicates that the text appears as the caption of a table	Core attributes plus: ALIGN — the alignment of the caption, either top or bottom; top is the default
<TABLE>	Marks the beginning and end of a table	Core attributes plus: ALIGN — floats the table to the left or right of text; deprecated in HTML 4.0 BORDER — specifies whether a border is displayed for a table BGCOLOR — the background color of the table; deprecated in HTML 4.0 CELLPADDING — the amount of space in pixels between the border of the cell and the cell content on all four sides CELLSPACING — the amount of space in pixels between the table cells on all four sides HEIGHT — the height of the table; deprecated in HTML 4.0 WIDTH — the width of the table, either to a fixed pixel width or percentage relative width

TABLE AP-7: HTML Table Elements (continued)

element	description	attributes
<TD>	Marks an individual table cell	Core attributes plus: ALIGN — the horizontal alignment for table cells within the table row VALIGN — the vertical alignment for table cells within the row BGCOLOR — the background color of the table row; deprecated in HTML 4.0 ROWSPAN — the number of rows spanned by a cell COLSPAN — the number of columns spanned by a cell
<TH>	Forces the contents of a cell to display as bold and centered	Core attributes plus: ALIGN — the horizontal alignment for table cells within the table row VALIGN — the vertical alignment for table cells within the row BGCOLOR — the background color of the table row; deprecated in HTML 4.0 ROWSPAN — the number of rows spanned by a cell COLSPAN — the number of columns spanned by a cell
<TR>	Marks a row of cells in a table	Core attributes plus: ALIGN — the horizontal alignment for table cells within the table row VALIGN — the vertical alignment for table cells within the row BGCOLOR — the background color of the table row; deprecated in HTML 4.0

TABLE AP-8: HTML Link Elements

element	description	attributes
<A>	Allows you to create a clickable hypertext anchor in a document; hypertext anchor can be text or an image	Core attributes plus: HREF — the target destination of the hypertext link NAME — names a fragment of the document TARGET — the window or frame in which the linked document displays
<BASE>	Sets the base URL or target for a page; this is an empty element	Core attributes plus: HREF — the absolute or relative original URL for the current document TARGET — the default window or frame in which links contained in the document display
<LINK>	Defines a relationship between the document and external resources, such as a style sheet	Core attributes plus: TYPE — the type of external resource HREF — the URL of the external resource

TABLE AP-9: HTML Inclusion Elements

element	description	attributes
<IMG>	Inserts an image into a Web page	Core attributes plus: WIDTH — specifies the width of the image in pixels HEIGHT— specifies the height of the image in pixels SRC — the URL that points to the image file; attribute is required ALIGN — allows you to wrap text around the image; valid values are left, middle, and right ALT — allows you to specify an alternate string of text if the image cannot be displayed by the browser BORDER — the border for the image; set this attribute to zero (0) to remove a hypertext border on an anchor image HSPACE — the horizontal white space in pixels on the left and right sides of an image VSPACE — the vertical white space in pixels on the top and bottom of an image

TABLE AP-10: Style Sheet Elements

element	description	attributes
<STYLE>	Used within the Head section to contain CSS style rules	TYPE — specifies the type of style language; for CSS, use text/CSS as the value

TABLE AP-11: HTML Formatting Elements

element	description	attributes
<B>	Boldfaces text	Core attributes
<BASEFONT> **Deprecated**	Allows you to set a default size for the body text in the document	COLOR — the default text color FACE — the default text face SIZE – the default text size for the document from 1 to 7; the normal browser default is size 3
<CENTER> **Deprecated**	Centers text or images horizontally on the page	None
<FONT> **Deprecated**	Allows you to specify the font size for any string of text; range of sizes is 1 to 7, with 3 being the default	SIZE — sets the font size COLOR — sets the text color FACE — sets the font typeface
<HR>	Inserts a horizontal rule on the page; this is an empty element	Core attributes plus: WIDTH — the length of the rule in pixels SIZE — the height of the rule in pixels ALIGN — horizontal rule alignment; default is center NOSHADE — turns off the default 3-D shading of the rule
<I>	Italicizes text	Core attributes
<TT>	Specifies monospace text, usually in Courier	Core attributes
<U> **Deprecated**	Underlines text	Core attributes

element	description	attributes
<FRAME>	Defines specific information for each frame in the frameset	Core attributes plus: FRAMEBORDER — the width of the frame's border MARGINHEIGHT — the margin height in pixels MARGINWIDTH — the margin width in pixels NORESIZE — prevents the user from resizing the frame by dragging the frame border NAME — sets a targeting name for the frame SCROLLING — determines whether scroll bars appear SRC — specifies the sources HTML file for the frame's content
<FRAMESET>	Defines the column and row characteristics of the frames in the frameset	COLS —separates the frameset into columns ROWS — separates the frameset into rows Both of these attributes need percentage or pixel values to specify the frame width or height
<NOFRAME>	Contains content that is viewable by browsers that do not support frames	Core attributes

Web Design

Numeric and Character Entities

TABLE AP-13: Numeric and Character Entities

character	character entity	numeric entity	description
"	&quot;	&#34;	Quotation mark
#		&#35;	Number sign
$		&#36;	Dollar sign
%		&#37;	Percent sign
&	&amp;	&#38;	Ampersand
'		&#39;	Apostrophe
(		&#40;	Left parenthesis
)		&#41;	Right parenthesis
*		&#42;	Asterisk
+		&#43;	Plus sign
,		&#44;	Comma
-		&#45;	Hyphen
.		&#46;	Period (fullstop)
/		&#47;	Solidus (slash)
0		&#48;	Digit 0
1		&#49;	Digit 1
2		&#50;	Digit 2
3		&#51;	Digit 3
4		&#52;	Digit 4
5		&#53;	Digit 5
6		&#54;	Digit 6
7		&#55;	Digit 7
8		&#56;	Digit 8
9		&#57;	Digit 9
:		&#58;	Colon
;		&#59;	Semicolon
<	&lt;	&#60;	Less than
=		&#61;	Equals sign

character	character entity	numeric entity	description
>	&gt;	&#62;	Greater than
?		&#63;	Question mark
@		&#64;	Commercial at
A - Z		A - Z	Uppercase letters A-Z
[		&#91;	Left square bracket
\		&#92;	Reverse solidus (backslash)
]		&#93;	Right square bracket
^		&#94;	Caret
_		&#95;	Horizontal bar (underscore)
`		&#96;	Acute accent
a-z		a - &#122	Lowercase letters A-Z
{		&#123;	Left curly brace
|		|	Vertical bar
}		&#125;	Right curly brace
~		&#126;	Tilde
			Non-breaking space
¡	&iexcl;	&#161;	Inverted exclamation mark
¢	&cent;	&#162;	Cent sign
£	&pound;	&#163;	British Pound sign
¤	&curren;	&#164;	Currency sign
¥	&yen;	&#165;	Yen sign
¦	&brvbar;	&#166;	Broken vertical bar
§	&sect;	&#167;	Section sign
¨	&uml;	&#168;	Spacing diaeresis
©	&copy;	&#169;	Copyright sign
ª	&ordf;	&#170;	Feminine ordinal indicator
«	&laquo;	&#171;	Left-pointing double angle quotation mark
¬	&not;	&#172;	Not sign
	&shy;	&#173;	Soft hyphen
®	&reg;	&#174;	Registered trademark sign
¯	&macr;	&#175;	Macron overline
°	&deg;	&#176;	Degree sign
±	&plusmn;	&#177;	Plus-or-minus sign

TABLE AP-13: Numeric and Character Entities (continued)

character	character entity	numeric entity	description
²	&sup2;	&#178;	Superscript digit 2
³	&sup3;	&#179;	Superscript digit 3
´	&acute;	&#180;	Acute accent
µ	&micro;	&#181;	Micro sign
¶	&para;	&#182;	Paragraph sign
·	&middot;	&#183;	Middle dot
¸	&cedil;	&#184;	Cedilla
¹	&sup1;	&#185;	Superscript digit 1
º	&ordm;	&#186;	Masculine ordinal indicator
»	&raquo;	&#187;	Right-pointing double angle quotation mark
¼	&frac14;	&#188;	Fraction one-quarter
½	&frac12;	&#189;	Fraction one-half
¾	&frac34;	&#190;	Fraction three-quarters
¿	&iquest;	&#191;	Inverted question mark
À	&Agrave;	&#192;	Capital letter A with grave
Á	&Aacute;	&#193;	Capital letter A with acute
Â	&Acirc;	&#194;	Capital letter A with circumflex
Ã	&Atilde;	&#195;	Capital letter A with tilde
Ä	&Auml;	&#196;	Capital letter A with diaeresis
Å	&Aring;	&#197;	Capital letter A with ring above
Æ	&Aelig;	&#198;	Capital letter AE
Ç	&Ccedil;	&#199;	Capital letter C with cedilla
È	&Egrave;	&#200;	Capital letter E with grave
É	&Eacute;	&#201;	Capital letter E with acute
Ê	&Ecirc;	&#202;	Capital letter E with circumflex
Ë	&Euml;	&#203;	Capital letter E with diaeresis
Ì	&Igrave;	&#204;	Capital letter I with grave
Í	&Iacute;	&#205;	Capital letter I with acute
Î	&Icirc;	&#206;	Capital letter I with circumflex

character	character entity	numeric entity	description
Ï	&Iuml;	&#207;	Capital letter I with diaeresis
Ð	&ETH;	&#208;	Capital letter ETH
Ñ	&Ntilde;	&#209;	Capital letter N with tilde
Ò	&Ograve;	&#210;	Capital letter O with grave
Ó	&Oacute;	&#211;	Capital letter O with acute
Ô	&Ocirc;	&#212;	Capital letter O with circumflex
Õ	&Otilde;	&#213;	Capital letter O with tilde
Ö	&Ouml;	&#214;	Capital letter O with diaeresis
x	&times;	&#215;	Multiplication sign
Ø	&Oslash;	&#216;	Capital letter O with stroke
Ù	&Ugrave;	&#217;	Capital letter U with grave
Ú	&Uacute;	&#218;	Capital letter U with acute
Û	&Ucirc;	&#219;	Capital letter U with circumflex
Ü	&Uuml;	&#220;	Capital letter U with diaeresis
Ý	&Yacute;	&#221;	Capital letter Y with acute
þ	&THORN;	&#222;	Capital letter THORN
ß	&szlig;	&#223;	Sz ligature
à	&agrave;	&#224;	Small letter a with grave
á	&aacute;	&#225;	Small letter a with acute
â	&acirc;	&#226;	Small letter a with circumflex
ã	&atilde;	&#227;	Small letter a with tilde
ä	&auml;	&#228;	Small letter a with diaeresis
å	&aring;	&#229;	Small letter a with ring above
æ	&aelig;	&#230;	Small letter ae
ç	&ccedil;	&#231;	Small letter c with cedilla
è	&egrave;	&#232;	Small letter e with grave
é	&eacute;	&#233;	Small letter e with acute
ê	&ecirc;	&#234;	Small letter e with circumflex
ë	&euml;	&#235;	Small letter e with diaeresis
ì	&igrave;	&#236;	Small letter i with grave
í	&iacute;	&#237;	Small letter i with acute
î	&icirc;	&#238;	Small letter i with circumflex
ï	&iuml;	&#239;	Small letter i with diaeresis

Web Design

Web Design

TABLE AP-13: **Numeric and Character Entities (continued)**

character	character entity	numeric entity	description
ð	&eth;	&#240;	Small letter eth
ñ	&ntilde;	&#241;	Small letter n with tilde
ò	&ograve;	&#242;	Small letter o with grave
ó	&oacute;	&#243;	Small letter o with acute
ô	&ocirc;	&#244;	Small letter o with circumflex
õ	&otilde;	&#245;	Small letter o with tilde
ö	&ouml;	&#246;	Small letter o with diaeresis
÷	&divide;	&#247;	Division sign
ø	&oslash;	&#248;	Small letter o with stroke
ù	&ugrave;	&#249;	Small letter u with grave
ú	&uacute;	&#250;	Small letter u with acute
û	&ucirc;	&#251;	Small letter u with circumflex
ü	&uuml;	&#252;	Small letter u with diaeresis
ý	&yacute;	&#253;	Small letter y with acute
þ	&thorn;	&#254;	Small letter thorn
ÿ	&yuml;	&#255;	Small letter y with diaeresis

Web Design

CSS
Reference

Objectives

► **Alphabetical CSS property reference**
► **CSS properties by category**
► **CSS measurement units**

This appendix includes CSS property descriptions, sorted both alphabetically and by category. For more detailed information, visit the World Wide Web Consortium Web site at *www.w3.org*.

Web Design

Alphabetical CSS Property Reference

TABLE AP-14: Common CSS Properties

notation	definition
< >	Words between angle brackets specify a type of value; for example, **<color>** enters a color value such as red
I	A single vertical bar between values means one or the other must occur; for example, **scroll I fixed** means choose scroll or fixed
II	Two vertical bars separating values means one or the other or both values can occur; for example, **<border-width> II <border-style> II <color>** means any or all of the three values can occur
[ ]	Square brackets group parts of the property value together; for example, **none I [underline II overline II line-through II blink]** means the value either is none or one of the values within the square brackets

TABLE AP-15: Complete list of CSS Properties

property	values	default	applies to
Background (Shorthand property)	<background-color> II <background-image> II <background-repeat> II <background-attachment> II <background-position>	No default for shorthand properties	All elements
Background-attachment	scroll I fixed	Scroll	All elements
Background-color	color name or hexadecimal value I transparent	Transparent	All elements
Background-image	<url> I none	None	All elements
Background-position	[<percentage> I <length>]{1,2} I [top I center I bottom] II [left I center I right]	0% 0%	Block-level and replaced elements
Background-repeat	repeat I repeat-x I repeat-y I no-repeat	Repeat	All elements
Border (Shorthand property)	<border-width> II <border-style> II <color>	No default for shorthand properties	All elements
Border-bottom	<border-bottom-width> II <border-style> II <color>	No default for shorthand properties	All elements
Border-bottom-width	thin I medium I thick I <length>	Medium	All elements
Border-color	<color>	Value of the 'color' property	All elements

property	values	default	applies to
Border-left (Shorthand property)	<border-left-width> || <border-style> || <color>	No default for shorthand properties	All elements
Border-left-width	thin | medium | thick | <length>	Medium	All elements
Border-right (Shorthand property)	<border-right-width> || <border-style> || <color>	No default for shorthand properties	All elements
Border-right-width	thin | medium | thick | <length>	Medium	All elements
Border-style	none | dotted | dashed | solid | double | groove | ridge | inset | outset	None	All elements
Border-top (Shorthand property)	<border-top-width> || <border-style> || <color>	No default for shorthand properties	All elements
Border-top-width	thin | medium | thick | <length>	Medium	All elements
Border-width (Shorthand property)	[thin | medium | thick | <length>]	No default for shorthand properties	All elements
Clear	none | left | right | both	None	All elements
Color	<color>	Browser specific	All elements
Display	block | inline | list-item | none	Block	All elements
Float	left | right | none	None	All elements
Font (Shorthand property)	[<font-style> || <font-variant> || <font-weight>] <font-size> [/ <line-height>] <font-family>	No default for shorthand properties	All elements
Font-family	Font family name (such as Times) or generic family name (such as sans-serif)	Browser specific	All elements
Font-size	<absolute-size> | <relative-size> | <length> | <percentage>	Medium	All elements
Font-style	normal | italic | oblique	Normal	All elements
Font-variant	normal | small-caps	Normal	All elements
Font-weight	normal | bold | bolder | lighter | 100 | 200 | 300 | 400 | 500 | 600 | 700 | 800 | 900	Normal	All elements
Height	<length> | <percentage> | auto	Auto	Block-level and replaced elements
Letter-spacing	normal | <length>	Normal	All elements
Line-height	normal | <number> | <length> | <percentage>	Normal	All elements

Web Design

TABLE AP-15: **Complete list of CSS Properties (continued)**

property	values	default	applies to
List-style (Shorthand property)	<keyword> II <position> II <url>	No default for shorthand properties	Elements with 'display' value 'list-item'
List-style-image	<url> I none	None	Elements with 'display' value 'list-item'
List-style-position	inside I outside	Outside	Elements with 'display' value 'list-item'
List-style-type	disc I circle I square I decimal I lower-roman I upper-roman I lower-alpha I upper-alpha I none	Disc	Elements with 'display' value 'list-item'
Margin (Shorthand property)	[<length> I <percentage> I auto]	No default for shorthand properties	All elements
Margin-bottom	<length> I <percentage> I auto	0	All elements
Margin-left	<length> I <percentage> I auto	0	All elements
Margin-right	<length> I <percentage> I auto	0	All elements
Margin-top	<length> I <percentage> I auto	0	All elements
Padding	<length> I <percentage>	0	All elements
Padding-bottom	<length> I <percentage>	0	All elements
Padding-left	<length> I <percentage>	0	All elements
Padding-right	<length> I <percentage>	0	All elements
Padding-top	<length> I <percentage>	0	All elements
Text-align	left I right I center I justify	Browser specific	Block-level elements
Text-decoration	none I [underline II overline II line-through II blink]	None	All elements
Text-indent	<length> I <percentage>	0	Block-level elements
Text-transform	capitalize I uppercase I lowercase I none	None	All elements
Vertical-align	baseline I sub I super I top I text-top I middle I bottom I text-bottom I <percentage>	Baseline	Inline elements
White-space	normal I pre I nowrap	Normal	Block-level elements
Width	<length> I <percentage> I auto	Auto	Block-level and replaced elements
Word-spacing	normal I <length>	Normal	All elements

CSS Properties by Category

TABLE AP-16: **CSS Font and Text Properties**

property	values	default	applies to
Color	<color>	Browser specific	All elements
Font (Shorthand property)	[<font-style> II <font-variant> II <font-weight>] <font-size> [/ <line-height>] <font-family>	No default for shorthand properties	All elements
Font-family	Font family name (such as Times) or generic family name (such as sans-serif)	Browser specific	All elements
Font-size	<absolute-size> I <relative-size> I <length> I <percentage>	Medium	All elements
Font-style	normal I italic I oblique	Normal	All elements
Font-variant	normal I small-caps	Normal	All elements
Font-weight	normal I bold I bolder I lighter I 100 I 200 I 300 I 400 I 500 I 600 I 700 I 800 I 900	Normal	All elements
Letter-spacing	normal I <length>	Normal	All elements
Line-height	normal I <number> I <length> I <percentage>	Normal	All elements
Text-decoration	none I [underline II overline II line-through II blink]	None	All elements
Text-indent	<length> I <percentage>	0	Block-level elements
Text-transform	capitalize I uppercase I lowercase I none	None	All elements
Vertical-align	baseline I sub I super I top I text-top I middle I bottom I text-bottom I <percentage>	Baseline	Inline elements
Word-spacing	normal I <length>	Normal	All elements

Web Design

TABLE AP-17: CSS Box Properties

property	values	default	applies to
Margin (Shorthand property)	[<length>	<percentage>	auto]	No default for shorthand properties	All elements
Margin-bottom	<length>	<percentage>	auto	0	All elements
Margin-left	<length>	<percentage>	auto	0	All elements
Margin-right	<length>	<percentage>	auto	0	All elements
Margin-top	<length>	<percentage>	auto	0	All elements
Padding	<length>	<percentage>	0	All elements
Padding-bottom	<length>	<percentage>	0	All elements
Padding-left	<length>	<percentage>	0	All elements
Padding-right	<length>	<percentage>	0	All elements
Padding-top	<length>	<percentage>	0	All elements
Border (Shorthand property)	<border-width> || <border-style> || <color>	No default for shorthand properties	All elements
Border-bottom (Shorthand property)	<border-bottom-width> || <border-style> || <color>	No default for shorthand properties	All elements
Border-bottom-width	thin	medium	thick	<length>	Medium	All elements
Border-color	<color>	Value of the 'color' property	All elements
Border-left (Shorthand property)	<border-left-width> || <border-style> || <color>	No default for shorthand properties	All elements
Border-left-width	thin	medium	thick	<length>	Medium	All elements
Border-right (Shorthand property)	<border-right-width> || <border-style> || <color>	No default for shorthand properties	All elements
Border-right-width	thin	medium	thick	<length>	Medium	All elements
Border-style	none	dotted	dashed	solid	double	groove	ridge	inset	outset	None	All elements

TABLE AP-17: CSS Box Properties (continued)

property	values	default	applies to
Border-top (Shorthand property)	<border-top-width> II <border-style> II <color>	No default for shorthand properties	All elements
Border-top-width	thin I medium I thick I <length>	Medium	All elements
Border-width (Shorthand property)	[thin I medium I thick I <length>]	No default for shorthand properties	All elements
Clear	none I left I right I both	None	All elements
Float	left I right I none	None	All elements
Height	<length> I <percentage> I auto	Auto	Block-level and replaced elements
Width	<length> I <percentage> I auto	Auto	Block-level and replaced elements

TABLE AP-18: CSS Background Properties

property	values	default	applies to
Background (Shorthand property)	<background-color> II <background-image> II <background-repeat> II <background-attachment> II <background-position>	No default for shorthand properties	All elements
Background-attachment	scroll I fixed	Scroll	All elements
Background-color	color name or hexadecimal value I transparent	Transparent	All elements
Background-image	<url> I none	None	All elements
Background-position	[<percentage> I <length>]{1,2} I [top I center I bottom] II [left I center I right]	0% 0%	Block-level and replaced elements
Background-repeat	repeat I repeat-x I repeat-y I no-repeat	Repeat	All elements

TABLE AP-19: CSS Classification Properties

property	values	default	applies to
Display	block I inline I list-item I none	Block	All elements
List-style (Shorthand property)	<keyword> II <position> II <url>	No default for shorthand properties	Elements with 'display' value 'list-item'
List-style-image	<url> I none	None	Elements with 'display' value 'list-item'
List-style-position	inside I outside	Outside	Elements with 'display' value 'list-item'
List-style-type	disc I circle I square I decimal I lower-roman I upper-roman I lower-alpha I upper-alpha I none	Disc	Elements with 'display' value 'list-item'
White-space	normal I pre I nowrap	Normal	Block-level elements

CSS Measurement Units

TABLE AP-20: CSS Measurement Properties

unit	code abbreviation	description
Centimeter	cm	Standard metric centimeter
Em	em	The width of the capital M in the current font, usually the same as the font size
Ex	ex	The height of the letter x in the current font
Inch	in	Standard U.S. inch
Millimeter	mm	Standard metric millimeter
Relative	For example: 150%	Sets a font size relative to the base font size; 150% equals one-and-one-half the base font size
Pica	pc	Standard publishing unit, equal to 12 points
Pixel	px	The size of a pixel on the current display
Point	pt	Standard publishing unit; there are 72 points in an inch

Glossary

Absolute path Points to the computer's root directory.

Active white space White space used deliberately as an integral part of your design that provides structure and separates content.

Animated GIF A Graphics Interchange Format (GIF) file that is capable of storing multiple images along with timing information about the images. This means that you can build animations consisting of multiple static images that play continuously, creating the illusion of motion.

ASCII The American Standard Code for Information Interchange (ASCII) is the most common format for text files. HTML files are ASCII text files.

Banding An effort to match the closest colors from the GIF's palette to the original colors in the photo.

Bandwidth The amount of data that can travel through a communications channel in a given amount of time.

Banner On a Web page, it is a graphic or text image that either announces the name of the Web site or sponsoring company or is an advertisement on the page.

Browser-safe colors The 216 colors shared by PCs and Macintoshes. These colors display properly across both platforms without dithering.

Cache The browser's temporary storage area for Web pages and images. There are two types of cache: memory cache and hard drive cache.

Canvas area The part of the browser window that displays the content of the Web page.

Cascading Style Sheets (CSS) A style language, created by the W3C, that allows complete specifications of style for HTML documents. CSS allows HTML authors to use over 50 properties that affect the display of Web pages. CSS style information is contained either within an HTML document or in external documents called style sheets.

Cell-level attribute Property or characteristic that, when placed in the beginning <TD> tag, affects only the contents of one cell. Cell-level attributes take precedence over row-level attributes.

CGI *See Common Gateway Interface.*

CGI script An application program that runs in the Common Gateway Interface (CGI). CGI scripts often are used to collect data that a user has entered in an HTML form and then pass it to an application for processing.

Client Software that communicates with a server. In the Web environment, the Web browser is client software.

Color channel One of the three basic colors in the RGB color space: red, green, or blue.

Color depth The amount of data used to create color on a display. The three common color depths are 8-bit, 16-bit, and 24-bit. Not all displays support all color depths.

Common Gateway Interface (CGI) The communications bridge between the Internet and the server. Using programs called scripts, CGI can collect data sent by a user via the Hypertext Transfer Protocol (HTTP) and transfer it to a variety of data-processing programs including spreadsheets, databases, or other software running on the server.

Complete URL A complete Uniform Resource Locator (URL) is an address of documents and other resources on the Web that includes the protocol the browser uses to access the file, server, or domain name; the relative path; and the filename.

Contextual links Allow users to jump to related ideas or cross-references by clicking the word or item that interests them.

CSS *See Cascading Style Sheets.*

Declaration When creating style sheets, part of the style rule that details the exact property values.

Deprecated elements Elements that the W3C has identified as obsolete in future releases of HTML.

Digital Subscriber Line (DSL) Technology that allows voice and high-speed Internet access on the same line, currently available to only a relatively small percent of all the households in the U.S.

Dithering This color-mixing process occurs when a browser encounters a color on a Web page that it does not support. The browser is forced to mix the color. The resulting color may be grainy or unacceptable.

Domain name An identifying name for an organization on the Internet. The domain name is an alias for the actual numeric IP address of the server that hosts the Web site. The domain name also is part of the Uniform Resource Locator (URL) address.

Dots per inch (DPI) A measure of screen resolution, the sharpness of a computer display. Also used to refer to the resolution capability of a computer printer.

DPI *See Dots per inch.*

DSL *See Digital Subscriber Line.*

Extensible Hypertext Markup Language (XHTML) A draft specification from the W3C for the recasting of HTML 4.0 as an application of the Extensible Markup Language (XML).

Extensible Markup Language (XML) A meta-language that allows you to create elements that meet your information needs, which significantly distinguishes it from the predefined elements of HTML. XML provides a format for describing structured data that can be shared by multiple applications across multiple platforms.

Extensible Style Language (XSL) A style language created by the W3C for use with the Extensible Markup Language (XML).

External style sheets ASCII text files that contain style rules written in CSS. External style sheets can be used to set styles for a large number of HTML documents.

Extranet A private part of a company's intranet that uses the Internet to share securely part of an organization's information.

Feature cell The table cell that contains the prominent article or most important information on the page. It should be the focus of the page and, therefore, in the visual center of the page.

File Transfer Protocol (FTP) A standard communications protocol for transferring files over the Internet.

Fixed resolution design Designing option used so that a Web page can be viewed at different screen resolutions; as the screen resolution changes, negative background white space on the right side of the page fills in the remainder of the screen and the content remains aligned to the left side of the page.

Flexible resolution design A Web page that has been designed to adapt to different screen resolutions. As the screen resolution changes, the white space between the columns expands to accommodate the varying screen width.

Font A typeface in a particular size, such as Times Roman 24-point.

Fragment A logical segment of an HTML document. You can name the segment using a fragment identifier.

Fragment identifier The use of the <A> element and NAME attribute to name a segment of an HTML file. You then can reference the fragment name in a hypertext link.

Frames Multiple, independently, and simultaneously controllable sections on a Web page.

Frameset A framed set of pages that contains independent frames.

Frameset document An HTML document that instructs the browser to arrange specific HTML files and divide up the page.

FTP *See File Transfer Protocol.*

FTP client A graphical software program that simplifies the task of transferring files using FTP.

GIF *See Graphics Interchange Format.*

Global attribute Property or characteristic that, when placed in the initial <TABLE> tag, affects the entire table.

Graphics Interchange Format (GIF) The Graphic Interchange Format (GIF) is designed for online delivery of graphics. The color depth of GIF is 8-bit, allowing a palette of no more than 256 colors. The GIF file format excels at compressing and displaying flat color areas, making it the logical choice for line art and graphics with simple colors.

Grid A layout device that organizes the Web page, providing visual consistency.

Hexadecimal number A base-16 numbering system that uses the numbers 0–9 and then the letters A–F. Hexadecimal numbers are used to express RGB color values in HTML.

High color 16-bit color depth.

HTML See *Hypertext Markup Language.*

HTTP See *Hypertext Transfer Protocol.*

Hypermedia The linking of different types of media on the World Wide Web.

Hypertext A nonlinear way of organizing information. When you are using a hypertext system, you can skip from one related topic to another, find the information that interests you, and then return to your starting point or move on to another related topic of interest.

Hypertext Markup Language (HTML) A standard language for specifying document structure.

Hypertext Transfer Protocol (HTTP) Set of rules for exchanging files on the Web. Using programs called scripts, CGI can collect data sent by a user via HTTP and transfer it to a variety of data processing programs including spreadsheets, databases, or other software running on the server.

Integrated Services Digital Network (ISDN) A set of standards for digital transmission over telephone lines to provide high-speed Internet access. Generally available from the phone company, requires special adapters in place of a standard modem.

Interlacing The gradual display of a graphic in a series of passes as the data arrives in the browser. Each additional pass of data creates a clearer view of the image until the complete image is displayed. You can choose an interlacing process when you are creating GIFs.

Internet Service Provider (ISP) A company that provides Internet access and Web site hosting services to individuals and organizations.

Intranet A private collection of networks contained within an organization. Intranet users gain access to the Internet through a firewall that prevents unauthorized users from getting into the intranet.

ISDN See *Integrated Services Digital Network.*

ISP See *Internet Service Provider.*

Joint Photographic Experts Group (JPEG or JPG) A file format, commonly shortened to JPG, designed for the transfer of photographic images over the Internet. JPGs are best for photos and images that contain feathering, complex shadows, or gradations.

JPEG See *Joint Photographic Experts Group.*

JPG See *Joint Photographic Experts Group.*

Kerning The printer's term for adjusting the white space between letters.

Landscape oriented Viewing or printing a page positioning the length or longer side on the horizontal axis.

Leading The vertical white space between lines of type. You can adjust leading with the CSS line-height property.

Lossless compression A file compression method that reduces file size without the loss of any data. GIF and PNG are lossless file formats.

Lossy compression A file compression method that discards some data to gain a smaller file size. The difference in quality of the resulting file is not that noticeable on a computer display. JPG is a lossy file format.

Markup language A structured language that lets you identify common elements of a document such as headings, paragraphs, and lists.

Meta-language A language that lets you describe the characteristics of a markup language. The Extensible Markup Language (XML) is a meta-language.

Nondithering Web colors The basic Web palette that contains 216 nondithering colors. The 216 colors are shared by PCs and Macintoshes and often are called browser-safe colors.

Page template A form that you can use to standardize the placement of objects, images, and text on your pages throughout the Web site.

Page turners Let you move either to the previous or next page in the collection.

Parser A program built into a browser that interprets the markup tags in an HTML file and displays the results in the canvas area of the browser interface.

Partial URL A Uniform Resource Locator (URL) that omits the protocol and server name, and only specifies the path to the file relative to one another on the same server.

Passive white space Blank areas that border the screen or are the result of mismatched shapes.

Pixel The unit of measurement on a computer display. The number of pixels on the display is based on the screen resolution chosen by the user. Pixels are a valid measurement unit in Cascading Style Sheets, abbreviated as "px."

Plug-ins Helper applications that assist a browser in rendering a special effect.

PNG *See Portable Network Graphic.*

Point A printing measurement unit, equal to 1/72 of an inch. Points are a valid measurement unit in Cascading Style Sheets, abbreviated as "pt."

Points of Presence (POP) Dial-up access points to your service provider's network. Your service provider should have at least one POP available so you can dial a local number to get access. Major ISPs such as AT&T have POPs throughout the United States, where a local ISP only will cover the area that includes their subscriber base.

POP *See Points of Presence.*

POP3 *See Post Office Protocol 3.*

Portable Network Graphic (PNG) A graphics file format for the Web that supports many of the same features as GIF.

Post Office Protocol 3 (POP3) A client/server protocol that allows an Internet server provider to receive and hold e-mail.

Progressive formats The gradual display of a graphic in a series of passes as the data arrives in the browser. Each additional pass of data creates a clearer view of the image until the complete image is displayed. *See Interlacing.*

Relative paths Tell the browser where a file is located relative to the document the browser currently is viewing.

RGB color value The three basic colors of red, green, and blue that computers use to display color.

Root directory In a computer file system, it is the directory that includes all the other directories on the disk. Indicated by a leading slash in the file path, for example: */graphics/logo.gif.*

Row-level attribute Property or characteristic that, when placed in the beginning <TR> tag, affects the entire row.

Screen resolution The horizontal and vertical height and width of the computer screen in pixels. The three most common screen resolutions (traditionally expressed as width × height) are 640 × 480, 800 × 600, and 1024 × 768.

Secure Sockets Layer (SSL) Communications software that allows transmission of encrypted secure messages over the Internet.

Selector When creating style sheets, the part of the style rule that determines the element to which the rule is applied.

Server The name for a computer that runs server software. Server software allows other computers, called clients, to interact with the server to access data. In the Web environment, servers answer requests from client Web browsers for HTML pages and other data.

SGML *See Standard Generalized Markup Language.*

Shareware Software that is distributed free so users can try before they buy. Users then can register the software for a relatively small fee compared with software produced commercially. Individuals or very small software companies usually develop shareware, so registering the software is important.

Site specification The design document for your site.

Sniffer A program that monitors Internet traffic. Sniffers can determine browser type, manage traffic, and also either legitimately or illegitimately capture data transmitted on the Web.

SSL *See Secure Sockets Layer.*

Standard Generalized Markup Language (SGML) A standard system for specifying document structure using markup tags.

Streaming A server-based technology that transmits audio or video content in a continuous stream to the user, allowing the content to be played while it is downloading, rather than waiting to download a complete file.

Structured Query Language (SQL) A programming language that lets you select information from a database.

Style sheet An ASCII text file that contains style information for HTML documents, written in either Cascading Style Sheets (CSS) or Extensible Style Language (XSL) can state sets of rules.

SQL *See Structured Query Language.*

T1 High-speed digital line system commonly used in ISP connections in the United States.

Text images Text created as graphics, usually as labels within the graphic.

Transparent spacer GIF A single-pixel graphic of just one color that is specified as transparent.

True color display 24-bit images that can contain almost 17 million different colors.

Typeface A design for a set of characters; the name of type family, such as Times Roman or Futura Condensed.

Uniform Resource Locator (URL) The global address of documents and other resources on the Web.

Value When creating style sheets, the part of the declaration that contains the precise specification of the property.

W3C *See World Wide Web Consortium.*

Web palette The 216 nondithering colors that are shared by PCs and Macintoshes.

Web-hosting service Commercial service that provides Web server space only and may be more capable of hosting a more complex commercial site. This service does not include Internet access.

Web Server A computer connected to the Internet that runs server software. The software lets the computer use the Hypertext Transfer Protocol to serve HTML files to Web browser clients.

World Wide Web (WWW) The most popular part of the Internet, consists of documents or Web pages stored on the Internet connected by Hypertext Transfer Protocol (HTTP).

World Wide Web Consortium (W3C) Founded in 1994 at the Massachusetts Institute of Technology to standardize HTML. The W3C, led by Tim Berners-Lee, sets standards for HTML and provides an open, nonproprietary forum for industry and academic representatives to add to the evolution of HTML.

XHTML *See Extensible Hypertext Markup Language.*

XML *See Extensible Markup Language.*

XSL *See Extensible Style Language.*

Web Design

Index

Index

Index

Index